'ERRATA'

Page 20; 3rd paragraph; beginning of 5th line; ch...

Page 40; 2nd paragraph; 8th line broken from th...

Page 68; 1st paragraph; 4th line. Between the words: "found chapter", insert "in".

Pages 106-107; All three paragraphs should be at the beginning of chapter 6, before verse 1.

Page 118; Starting with the words at the end of the third line of the first paragraph: 'it will be clear....' The rest of the paragraph and the following should be at the beginning of Chapter 7, before verse 1.

Page 125; End of seventh line; insert 'of' after 'consequences'.

Page 154; First two lines on the page should be amended to read: 'which will occasion a plague of locust, and being like scorpions will sting and torment the people for five months (Chapter 9:1-11). The sixth' ....

Page 156; Third paragraph, end of line four; should read: 'such a day'.

Page 173; First paragraph, third line, change '146', for '27', to read: 'circa 27 BC'.

Page 177; First line, second word; delete 's' from 'fails'.

Page 193; The last paragraph should be at the beginning of Chapter 15, before verse 1.

Page 199; The last paragraph should be at the beginning of chapter 16, before verse 1.

Page 203; First paragraph, fifth line; 'will' should follow 'they' in fourth line.

Page 208; First paragraph, first line. Delete the definite article "the", between the words: "and" & "immoral".

Page 210; The last paragraph should be at the beginning of Chapter 17, before verse 1.

Pages 220-221; The last paragraph should be at the beginning of Chapter 18, before verse 1.

Page 236; The last paragraph should be at the beginning of chapter 19, before verse 1.

Page 264; First paragraph; fourth line; 'hell' should read 'hades', and delete 'Gehenna'.

Pages 265-266; The last three paragraphs, beginning on page 265, should be at the beginning of chapter 21, before verse 1.

Pages 290-291; The last paragraph on pages 290-291, should be at the beginning of Chapter 22, before verse 1.

Page 293; Last paragraph, second line, insert 'be' after 'will'.

THE REVELATION OF JESUS CHRIST

THE REVELATION OF JESUS CHRIST

A Verse-by-Verse Study

by
Tom H Ratcliffe

Christian Year Publications

ISBN-13: 978 1 872734 59 0

Copyright © 2021 by Christian Year Publications
40 Beansburn, Kilmarnock, Scotland

All rights reserved. No part of this publication may be reproduced, stored in a retrievable system, or transmitted in any form or by any other means – electronic, mechanical, photocopy, recording or otherwise – without prior permission of the copyright owner.

Typeset by John Ritchie Ltd., Kilmarnock
Printed by Bell & Bain Ltd., Glasgow

Contents

Acknowledgements 7
Introduction 9
Chapter 1 12
Chapter 2 35
Chapter 3 64
Chapter 4 90
Chapter 5 99
Chapter 6 108
Chapter 7 119
Chapter 8 126
Chapter 9 135
Chapter 10 143
Chapter 11 148
Chapter 12 160
Chapter 13 170
Chapter 14 182
Chapter 15 194
Chapter 16 200
Chapter 17 211

Chapter 18 222
Chapter 19 237
Chapter 20 252
Chapter 21 267
Chapter 22 292
Bibliography 314

Acknowledgements

I could not have undertaken this work or achieved anything without the moment by moment guidance and help of the Holy Spirit of God. Any blessing which accrues to the saints of God from using the book in their studies will occasion praise and thanksgiving to God alone through our Lord Jesus Christ.

I am indebted to all the dear saints of God who prayerfully encouraged me to compile, in book form, all my jottings on the book of: *The Revelation of Jesus Christ.*

I deeply appreciate the valued help of my daughter, Mrs. Naomi Douglas, in preparing the manuscript ready for the Printers.

My special thanks to dear Muriel, my beloved wife, for her encouragement and patient endurance of loneliness for hours on end, as I locked myself away in my study.

I acknowledge, with thanks, the help of the Printers and Publishers to get the book into the public domain.

Introduction

This little work is the product of much prayer and time spent in the sanctuary before the Lord. It is the result of a long-held exercise, occasioned by an earnest desire for all the saints of God, young and old, to avail themselves of the blessings God has promised to all who read, hear, and keep the things written in: *The Revelation of Jesus Christ*.

Some readers may already have the little book with the title: *John's Letters to the Seven Churches,* covering the first three chapters of: *The Revelation of Jesus Christ*. For the benefit of readers who have not had sight of the little book, the complete text is included in this study as the first three chapters.

Many dear saints of God mistakenly believe the book: *The Revelation of Jesus Christ* is not for them, claiming the teaching is far too complex for the ordinary person to understand. On this latter point, we must never forget that every child of God is indwelt with the Holy Spirit of God. This enables us to understand what God has been pleased to reveal to us from His Word by the Holy Spirit. *Eye hath not seen, nor ear heard, neither have entered into the heart of man, the things which God hath prepared for them that love Him; but God hath revealed them unto us by His Spirit; for the Spirit searcheth all things, yea, the deep things of God* (1 Corinthians 2:9-10).

We shall see that the book covers three periods of time.

1) Chapter One has to do with all that is past.

2) Chapters Two and Three relate to all that is current, i.e., today, being the day of God's grace to the world, which commenced on the Day of Pentecost (Acts 2:1-4), and will end with the rapture of the church to heaven (1 Corinthians 15:51-53 and 1 Thessalonians 4:16-17).

3) All that we read from Chapter Four through to the end of the book are details of events which are still prophecy.

Unless we understand and accept the teaching about the rapture of the church to glory, referred to above, we shall not be able to comprehend the grand design of God's majestic objective and His divine movements toward the glorious exaltation of His Beloved Son as King of kings and Lord of lords.

Readers will note in their studies that the greater part of the book of: *The Revelation of Jesus Christ* covers the period known as the time of tribulation. At this time, God's governmental judgments will impact upon the entire world, being the fulfilment of the 70th week of years, as prophesied by Daniel in his book, Daniel 9:27. The last half of the said week, i.e., three and a half years, will be as the Lord Jesus defined it, a time of *great tribulation* (Matthew 24:21), when the nation of Israel will experience the greatest of all trials it has ever known. All the saints of God should comfort their hearts with the knowledge that when that grievous time falls upon the world, they will be in glory (Revelation 3:10), and spectators of all events happening on earth.

The book presents an accurate overview of what God, by His Spirit, has been pleased to reveal to us of His future dealings with mankind, through our Lord Jesus Christ. Great care has been taken to make clear the difference between what is symbolic and what is actual in the fulfilment of God's judgments.

The writer has taken full advantage of the ministry of spiritual worthies of yesteryear. The titles of their spiritual tomes are given at the end of the book.

May all who take up this volume to read as a help in their studies of God's Word be richly blessed in their souls and gain an expanded, enhanced, and enriched spiritual understanding of all God's ways through Christ.

Chapter 1

The noun REVELATION means Unveiling. In this book, God is unveiling the Lord Jesus Christ and His plans for this world. So, this book is not only the final book of the Bible, it is also the book of final things. It is a book of Judgments, and about the unveiling of the One who will execute those Judgments.

What we have in the first chapter is an introduction to the entire book. In this Chapter 1, we have the things which have been, i.e., passed into history. In Chapters 2 and 3, we have the current history of the church, i.e., the things that are; and in Chapter 4 through to Chapter 22, we have the record of all the things which shall be hereafter. The book reveals the events which will occur during Daniel's 70th week, the last of a period of 70 weeks of years, a prophecy revealed to Daniel by the angel Gabriel, detailed in Daniel 9:21-27. In Jeremiah 30:7, the week is spoken of as: *the time of Jacob's trouble.* The last half of the week is referred to by the Lord Jesus Himself as a time of: *great tribulation* (Matthew 24:21).

The book details the rise and fall of the world's last Gentile ruler, called the Beast; also, the False Prophet who is a Jew and called the Antichrist, plus details of their final doom (Revelation 20:10). This book also sets out the eternal destiny of all mankind, saved and unsaved; it is, therefore, the Book of Destiny. God gave this book to the Lord Jesus; the Lord Jesus then gave it to an angel; the angel gave it to John, and John gave it to the seven churches. No other book of the Bible was so given; thus, the manner of its giving adds divine gravitas to all that is written. God's objective was to show to His servant all things that must shortly come to pass, from the beginning to the end.

> **v. 1.** *The Revelation of Jesus Christ, which God gave unto Him, to shew unto His servants things which must shortly come to pass; and He sent and signified it by His angel unto His servant John.*

The first five words in verse 1 give us the correct title of the book: *The Revelation* (Unveiling) *of Jesus Christ*. It is not the book of John the divine, as given in some Bibles.

Our Lord veiled His official glory when here as Son of Man, but His unparalleled moral glory, which was evident day by day, was apparent for all to see. On earth, our Lord was the lowly, suffering Lamb, born in a stable, harassed by Satan, rejected by His own people, mocked, ridiculed, and hated by the world. He was assaulted, falsely accused, nailed to a cross, and then buried in a borrowed tomb. However, in this unveiling, the Lord Jesus is seen in an entirely different light. We see the power of His glory, the authority of His Word, and the righteousness of His judgments on the saved and unsaved. The Lord is going to see the fruit of the travail of His soul and be eternally satisfied (Isaiah 53:11).

> **v. 2.** *Who* (John) *bare record of the Word of God, and of the testimony of Jesus Christ, and of all things that he saw.*

John faithfully testified to the Word of God; secondly, to the Testimony of Jesus Christ, and, thirdly, he faithfully testified to all that he saw.

John was, for the entire period of the unveiling, wholly taken up by the Holy Spirit of God. Furthermore, all that is recorded happened on the one Lord's Day (verse 10). Just as John confirmed the truthfulness and accuracy of all he wrote about in his Gospel (John 21:24), so with equal integrity, he recorded all he saw and heard of the unveiling of the Lord Jesus while on the Isle of Patmos.

> **v. 3.** *Blessed is he that readeth, and they that hear the words of this prophecy, and keep those things which are written therein; for the time is at hand.*

This is the only book in the Bible which promises a blessing to all who read and keep (*believe*) the words written. The assured blessing is given at the beginning here in verse 3; also, at the end of the book in Chapter 22:7. So, I ask myself, why are so many dear Christians reluctant to study the book, a book so full of blessings? See also Revelation 14:13; 16:15; 19:9; 20:6; and 22:14.

The words of this prophecy. This confirms that much of what is recorded has yet to happen. Albeit, John says that the time is at hand, or near. John was 90-95 years old when exiled to the Isle of Patmos by Emperor Domitian. So, it is now well over 1900 years since the words, *the time is at hand,* were written. Just as God's ways are not our ways and His thoughts are not our thoughts, so, His time is not our time. However, when specific periods of time are mentioned in the Bible, we should take note and ask ourselves: Are they literal or figurative periods of time?

Peter's words that, *one day is with the Lord as a thousand years, and a thousand years as one day* (2 Peter 3:8), signify that in the eternal state with God, where there is no night (Revelation 21:25), time does not feature; instead of time we have eternity. So, the statement *a thousand years* is figurative, confirming that eternity is without measure. However, when we read in Revelation 20:2 that Satan will be bound for one thousand years, we must understand that the period referred to is literal. The saints will reign with Christ for the one thousand year period as recorded in Chapter 20, verses 4 and 6.

In verse 7 of Chapter 20, we read that after the one thousand years, Satan will be loosed out of his prison. For this statement to be meaningful and correctly understood, we must accept the time given as literal. If, as some erroneously think, the millennial reign of Christ is figurative, how should we understand Chapter 20 verse 7, which clearly states that Satan will be released after 1,000 years? Surely, the one-thousand-year reign of Christ is literal.

On his release, Satan will deceive all the nations of the earth by gathering them around the beloved city (*Jerusalem*) to war against the saints. But fire will come down from God out of heaven to devour all the enemies of Christ (Revelation 20:9). So, here in verse 3, it is God's time, the time for the unveiling of all that we read from Chapter 4 to Chapter 22. *The time is at hand* (near).

> **v. 4.** *John to the seven churches which are in Asia* (Turkey): *Grace be unto you and peace, from Him which is, and which was, and which is to come; and from the seven Spirits which are before His throne.*

The seven churches were and are, in testimony and character, representative of all the churches from the time of John's exile to the second coming of Christ when He will come with power and great glory with His saints, as recorded in Jude, verses 14-15. In Jude, the number 10,000 is figurative of an innumerable company. The reason the figure 10,000 is given is that it is the highest numeral which can be expressed in the Greek language; accordingly, Scripture gives us multiples of tens of thousands.

Grace be unto you, and peace. Grace is the source of all blessing from God our Father through our Lord Jesus Christ (2 Corinthians 8:9). Peace applies to our happy and rightful state before God; it is: *the peace of God which passeth all understanding* (Philippians 4:7). One can never know the peace of God until one knows the grace of God which comes through faith in the Lord Jesus Christ.

From Him which is; has reference to our Lord's omnipotent, independent, unchangeable existence, the self-existing One. To Israel, He was the *I AM THAT I AM* (Exodus 3:14). The power of such a divine title was demonstrated on the occasion when officers of the chief priests, together with Pharisees, and Judas who betrayed Him, came to arrest the Lord Jesus. In declaring it was Jesus the Nazarene whom they sought, Jesus replies: *I AM.* And immediately, *they went backward, and fell to the ground* (John 18:5-6). We wonder at the infinite mercy and grace of the Lord Jesus to allow such brigands to arise and pursue their nefarious objective!

From Him ... which was, intimates Jehovah's relation to the past. *From Him ... which is to come,* declares His inseparable connection with all that is future, i.e., the Unveiling.

And from the seven Spirits which are before His throne. Clearly, there are not seven Spirits of God. The seven refers to the seven attributes of Jehovah which fully define the character and function of the Spirit of God as given in Isaiah 11:2, where we read about, The spirit of the Lord Jehovah, the spirit of wisdom, the spirit of understanding, the spirit of counsel, the spirit of might, the spirit of knowledge, and the spirit of the fear (*reverence*) of the Lord. That the Spirits are *before His throne* implies that the divine attributes of God's Spirit are ever ready to be exercised, as and when the occasion demands.

> **v. 5.** *And from Jesus Christ, who is the faithful witness, and the first begotten of the dead, and the prince of the kings of the earth. Unto Him that loved us, and washed us from our sins in His own blood.*

Here we have a three-fold title.

i. *Faithful witness*. Being in stark contrast to preceding Old Testament witnesses. The Lord Jesus said to Pilate: *for this cause came I into the world, that I should bear witness unto the Truth* (John 18:37).

ii. *First begotten of* (from among) *the dead*. The Lord was the first Man to rise from among the dead with a glorified body. Firstborn signifies He was the first in time of the coming harvest of all who have died in Christ. Being the firstfruit, implies that He is the first in rank of all who will rise from among the dead to enter the glory of heaven (1 Corinthians 15:20). Our Lord was the first of a new race, a new creation, God's family.

We have three resurrections recorded in the Gospels, but not one of the individuals was raised with a glorified body; they were raised with their natural body, to die again. Firstly, the widow of Nain's son, Luke 7:14; secondly, Jairus' daughter, Luke 8:54; and, thirdly, Lazarus, John 11:43-44.

iii. *The Prince of the kings of the earth*. In resurrection, our Lord said, *All power is given unto Me in heaven and in earth* (Matthew 28:18). Everything in the universe belongs to Christ. He has purchased it with His blood (Matthew 11:27). As a Prince, He is first in authority, power, rank, status, and position. No one is more supreme than He. He is the omnipotent One. The title *Prince* confirms our Lord's association with all on earth who recognise the supremacy of His being. He has: *washed us from our sins in His own blood;* not the blood of beasts. The efficacy of the blood of Jesus Christ will impact on all that God has purposed for the establishment of His new creation.

> **v. 6.** *And hath made us kings* (a kingdom) *and priests unto God and His Father; to Him be glory and dominion for ever and ever. Amen.*

As members of God's family, we are a kingdom of priests, and as saints of God we belong to the heavenly Kingdom of which the Lord Jesus is Sovereign, being King of kings, and Lord of lords. The character in which we shall rule and reign with Christ over the earth is given as priests. Why priests? you may ask. Peter wrote: *Ye…are built up a spiritual house, an holy priesthood, to offer up spiritual sacrifices, acceptable to God by Jesus Christ* (1 Peter 2:5). Throughout eternity, we shall be worshippers of God through Jesus Christ.

To Him be glory and dominion for ever and ever. Amen. The outburst of praise from John signifies his apprehension of the magnitude of the redemptive work of Christ, and its impact upon the whole of creation. John cannot refrain from attributing glory and dominion to the One who loves us, and washed us from our sins in His precious blood. The, *Amen,* at the conclusion of John's doxology, is a solemn asseveration of the truth stated.

As successive disclosures of our Lord's rich character deepen, so the doxologies increase in their fulness. Here in verse 6, the fulness is two-fold, glory and dominion. In Chapter 4:11, the fulness is three-fold, glory, honour, and power. In Chapter 5:13, the fulness is four-fold, blessing, honour, glory, and power. But, in Chapter 7:12, the fulness is seven-fold (perfection), blessing, glory, wisdom, thanksgiving, honour, power, and might. It is beyond human ken to comprehend the fulness and richness of the character of our Lord in glory: *For in Him dwelleth all the fulness of the Godhead bodily* (Colossians 2:9).

> **v. 7.** *Behold, He cometh with clouds; and every eye shall see Him, and they also which pierced Him: and all kindreds of the earth shall wail because of Him. Even so, Amen.*

Behold, He cometh with clouds. This verse refers to the second coming of the Lord Jesus to the world, about which Paul wrote in his epistle to Titus: *Looking for that blessed hope, and the glorious appearing of the great God and our Saviour Jesus Christ* (Titus 2:13). The Lord Jesus will be prominent and visible for all to see and wonder. The saints of God coming with the Lord Jesus will be enveloped in the great cloud of the glory of Christ.

Every eye shall see Him, and they also which pierced Him. Here, we have a description of the revelation of the Lord Jesus Christ to the world. It will be His second coming, but this time it will be with all His redeemed saints, with power and great glory, as confirmed by the Scriptures; Zechariah 14:5; Colossians 3:4; Jude 14, and Revelation 19:11-14. The reference to those who pierced Him, includes not only the Roman soldiers, but also those reprobate and unregenerate of the Jewish nation.

However, seven years earlier, at the very least - the actual period of time may well be greater - the Lord will have come to the clouds and raptured away to glory all the saints of God, from the time of Adam to the end of the current day of His Mercy and Grace to the world. The event will not be witnessed by the ungodly world; albeit, the world will awake to realise that a vast company of people have disappeared from this scene. It is most likely that millions of souls will suddenly become aware that they are eternally lost. They will reflect on the many opportunities they had to repent of their sins and put their faith and trust in the Lord Jesus Christ; thus, they will forever rue the day they rejected God's offer of a free salvation. The great event of the rapture of the saints to heaven is confirmed in the following Scriptures, John 14:3; 1 Corinthians 15:23; Philippians 3:20-21; 1 Thessalonians 4:15-17. The dead in Christ will rise first, then we which are alive and remain will be caught up and changed into the likeness of our blessed Saviour, to be with Him throughout the golden ages of eternity.

When the Lord comes with His saints, every eye shall see Him, including those which pierced Him. The last sight ungodly men had of the Lord Jesus here on earth was when He hung upon a cruel cross, with a crown of thorns upon His head, nails through His hands and feet, and blood flowing from His wounded body. The next time the world sees the Lord Jesus will be when He comes with majesty, power, and great glory, with tens of thousands of His saints (Jude 14).

All kindreds of the earth shall wail because of Him. There is little doubt that those who are referred to here comprise the faithful remnant of the tribes of Judah and Benjamin which will have come through great tribulation, together with the ten tribes who were scattered throughout the world, together with the Gentile nations. All will mourn and be grief-stricken with a profound sense of guilt on seeing the One whom they rejected as the Messiah, now the Lord of glory, power, dominion and might. Then will come to pass the fulfilment of the Scripture in Romans 11:26: *And so all Israel shall be saved: as it is written, There shall come out of Sion the Deliverer, and shall turn away ungodliness from Jacob.*

Millions of the nations of the world who will have survived the cataclysmic judgments of Almighty God will likewise see the Lord when He comes with tens of thousands of His saints.

Even so, Amen; is a double affirmation of the Spirit's seal to this striking, prophetic testimony. *Even so* (yes), is in Greek, but *Amen,* is in Hebrew. It is for both Gentile and Jew throughout the world to understand the importance of this prophetic testimony.

> **v. 8.** *I am Alpha and Omega, saith the Lord, which is, and which was, and which is to come, the Almighty.*

The words: *the beginning and the ending,* in the KJV and other versions of the Bible, are an unwarranted interpolation. The subject of the verse is the communication God has made through His Son, hence the titles: *Alpha and Omega.* The titles, *beginning and ending,* have reference to God's calendar of events in relation to this world and the people in it; such titles are correctly found in Revelation 21:6 and 22:13.

Alpha and Omega are the first and last letters of the Greek alphabet, an example of all the alphabets which make up the lexicons of human language in which we have the fullest expression and complete definition and revelation of the Godhead. The declaration of these divine titles, the renown of the speaker and the nature of what He discloses demand our close attention. God Himself is the speaker as He announces His own titles and glories. God is the source and the origin of all truth revealed through His Son, Jesus Christ. Furthermore, the beginning of all divine testimony is in God and ends in Christ. All honour and glory will centre in God the Alpha and Omega. Everything necessary to be known about God and the Godhead has been recorded for man's blessing. No matter what depths of knowledge man may plumb, he can know nothing beyond what God has revealed through His Word.

Which is; has reference to our Lord's independent, unchangeable self-existing, eternal being, the ever great, unique 'I AM.'

Which was; intimates Jehovah's relation to the past, His eternal existence, as with Melchizedek, without beginning and without ending (Hebrews 7:3).

Which is to come; declares His inseparable connection with all that is future. *The Almighty,* such a title is full of divine strength and power, implying that God, who is without equal, is Almighty in sustaining His people, and Almighty in judgment upon His enemies.

> **v. 9.** *I John, who also am your brother, and companion in tribulation, and in the kingdom and patience of Jesus Christ, was in the isle that is called Patmos, for the Word of God, and for the testimony of Jesus Christ.*

Because of his faithful testimony of Jesus Christ, John was exiled to the Isle of Patmos, in the Aegean Sea, by Emperor Domitian. John was a brother in Christ to all believers in the churches to which he was to write. He was not a brother to unbelievers. The great lie of Satan today is that all men are brothers, and that God is the Father of all. The Lord Jesus had to tell the Pharisees: *Ye are of your father the devil* (John 8:44), confirming they were neither God's children, nor His sons.

And companion in tribulation. John readily identified with all who were suffering for Christ's sake. John, by his words, was confirming his belief that no matter how much he might be called upon to suffer at the hand of men for Christ, nothing could possibly separate him from the love of God in Christ Jesus (Romans 8:38-39). Do we have that assurance?

And in the kingdom and patience of (in) Jesus; relates to the present time. We are not yet in the kingdom of power with Christ, but we are in the kingdom and patience with, and in, Jesus Christ. While awaiting our Lord's coming to call His saints to Himself, we shall experience suffering and trial from the world. So, we must not be surprised by the world's hostility toward us (John 15:18). The Lord's word to His disciples was: *In the world ye shall have tribulation: but be of good cheer; I have overcome the world* (John 16:33).

> **v. 10.** *I was in the Spirit on the Lord's Day, and heard behind me a great voice, as of a trumpet.*

Being in the Spirit implied that John's heart, mind, and soul were wholly taken over by the Holy Spirit. No other thought would occupy his mind, no other word or sound would enter his ears, no other sight would fill his eyes, no other feeling would enter his heart, save what would come to him by the Spirit of God. So, John was the perfect vessel to have revealed to him the unveiling of the Jesus Christ.

John *heard behind* him *a great voice, as of a trumpet.* His back was to the churches and his face toward the kingdom. John was called to look back and take account of the state of the churches: *the things that are.* It was a matter of great public importance which had to be communicated to the churches. The voice, being as *of a trumpet,* would imply the loudest possible, unmistakable voice of the Lord, to leave none in doubt as to the divine origin, power, authority, and reliability of the communication.

> **v.11.** *Saying, I am Alpha and Omega, the first and the last: and, What thou seest, write in a book, and send it unto the seven churches which are in Asia; unto Ephesus, and unto Smyrna, and unto Pergamos, and unto Thyatira, and unto Sardis, and unto Philadelphia, and unto Laodicea.*

The words in this verse: *I am Alpha and Omega, the first and the last,* are an unfortunate interpolation; but in verses 8 and 17, they fit beautifully within the context. When man alters what is written in the inspired Word of God, he spoils and corrupts the text. In this verse, the Lord is not speaking about communication, i.e., Alpha and Omega, neither is He speaking about His Origin and Omnipotence, i.e., first and last; but He is advising John to write what he sees, and to send the letters to the seven churches.

What thou seest, write in a book. What John wrote was not to be put into a drawer, filed away or hidden where no one could read it. The written book was to be given and acted upon by the seven churches. Sadly, there are so many Christians today who, to their spiritual loss, never read or study the book of the Revelation of Jesus Christ. To them, it is a closed book. They overlook the fact that it is the only book in the Bible where, in the first and last chapters, a blessing is assured to all who read, hear, and act upon its teaching. We know that in the dark ages of Roman Catholicism to possess and/or read the Bible was an offence punishable by death. Such was the cruelty of man's religion, void of the love of God. We also know that the seven churches listed are in Turkey. Today, Turkey is a 100% Islamic country, and intolerant of Christian teaching.

v. 12. *And I turned to see the voice that spake with me. And being turned, I saw seven golden candlesticks.*

From verse 12 to verse 20, we have what John saw and heard when he turned to see the voice that spoke to him. It was the vision of the glory of Christ's person in the midst of the seven golden candlesticks (Lampstands). Verse 20 tells us that the seven golden candlesticks (Lampstands): *are the seven churches*. Gold, being the most precious of all metals, speaks of divine righteousness as seen in Christ. The churches, in their testimony, were to reflect the divine righteousness of Christ. In the symbol of the seven golden lampstands we have the completeness and perfection of the church on earth as seen by God in Christ. Alas, we know that the church in testimony, did not and does not reflect such divine perfection. The lampstands represent separate churches, each responsible to be a witness of the love of God to the world, to be a light in the world of spiritual and moral darkness. We may ask ourselves as members of the church of God; are we bright, faithful, and active enough, in the power of the Holy Spirit, to have a spiritual and moral impact upon the local community where we live?

> **v. 13.** *And in the midst of the seven candlesticks one like unto the Son of Man, clothed with a garment down to the foot, and girt about the paps* (breasts), *with a golden girdle* (sash).

In the midst of the seven candlesticks. The Lord is walking in the midst of the candlesticks as a judge. The subject of the entire book is judgment; acceptance of this fact will greatly help in our understanding of the unveiling of the Lord Jesus. As 'Son of Man' He quickens the dead, physically and spiritually, and because God will have Him honoured in the very nature in which man outraged Him, God has determined that the Lord, as Son of Man, will execute the final judgments on unregenerate man at the Great White Throne (Acts 17:31 and Revelation 20:11-15).

Clothed in a garment down to the foot. Although we are not told the fashion of the garment nor its colour, we may safely assume the garment to have been after the pattern of the Ephod (Exodus 28:6-7), and in all probability white, similar to the garment Aaron wore as High priest on the great day of atonement (Leviticus 16). The flowing garment was not girded about the loins, but left free to signify the dignity of the priestly judgment which the Lord was freely exercising, for He walked in the midst of the seven churches as the *Son of Man*. The Lord's feet were uncovered that John might understand the Lord's response to all who had trodden His name under foot. Ref. verse 15.

Girt about the paps (breasts) with a golden girdle. The girdle worn by Aaron the High Priest, when wearing his garments of glory and beauty, was multi-coloured (Exodus 39:5); but here the girdle is golden, and worn about the breasts, signifying the Lord being ready to exercise divine judgment in righteousness. Gold in Scripture speaks of divine righteousness.

> **v. 14.** *His head and his hairs were white like wool, as white as snow; and His eyes were as a flame of fire.*

The whiteness of His head and hair were indicative of the perfection, maturity, and fulness of the divine attributes residing in the Head of Christ; His holy thoughts, His divine wisdom, His pure, righteous, and inscrutable perfection in judgment; all in alignment with the mind of God. Notice also, there is no diadem or crown, no mitre as if He were acting in gracious intercession, for He is about to pour out His governmental judgments upon the world.

And His eyes as a flame of fire. Who can escape the penetrating scrutiny of the all-seeing divine eyes of judgment? All the nakedness, wickedness, and evil, man has sought to cover up, will be searched out, exposed, and judged.

> **v. 15.** *And His feet like unto fine brass, as if they burned in a furnace; and His voice as the sound of many waters.*

His feet as fine brass, as if they burned in a furnace. Undefiled feet that will tread down all opposing forces with unyielding ferocity and red-hot judgment. They tell us that the Lord God is a God of Justice and of Judgment. The Scriptures record that the ungodly have trodden underfoot the Son of God (Hebrews 10:29). However, with unbending, judicial strength, the Lord will tread down all His enemies under His feet (Hebrews 2:8). In the coming day of divine judgment everything that is unholy will be erased and stamped out for ever by God's anointed One; then shall righteousness dwell on the earth (2 Peter 3:13).

His voice as the sound of many waters. The loudest and continuous sound in nature is the sound of mighty waterfalls; e.g. Niagara Falls on the border between the U.S. and Canada; and the Victoria Falls between Zimbabwe and Zambia in Africa. The thunderous sound of the falling water blocks out all other sounds of nature. In the great day of judgment, only the Lord's voice will be heard above all the sounds of nature, including the sounds of waterfalls, as He pronounces His judgments.

> **v. 16.** *And He had in His right hand seven stars; and out of His mouth went a sharp two-edged sword; and His countenance was as the sun shineth in his strength.*

In His right hand, seven stars. Being in His right hand implies supreme authority, honour, and security. The stars speak of those with spiritual responsibility, who give light in the assembly of God's people. It is well to bear in mind that a star does not announce itself or boast of its light; it simply shines for others to discern and benefit from its shining. So, the function of a star in the assembly of God's people is to shine and guide the saints in these days of spiritual and moral darkness.

Out of His mouth went a sharp two-edged sword. The Word of God cuts open everything, nothing is any longer hidden. The Word exposes all, and distinguishes between right and wrong. Ref. Solomon and the baby (1 Kings 3:24-27). Thus, the Sword of His mouth not only separates right from wrong being two-edged, but it also pierces the conscience to effect moral and spiritual conviction, so discerning between good and evil.

And His countenance was as the sun shineth in his strength. When Saul, on his way to Damascus, was struck down, he later recorded that he saw a Light brighter than the mid-day sun. Nothing will be concealed from the One who is the Light of the world (morally and spiritually). Here, John was seeing the Lord in His shekinah (dwelling) glory. At the transfiguration, the favoured three were afraid when they entered the cloud of glory (Matthew 17:6 and Luke 9:34). Later, Peter writes: *we ... were eye witnesses of His majesty* (2 Peter 1:16). Today, we are privileged, by faith, to gaze upon Him.

> *Gazing on Thee, Lord in Glory;*
> *While our hearts in worship bow.*
> *There we read the wondrous story,*
> *Of Thy Cross, its shame and woe.*
>
> Miss. C. Thompson

In that coming day of glory, there will be no clouds to diminish the out-shining of His Person, nothing to conceal the dignity and glory of His enthronement in heaven.

v. 17. *And when I saw Him, I fell at His feet as dead. And He laid His right hand upon me, saying unto me, Fear not; I am the first and the last.*

John, who pillowed his head on his Master's bosom, who witnessed His shekinah glory, who out-ran Peter to the sepulchre, who worshipped Him as risen from the dead, and who witnessed with rapt gaze His ascension to glory, is now alone on the Isle of Patmos. Seeing the Lord in all His glory, so overwhelmed him that he fell at His feet as dead.

CHAPTER 1

John was not dead, but the glorious sight was so astonishingly breathtaking and unexpected, that he falls prostrate before Him.

Christ here is in the midst of the churches in the full display of the attributes that betoken His power and majesty: *He laid His right hand upon me.* It was more than a touch; it was the hand of power. The pressure of that hand in its life-giving energy and strength thrilled the disciple whom Jesus loved. *His right hand* speaks of honour, power, authority, and favour. When did we last experience the hand of the Lord Jesus upon us? It should be a daily experience. We might recall the occasion when the Lord put out His hand and touched the leper (Matthew 8:3). When Peter was about to drown in the Sea of Galilee, the Lord put out His hand and saved him (Matthew 14:31). The incident when Peter's mother-in-law was sick of a fever; the Lord took her by the hand and lifted her up and she recovered to good health (Mark 1:31). Then there was the occasion when the Lord took Jairus' daughter by the hand, and immediately she was restored to full life (Luke 8:54). We should cherish the touch of the Master's hand from time to time, to lift us up, to encourage, strengthen, and guide us.

Fear not; I am the first and the last. We should have no fear in this life with our faith secured in One with such a divine title. The *first and the last,* is a title of Jehovah which the Lord claimed 3 times for Himself, ref. Isaiah 41:4; 44:6; and 48:12. The Lord here in Revelation likewise claims the title 3 times; 1:17; 2:8; and 22:13. *First and last* has to do with Christ personally. He was foremost in time, order, place, and importance. The title, *first,* emphasises the absolute supremacy of the eternal, self-existing One. As the first, He is before all, above all, and from Whom all things proceed. As the last, nothing will follow once the final judgments on this creation are enacted. Finally, the glorified Son of Man, the Lord

Jesus, will surrender all to His Father, that God may be all in all (1 Corinthians 15:24 and 28).

v. 18. *I am He that liveth, and was dead; and, behold, I am alive for evermore, Amen; and have the keys of hell and of death.* (N.B. The destinies should be reversed, as death comes before the destiny of the soul).

The risen Lord assures John that He is truly alive. That should be the message in every gospel preaching, to leave souls in no doubt that we believe in a Living Christ; One who died for our sins, but now is alive for evermore at the right hand of the Throne of God, who alone is able to save to the uttermost all who come unto God by Him (Hebrews 7:25).

The keys of death and of hades. Having the keys of death and hades confirms that our Lord has total control of all the souls of mankind, saved and unsaved, who have passed this life. Spiritism and necromancy can never interfere with the souls of men and women who have left this scene through death. The Lord holds all souls secure against the day of divine judgment. The greatest mimic in this creation is Satan, who ably mimics the voices of individuals who have departed this life; and he does so through the practice of spiritism and necromancy by unregenerate souls.

v. 19. *Write the things which thou hast seen, and the things which are, and the things which shall be hereafter.*

This verse makes clear the importance of seeing there are three divisions of the book of the Revelation. The three divisions have already been referred to in verse 8, they are things which were, are, and shall be; they do not over-lap. They are complete, distinct, successive phases of church history, through to the end.

CHAPTER 1

Chapter 1.   Things already seen (past).

Chapters 2 and 3. The things which are now (current).

Chapters 4–22.   The things which shall be hereafter (prophecy).

So vital, important, and overwhelming will be the unveiling of the Lord Jesus that John is told to write down everything he sees and hears. When we catch our first glimpse of our Lord in glory, we too shall be caught up in wonder, love, and praise. Our praise will be in unison with the denizens of heaven, which will echo throughout the heavenly courts for all eternity.

Thus, everything John saw and heard on the Isle of Patmos, is now recorded for our instruction. John was given a sight of our Lord clothed in His judicial garments. This is how He will be arrayed when seated on the Great White Throne, to judge and pass sentence on all whose names are not found written in the Lamb's Book of Life (Revelation 20:11-15).

> **v. 20.** *The mystery of the seven stars which thou sawest in My right hand, and the seven golden candlesticks. The seven stars are the angels of the seven churches; and the seven candlesticks which thou sawest are the seven churches.*

The mystery of the seven stars. The word *mystery* in the New Testament signifies what is secret until revealed; when the mystery is revealed, it is no longer a secret. All teaching in the Bible is a mystery to unbelievers, as for example the seven mysteries of the Kingdom of Heaven in Matthew 13. In 2 Thessalonians 2:7 we read: *for the mystery of iniquity doth already work, only he* (the Holy Spirit) *who now letteth will let, until he be taken out of the way.* The secret working of evil will continue until it is fully ripe, and the man of sin fully revealed. The seven stars are in the Lord's right hand in verse 16, but they are on His right hand here in verse 20 (here the Greek word is *on*, not *in*). *In His hand,* suggest our security in Christ; but: *on His hand,* has to do with the display in testimony of our relationship with Christ.

The stars are the angels of the seven churches; they represent the spiritual and responsible element of a church and may not be just one person; it may be several who are spiritually mature, and recognised as stars by the saints; but such persons do not exalt themselves, neither would they be appointed by others. It would be presumptuous for any to claim to be a star. It is the saints of God in a church who spiritually discern the luminaries; such do not announce their spiritual responsibilities, they humbly exercise them as led by the Holy Spirit. Like stars, they simply shine as navigators, leading the saints with love along the path of faith. Accordingly, the angels are messengers who bring the truth of the Word of God to the saints.

The seven candlesticks are the seven churches. All seven churches were in the country of Turkey which today is a 100% Islamic country. There were, of course, many other churches in Turkey and elsewhere, but clearly the Spirit of God identified seven in the one country, being representative of the spiritual character of the church universal, down through the centuries.

I know there are some who do not accept what the ancient, godly fathers of yesteryear taught regarding *dispensational teaching*. But can we dispute what the Lord God said in Genesis 3:15: *and I will put enmity between thee and the woman, and between thy seed and her seed; it shall bruise thy head, and thou shalt bruise his heel.* Surely it spoke of a dispensation 4,000 years later. Furthermore, we have the Lord's Olivet discourse in Matthew 24 and 25; all full of dispensational teaching; and there are many other examples throughout the Scriptures. So, here we have the seven churches which the Spirit of God presents to us as characteristic of their spiritual state, both current and down through the centuries, from A.D. 95 to the present day and beyond. With the Lord's help, we are going to look at the spiritual interpretation and significance of the letters, and to see in them a panorama of church history from the time John wrote the letters (circa A.D. 95), to the present day and beyond. We shall also see that the spiritual characteristics of each church exist in any moment of time within the said historical framework.

The meanings of the names of the seven churches are significant and worthy of note.

Ephesus means, not lasting very long, short lived, most desirable; representing the apostolic church of the first century. The church had lost all evidence of the first love which initially drew it to Christ.

Smyrna means, anointed for burial, suffering, bitterness, myrrh, mourning; representing the church from Pentecost to the beginning of the 4th Century. The church was cruelly persecuted throughout the reign of ten tyrannical Roman Emperors.

Pergamos means, fortified and married, because the church became divorced from Christ and married to the political world. It happened when Constantine succeeded Diocletion as emperor of the Roman empire. Features of the church continued from the 4th through to the 16th Century.

Thyatira means, a continual sacrifice. In the Roman church, Christ is continually offered in the sacraments as a sacrifice. From the 6th Century, the church with her idolatry and iconology continues through to the present day and beyond.

Sardis means, incomplete, of the flesh; representing the church from the period of the Reformation to the present day. Not wholly separated from Rome and the world.

Philadelphia means, brotherly love. The seed of this church was sown during the first century, and continues through to the present day. However, there was a spiritual awakening from the 18th Century onwards when the world experienced evangelical, missionary movements by the Spirit of God, resulting in a great spiritual awakening. Today the true church is bound together by divine love for the Lord Jesus, and for one another.

Laodicea means, the opinion of the people shall rule. The authority of the Word of God was disregarded. The church was governed and controlled by the will of the people, rather than by God.

Chapter 2

Letter to **Ephesus** 1 - 7

> **v. 1.** *Unto the angel of the church of Ephesus write; these things saith He that holdeth the seven stars in His right hand, Who walketh in the midst of the seven golden candlesticks.*

The angel referred to is not an angel of heaven, but rather one or more brothers responsible for the moral and spiritual wellbeing of the church. As such, they are the stars which the Lord holds in His hand. We see then that the angels are representative of the spiritual and moral state of a church, and responsible to exercise divine influence for the spiritual and moral well-being of the saints.

The stars are the church's light bearers. They derive their light from the Lord and, being subject to His power, they are sustained and controlled by Him. The fact that He holds the seven stars in His right hand confirms the security and honour bestowed upon them.

When Paul, forty plus years earlier, was inspired by the Holy Spirit to write his epistle to the Ephesian church, everything about the church was pleasing to the Lord. Paul's letter set out most profound truths, including the richest exposition of the counsels of God relating to Christ and His church. Alas, according to John's letter, the spiritual height of the church had plummeted.

It was at Ephesus (Acts 19) that Paul came across twelve disciples baptised with the baptism of John the Baptist but who had not received the Holy Spirit. The twelve disciples were then baptised according to Romans 6. Whereupon, Paul laid his hands upon them (*identified himself with them*) and they received the Holy Spirit, not by the hand of Paul, but by the hand of the Lord Jesus. The Ephesian church was established and prospered spiritually, being blessed with every spiritual blessing in the heavenlies, in Christ. Before Paul left Ephesus, he warned the saints that after his departure, grievous wolves (ungodly men) would enter in among them, not sparing the flock (Acts 20:29). Sadly, that is exactly what happened, as John's letter reveals. The church had lost the first love it had for God and for Christ and for the souls of men.

The Lord was walking in the midst of the seven churches in judgment; but today He deigns to be in the midst of individual churches, when the saints are gathered together unto His Name, for their blessing and joy (Matthew 18:20).

> **v. 2.** *I know thy works, and thy labour, and thy patience* (endurance), *and how thou canst not bear them which are evil: and thou hast tried them which say they are apostles, and are not, and hast found them liars.*

I know, is a statement repeated in each letter, implying the Lord's absolute and full knowledge of the spiritual conditions and circumstances of His people. Although there was decline in faithfulness with five of the seven churches, including Ephesus, our Lord loves to commend all traits of faithfulness, before He reproves.

Accordingly, the Lord commends the saints for their works, their labour, their patience, their godly judgment of evil, their endurance and the fact that they had not fainted. If John's record had not gone further, it might have been said, here is the testimony of a perfect church. Alas, we have in verse 4 the sad, judicial statement: *they had lost their first love*.

However, the spiritual diligence of the Ephesian saints enabled them to discern the falsehood of those who claimed to be apostles. An apostle is a messenger of the Lord. *So,* the saints did as John exhorts us to do today: *believe not every spirit, but try the spirits, whether they are of God* (1 John 4:1). The saints found that such false individuals betrayed themselves by their speech, behaviour, and habits. Accordingly, they would have been put out of the company of the saints.

> **v. 3.** *And hast borne, and hast patience, and for My name's sake hast laboured, and hast not fainted.*

The Lord knew all the activities of the saints, their self-sacrificing labour, and their endeavour to promulgate and protect the truth of Holy Scripture. He commended the church for its patience (*endurance*) against the forces of Satan. Divine patience must never be exercised toward those who commit evil, but judgment made in the fear of the Lord. We should never be indifferent about what is evil; the fight against it may be long, but we must never give up. The saints were commended for their patience, they had not fainted. We too should be marked by such divine features.

> **v. 4.** *Nevertheless, I have somewhat against thee, because thou hast left thy first love.*

We know from Galatians 5:22 that the first attribute of the Fruit of the Spirit is love. When the apostle Paul wrote to the Ephesian saints, he confirmed that he had heard of their love to all saints. Alas, that initial love for God, for the Lord Jesus, for the souls of men, and toward all saints, which overwhelmed them when they first owned Christ as their personal Saviour, was no longer active. Sadly, the love of God which was shed abroad in their hearts by the Holy Spirit was lying dormant. Having left their first love was the only censure against the church; albeit, it was most serious because it rendered their work sterile and fruitless.

The apostle Paul reminded the saints at Corinth that the exercise of any gift not motivated by the spirit of love would not bear fruit (1 Corinthians. 13:1-3, *et al.*). The saints had forgotten that the very kernel of Christianity is LOVE. The love which is shed abroad in their hearts by the Holy Spirit of God.

> **v. 5.** *Remember therefore from whence thou art fallen, and repent, and do the first works; or else I will come unto thee quickly, and will remove thy candlestick out of his place, except thou repent.*

The ministry of Christ and His church in the epistle to the Ephesian saints, forty plus years earlier, reached the highest level of divine revelation regarding to the counsels of God. The teaching was commensurate with the spiritual maturity of the church at the time. Sadly, legality had crept in and quenched the outflow of the love of God. The love and grace of God through our Lord Jesus Christ was no longer evident. It was vital the church actioned divine counsel, to: *remember* and *repent*. The church was to remember the moral and spiritual elevation they once occupied, when they were conscious of being blessed with every spiritual blessing in the heavenlies in Christ (Ephesians 1:3). They were to repent and judge the state of their hearts before the Throne of Grace.

Doing their first works; would refer to when they first came to Christ: *They continued steadfastly in the apostles' doctrine and fellowship, and in breaking of bread, and in prayers* (Acts 2:42). These activities would have been a testimony to the world of their calling of God. So, it should be with us today. Let us ask ourselves in the fear of the Lord, have we lost that love and desire to live our lives according to the truth of God's Word, and to enjoy the fellowship of saints, to remember the Lord Jesus in the Breaking of Bread, and to be before the Throne of God in prayer day by day? Oh, may we daily rehearse from our heart the words:

> *Keep us, Lord, O keep us cleaving,*
> *To Thyself and still believing,*
> *Till the hour of our receiving,*
> *Promised joys in heaven.*
>
> T. Kelly

Clearly, the saints at Ephesus had allowed to lapse some of the divine attributes of Christianity. If they failed to repent, the church, that once shone so brightly for the glory of God, would cease to be a spiritual light-bearer. The church at Ephesus would no longer exist. The threat to remove the candlestick (testimony) refers only to the church as God's light-bearer in the world.

v. 6. *But this thou hast, that thou hatest the deeds of the Nicolaitans, which I also hate.*

The Nicolaitans were guilty of quenching the activities of the Holy Spirit in the church. The name comes from *Nico*, meaning suppression, and *Laity* meaning the people. Void of divine authority, they assumed the role of rulers of the people in the Christian church. We have this situation in Christendom today, with man-appointed bishops, clergy, etc. controlling every activity in a church, from the lowest to the highest level, giving no place for the operation of the Holy Spirit of God in and through the saints. Nicolaitans disregarded the High Priestly office of the Lord Jesus. Let us likewise hate the practice and principles of the Nicolaitans.

> **v. 7.** *He that hath an ear, let him hear what the Spirit saith unto the churches; To him that overcometh will I give to eat of the tree of life, which is in the midst of the paradise of God.*

The injunction implies that Christians should ever have an open ear to hear and respond to the teaching of God's Word by the Holy Spirit, and not give ear to the philosophies of men. May our gracious Lord help us to open our ear morning by morning to hear as the instructed, ref. Isaiah 50:4. The overcomer is one who allows the Holy Spirit of God to take complete control of their life, so that his/her service will be motivated by the love of God. When Adam and Eve sinned, God preserved them from eating of the Tree of Life which was

in the midst of the garden (Genesis 2:9); otherwise, man would have lived for ever in sin. It is only when our lives are lived in the current of God's will that we shall experience the spiritual blessings and benefits derived from ingesting the precious Truth of God's Word. The spiritual food which will sustain and help us in our Christian pathway is Christ Himself; He is the Tree of Life. The Lord Jesus said: *I am the bread of life; he that cometh to Me shall never hunger; and he that believeth on Me shall never thirst…I am the living bread which came down from heaven; if any man eat of this bread, he shall live for ever … whoso eateth My flesh, and drinketh My blood, hath eternal life; and I will raise him up at the last day* (John 6:35; 51 and 54). These Scriptures relate to the appropriation of the death of Christ to our lives from day to day. They in no way relate to the occasions when we gather together to remember the Lord Jesus in the Breaking of Bread. As the apostle Paul put it so succinctly, *daily I die*, (1 Corinthians 15:31). Thus, he was spiritually sustained by applying the death of Christ to his life day by day. A lesson for us today.

In the midst of the Paradise of God. The paradise of God is the heavenly realm of eternal bliss, where all the divine attributes of honour, glory, dignity, and power, gravitate to that Blessed One who is the centre of God's counsel and purpose. It is a very precious experience to daily get fresh impressions of the glory of our blessed Saviour; it will happen when we meditate on Him, and when in spirit, our souls are transported to where He is at the right hand of the greatness on high (Philippians 2:9). What a glorious portion for the overcomer!

> *There Christ the centre of the throng,*
> *Shall in His glory shine;*
> *And not an eye, those hosts among,*
> *But sees His glory, Thine.*
>
> J. N. Darby

Letter to **Smyrna** 8-11

v. 8. *Unto the angel of the church in Smyrna write; These things saith the first and the last, which was dead, and is alive.*

Smyrna means suffering, anointed for burial, bitterness, myrrh, sorrow, mourning. It represents the church from Pentecost to the beginning of the 4th Century. In the Hebrew language, Smyrna is the same word as Myrrh. The Myrrh plant has the general appearance of having survived extremely hostile environmental conditions; it is the result of such conditions that the plant yields the precious, fragrant myrrh oil; as happened in the life of our blessed Lord when here on earth. A hostile environment around Him occasioned the constant outflow of a precious fragrance to God His Father, particularly on the Cross, when He endured the judgment of Almighty God against sin. Wherever we find Myrrh mentioned in the Bible, it more often than not is associated with suffering and death. The following references are a few examples of this unimpeachable fact.

Genesis 43:11. Jacob's gift to the ruler of all Egypt included Myrrh. Possibly unbeknown to Jacob, but his inclusion of Myrrh in his gift to the ruler of all Egypt was testimony to all the sufferings his son Joseph endured at the hands of his brothers, and while he was in prison in Egypt (Psalm 105:17-18). Joseph's life yielded a constant, sweet fragrance of love and devotion to Jehovah.

One third of the constituents of the holy anointing oil was Myrrh (*Exodus 30:23*). Not only did all the miracles, signs, and wonders, manifested by our Lord on earth occasion a sweet fragrance to God, His Father; but none more so than His atoning sufferings on the Cross.

In *Matthew 2:11*, we read, the gift of the Magi included Myrrh. The gold spoke of the glory of God in a Man (*Jesus*) after His own heart. The frankincense spoke of the precious fragrance that would daily ascend to the Throne of God from the life of the Lord Jesus. Again, the myrrh spoke of His sufferings as He answered to God for our sins and the sin of the world.

Mark 15:23. At the Cross, they offered the Lord Jesus vinegar mingled with Myrrh. Myrrh is a powerful analgesic which, if ingested, will numb one's senses and pain. Our blessed Lord would take nothing to numb His mind, senses, and will, in order to alleviate the pain from the injuries inflicted upon Him by man. Furthermore, nothing on earth could have relieved our Lord from the spiritual sufferings He experienced from the judgment which Almighty God poured out upon Him for the sin of the world and for our sins; such unmitigated judgment fell upon Him, instead of falling upon us (Isaiah 53:4-5).

John 19:39. When Joseph of Arimathaea took the body of Jesus from the Cross, he, together with Nicodemus, wrapped the body of Jesus in new, pure clothes, dressed with a mixture of Aloes and Myrrh. The action of Joseph and Nicodemus was carried out with profound love, respect, and honour for the Lord Jesus. At the time, Joseph and Nicodemus did not understand that no corrupting influence could possibly infect that Holy Body. The oil of Aloes was a preservative, the Myrrh was a fragrant oil which would neutralise any smell of decay; but, of course, there was no decay (Psalm 16:10).

There is not one word of censure in this letter, and notwithstanding the severity of their sufferings, the saints remained faithful to their high calling (Philippians 3:14). They knew from experience that: n*o chastening* (of the Lord) *for the present seemed to be joyous, but grievous: nevertheless afterward it yieldeth the peaceable fruits of righteousness unto them which are exercised thereby* (Hebrews 12:11). Furthermore, the Smyrnean saints would have known that our blessed Lord had Himself experienced tribulation to the utmost. Thus, He would assure His own of their security and strength in times of testing, for He said to His disciples: *In the world ye shall have tribulation: but be of good cheer; I have overcome the world* (John 16:33). We should never try to escape the trials which may befall us; to do so may prove to be a perilous pursuit.

These things saith the first and the last. The title, *first and the last*, is one of the grandest titles attached to our blessed Lord. As the *first*, He was before all time, He is above all and nothing could possibly have preceded Him. He is the first in rank, status, and order, the supreme One, paramount in all things: *That in all things He might have the pre-eminence* (Colossians 1:18). As the *last,* none can possibly follow the One in whom all God's purposes and counsels are planned and will be carried out and finalised. He is the completer of all things for all eternity.

Which was dead and is alive. For the Smyrnean saints, it would have been a comfort knowing they would never have to experience a death like that which our Lord passed through. God's judgment against sin was exhausted in His Son upon the Cross. Our Lord suffered and died for sin in our place. The divine approbation of God for the atoning work of His Son was confirmed by His resurrection from among the dead when, on the third day, God raised Him by the power of His glory. So, the One speaking to the Smyrnean saints is the Lord of Glory at the right hand of the greatness on high, alive for evermore. The great assurance for the Smyrnean saints was that they would never have to answer to God for their sins. The atoning blood of the Lord Jesus had cancelled out all guilt; they were justified by faith (Romans 5:1).

> **v. 9.** *I know thy works, and tribulation, and poverty, (but thou art rich) and I know the blasphemy of them which say they are Jews, and are not, but are the synagogue of Satan.*

In the authorised text, the plural noun, *works,* should be deleted; it is the sufferings of the saints which the Lord's letter highlights. The Lord was not indifferent to the sufferings of the Smyrnean church. The saints will have learnt that glory, reward, and peace, always follow godly sufferings. The Lord Jesus said to the two on the way to Emmaus: *Ought not Christ to have suffered these things, and to enter into His glory?* (Luke 24:26).

We also have the words of the apostle Paul: *For I reckon that the sufferings of this present time are not worthy to be compared with the glory which shall be revealed in us* (Romans 8:18).

An explanation for the sufferings of the Smyrnean church resided exclusively in the sovereignty of God; they were world-wide and the severest in the entire history of Christendom. However, we do know that today there are areas in the world where Christians are being sorely tried for their faith in Christ, even unto death. We acknowledge that these are pockets of severe persecution; but in the greater part of the so-called Christian world, saints enjoy reasonable liberty to serve, gather together, and worship the Lord free of fear. Nevertheless, we must not overlook the fact that as the current time of God's day of grace to the world draws to a close, persecution of the church in general will increase. It therefore behoves us to continue to pray for all saints who are currently suffering for their faithfulness in testimony.

The Lord Jesus warned His disciples that: *In the world ye shall have tribulation: but be of good cheer; I have overcome the world* (John 16:33). Today, we take comfort in those words. The poverty of the Smyrnean saints was in the things of the world; they were void of property and belongings, and possibly food, but they were rich in God, having been blessed with every spiritual blessing in the heavenlies in Christ.

Accordingly, the Smyrnean saints were following in the footsteps of the Lord Jesus Christ: *Who, when He was reviled, reviled not again; when He suffered, He threatened not; but committed Himself to Him that judgeth righteously* (1 Peter 2:23).

But are the synagogue of Satan. We frequently read in the Old Testament about the congregation of the Lord, but here, and in the letter to the angel of the Philadelphian church, reference is made to the congregation of Satan. The blasphemy of those who say they are Jews, and are not, confirms they keep company with, and are a synagogue of Satan. Today, there are many specious sects which exist under the umbrella of Christianity. Such sects deny fundamental truths of Holy Scripture relating to the Deity, Person, and Atoning work of the Lord Jesus Christ. As a consequence, they neither belong to, nor form part of the church of Christ.

> **v. 10.** *Fear none of those things which thou shalt suffer: behold, the devil shall cast some of you into prison, that ye may be tried; and ye shall have tribulation ten days: be thou faithful unto death, and I will give thee a crown of life.*

Whenever the Smyrnean saints were called upon to suffer physically, they did not despair, because, as the Lord Jesus had said: *Fear not them which kill the body, but are not able to kill the soul: but rather fear Him which is able to destroy both soul and body in hell* (Matthew 10:28). The main features of this verse are, fearlessness, suffering, imprisonment, tribulation, faithfulness, and a crown of life.

The term *ten days* is a figure of speech and refers to ten periods of time covered by ten tyrannical Roman Emperors, beginning with Nero in the first century, and concluding with Diocletian who died A.D. 312. The other eight emperors in order of their reign, were Domitian, who exiled John to the Isle of Patmos (circa A.D. 95), Trajan, Marcus Aurelius, Septimus Severus, Maximus, Decius, Valerian, Aurelian. Thus, it was the Roman emperors who inflicted severe persecutions upon the Smyrnean saints, but the more they suffered, the brighter shone the testimony of their service, love, devotion, and commitment to the will of God through Christ. It was true in Old Testament times and remains true today, that when God's people come under severe trial from the forces of evil, the testimony of their faith and commitment to God shines brighter as a beacon of light in this world of moral darkness.

In the Scriptures, the noun, *day,* can refer either to a 24-hour period or to a time of several days, weeks, months, or years. The context of the sentence in which the noun occurs will clearly indicate how the noun, *day,* should be understood. The seven days of creation were clearly 24-hour periods, as the Scripture says: *the evening and the morning were the first day, etc. etc.* (Genesis 1). There are many references in the Scriptures where day means a period of time, or the current time. In Zechariah 4:10; we read: F*or who hath despised the day of small things*. Luke 6:23 speaks of the day of great trial for the Jewish nation prior to the Lord coming to set up His Kingdom; and in 2 Corinthians 6:2, we read: *Behold, now is the day of Salvation*, which has reference to the present Day of Grace.

Be thou faithful unto death, and I will give thee a crown of life. A Christian man named Augustine first coined the phrase: *the blood of the martyrs is the seed of the church*. According to historical records, the church certainly grew numerically during the first three centuries of the current era; notwithstanding, it was a time of great persecution. The epistle to the Hebrews, chapter 11 verses 32–39 refer to the many who, for the testimony's sake, were faithful unto death. From that time forward down through the centuries, all who have suffered and died for their faith in our living Saviour will likewise receive a crown of life (dignity, honour, experience of eternal life in heaven).

During, and following the 1939–1945 World War, there was a great Christian awakening in this country. Churches, which were rarely more than a quarter filled, were regularly more than half filled week after week. Furthermore, there was a significant evangelical movement throughout the nation, with much spiritual blessing. However, from the 1960s onwards, when there began to be material prosperity and peace among civilised nations, there occurred a substantial decline in commitment to divine things in Christendom.

Many churches, chapels, gospel halls and the like, now lie redundant. Sadly, there are many sects which do not accept certain sections of the Bible as the inerrant Word of God; they follow only those parts of the Scriptures which coincide with their way of thinking. Furthermore, such sects appear to be prospering by an increase in numbers attending their gatherings. Alas, it is patently clear today that the spirit and character of the Laodicean church is already evident in Christendom as a whole. Read what the apostle Paul said, as recorded in Acts 20:28-30.

> **v. 11.** *He that hath an ear, let him hear what the Spirit saith to the churches; He that overcometh shall not be hurt of* (come into) *the second death* (in hell, Gehenna).

This potential life-saving injunction applies to all mankind. If heeded and acted upon in faith by man, it will ensure eternal life to the individual. The consequence of rejection and persistent unbelief is too awful to contemplate. Finally, we have the promise to the overcomer. To the church at Ephesus, the overcomer would achieve recovery through repentance, by doing the first works, and exercising their first love which they had lost. Here, the Smyrnean saints were found to be courageous unto death, and faithful to the Lord and His testimony. The expression, second death, stands in positive contrast to our first death should we be called home before the rapture of the saints to glory (1 Corinthians 15:51-57 & 1 Thessalonians 4:17). No God-fearing soul of Old Testament times and born-again Christian believers from New Testament times, including periods after the rapture of the saints, will experience the second death. However, all who appear for judgment before the Great

White Throne will suffer the second death which is Hell, Gehenna, the place of eternal punishment, the lake that burns with fire and brimstone for ever and ever (Revelation 20:11-15).

Letter to **Pergamos** 12–17.

> **v. 12.** *To the angel of the church in Pergamos write; These things saith He which hath the sharp sword with two edges.*

Pergamos means fortified and marriage. It was a church divorced from God, and being married to the political world was given over to spiritual idolatry and worldly strength. The spirit and function of the Pergamos church represented the church from the 4th through to the 16th Century; from the reign of Constantine to the Reformation. The Pergamos period of the church began in 313 A.D. when Constantine succeeded Diocletian. Constantine was mainly responsible for bringing an end to the severe affliction and oppression of the church; he did it by rescinding the edicts of persecution against Christians, which were so cruelly enforced by Diocletian and his predecessors. Alas, in the absence of such trials, the church no longer remained totally separate from the corruption of the world. The grave mistake Constantine made was to fuse Christianity with the political world. It is important to note there is no historical evidence that Constantine was or became a born-again Christian. It was during the time of Constantine's reign as Emperor of the Roman empire, that the church began to allow superstitious and idolatrous practices from the heathen world to be recognised, and abound. This was the beginning of Christendom, when Constantine declared Christianity to be the official religion of the Roman empire.

Thus, the stage was set for the advent of the Roman Catholic church, when Gregory I became its first pope in A.D. 590.

These things saith He which hath the sharp sword with two edges. It is the sword that separates the body from the soul, the flesh from the spirit, and separates that which is biblical from that which is not; it also isolates that which is right, from that which is wrong (Hebrews 4:12). When the Word of God is prayerfully studied, its truth will separate that which is spiritual from that which is carnal in our lives.

Note, the Sword is not sheathed, but drawn ready for instant work. The Sword also pierces the conscience to effect moral and spiritual conviction to discern between right and wrong.

> **v. 13.** *I know thy works, and where thou dwellest, even where Satan's seat* (throne) *is; and thou holdest fast My name, and hast not denied My faith, even in those days wherein Antipas was My faithful martyr, who was slain among you, where Satan dwelleth.*

The words *thy works* are an interpolation. The Lord acknowledges that the saints are living in the world under the influence of Satan, the place of his throne. It was a sorrowful situation in Pergamos because the church had forgotten her heavenly calling and character and had settled down in the world which crucified their Lord and Saviour. The main theme of this letter is that the church is dwelling (has settled down) where Satan's *throne* is established. It is a sad fact that there are many Christians today who have settled down in this world, much like Lot, as recorded in Genesis 13:11-12; and have forgotten the hope of their heavenly calling (Hebrews 3:1). However, the Lord commends the church for holding fast the Name of their Lord and Saviour Jesus Christ, and not denying the Christian faith. We too ought ever to be ready to stand up for, and defend the Name of our Redeemer whenever we hear it being taken in vain. Antipas was clearly a saint who stood up for his faith and testimony before the Roman hierarchy; and suffered an untimely death as a consequence; what an example! Antipas was given that divine accolade: *My faithful martyr* (witness), by the Lord Himself. Like Stephen (Acts 7:59), Antipas sealed his testimony with his blood.

> **v. 14.** *But I have a few things against thee, because thou hast there them that hold the doctrine of Balaam, who taught Balak to cast a stumbling block before the children of Israel, to eat things sacrificed unto idols, and to commit fornication.* (See Numbers, chapters 22-24).

In Pergamos, Satan was inside the church as a seducing and subtle serpent perverting the saints by false and seductive teaching. Much like the behaviour of Balaam whose name means: *destroyer of the people*, who caused Israel to sin. It is important to note that the church itself had not openly accepted false doctrine, but there were those in the church who held and promulgated the false doctrine of Balaam, which was the spirit of compromise, which exposed the children of Israel to disrepute through corruption, leading them to commit whoredom with the daughters of Moab, to worship and bow down to the gods of the Moabites, to join themselves to Baal-peor, and to eat things offered to idols; all of which should be emphatically eschewed by the saints of God. Thus, Balaam caused Israel to sin (Numbers 25:1-3 & 31:16).

> **v. 15.** *So hast thou also them that hold the doctrine of the Nicolaitanes, which thing I hate.*

The Nicolaitanes were people who dominated, ruled over, and controlled the worshippers. *Nico*, means to rule like the clergy; *laity*, means the people. What occurs in Christendom today is the Holy Spirit is displaced with man-appointed bishops, deacons and clergy, who direct what goes on in church buildings, most of which is vain repetition. Godly theologians believe that the Nicolaitanes were people who abused the grace of God, disregarded holy, moral standards of life, and combined the profession of Christianity with fleshly indulgences together with the impurities of Paganism. For these serious reasons, the Lord hated the doctrine of the Nicolaitanes, who were the servants of Satan. The angel (responsible element) of the church in Pergamos is not charged with holding the evil doctrines, but censured for not resisting the evil. To be indifferent to what is evil is dishonouring to God, it is a grave sin.

> **v. 16.** *Repent; or else I will come unto thee quickly, and will fight against them with the sword of My mouth.*

Repent means more than just saying sorry to the one offended. It means to exercise self-judgment, to reproach oneself for what one has said or done amiss, to be contrite and remorseful, to be full of guilt and regret, to humble oneself with godly sorrow, and be before the Throne of Grace with a sincere confession of failure. (See Psalm 51.) Whenever we sin wilfully, as David did, we should, in the privacy of our own home, get before the Mercy Seat, and make a full confession of the offence to God who, through the efficacy of the blood of Christ, will both forgive and cleanse (1 John 1:9). If we have a conscience about a sin or sins we have knowingly committed, to simply say: *forgive my sins*, is scarcely a full confession. As children of God, we should have the assurance that we have already been forgiven for all our past, present, and future sins committed unwittingly, so that, as the apostle Paul states: *Being justified by faith, we have peace with God* (Romans 5:1).

A full understanding of our justification by faith would preclude the need to regularly rehearse the words: *forgive my sins*. Furthermore, we should never meet together with God's children with a burden of unconfessed sin on our conscience; to do so would be gravely dishonouring to our blessed Saviour, for such matters as unconfessed sin should be confessed and repented of before the Lord at one's home, before we meet with the Lord's people. For one to meet with the Lord's people with a burden of unconfessed sin will adversely affect the liberty of the Holy Spirit to work for the blessing of the saints. Let us heed the injunction of the apostle Paul: *Grieve not the Holy Spirit of God* (Ephesians 4:30-32).

However, if the church did not repent, the Lord would not delay coming to them in judgment with the Sword of His mouth. The Sword of His mouth refers to the almighty, judging power of His Word: *For the word of God is quick, and powerful, and sharper than any twoedged sword, piercing even to the dividing asunder of soul and spirit, and of the joints and marrow, and is a discerner of the thoughts and intents of the heart* (Hebrews 4:12). If the Lord's judgment became necessary, it would be applied with the same objective as given in Ezekiel 36:22: *Thus saith the Lord God, I do not this for your sakes … but for Mine holy name's sake.*

> **v. 17.** *He that hath an ear, let him hear what the Spirit saith unto the churches; To him that overcometh will I give to eat of the hidden manna, and will give him a white stone, and in the stone a new name written, which no man knoweth saving he that receiveth it.*

Whilst the Spirit speaks to the churches, it is to individuals that the call to hear is made. The churches are not called to hear, but individuals; therefore, the Scripture says: *he that*, and, *let him*. Whenever there is failure in the church, it is not corporate recovery which is called for, but for individuals to be exercised about the failure, and then confess and repent before God at the Throne of Grace.

To him that overcometh will I give to eat of the hidden manna. The words:

to eat, in the A.V. are an unnecessary interpolation. The overcomer is one who eschews all forms of evil, the lust of the flesh, the lust of the eyes, and the pride of life (1 John 2:16). The manna which sustained Israel throughout their wilderness journeys was visible for all to see each morning. However, a golden pot, full of the manna, was sealed in the Ark of the Covenant for nearly 500 years (see 1 Kings 6:1). It was a constant reminder to Israel of Jehovah's rich and sustaining provision as they journeyed for 40 years through the wilderness. The spiritual significance for us today of eating the hidden manna is the personal, daily appropriation to our souls of the death of Christ, His ascension to glory, and His exaltation to the right hand of the throne of God. Our Lord, as the hidden manna, is unseen by the world, but visible to the eye of faith, and it is by faith that we feed upon Him.

In Pergamos there had been a tendency to eat things which had been offered to idols; so today the Lord says, I will feed you with spiritual food, the hidden manna which alone will sustain you in your Christian pathway. The hidden manna is, as we have said, Christ Himself in glory at the right hand of God His Father, and seen only by the eye of faith.

And will give him a white stone, and in the stone a new name written, which no man knoweth saving he that receiveth it. The white stone given will be a symbol, confirming that not only is the individual justified by faith before God, but is also a recognition of the Lord's particular pleasure in the faithfulness of his testimony here on earth. In biblical days and since, a host's appreciation of a guest would have been noted by the giving of a white stone with the guest's name written upon it.

In courts of law, whenever a white stone was given, it confirmed a person's acquittal; but a black stone would confirm a person's guilt and condemnation. In heaven, only the recipient of the white stone will know the meaning and significance of his new name written upon the stone. The new name will convey a precious expression of the Lord's personal delight in the redeemed soul; a secret disclosure of His inestimable pleasure in the overcomer, which will endure for all eternity. Every child of God in heaven will receive a white stone with his new name written upon it.

Letter to **Thyatira** 18–29

> **v. 18.** *Unto the angel of the church in Thyatira write; These things saith the Son of God, who hath His eyes like unto a flame of fire, and His feet are like fine brass.*

Thyatira means a continual sacrifice. The vast majority of godly and eminent expositors of the Bible recognise the church of Thyatira as a pattern of the current Roman Catholic church, in which Christ is continually offered as a sacrifice in the sacraments. This letter is the longest of the seven, and details the history of the first of the last four churches whose character will continue to the second coming of Christ to the world; this time with power and great glory with all His redeemed (Matthew 24:30). However, there was no recognised Roman Catholic church until the Pope was acknowledged as the head of Christendom in the 7th Century. Thyatira represents a specific character of the church from the 7th Century through to the end of this age.

The title, 'Son of God' is nowhere else found in this book; thus, its occurrence here is significant and worthy of note, primarily because it emphasises the deity of the Lord Jesus. The Roman church accustoms people to think more of the Lord Jesus as the son of Mary, rather than as the Son of God, and to give pre-eminence to Mary above the Lord Jesus. Furthermore, this church had given a superior place to the evil woman

(*Jezebel*), and accommodated her teachings and principles of corruption. Thus, the Lord introduces Himself in the full force and power of His deity as the Son of God who is supreme, unique, over and above all beings, including things in creation (Ephesians 4:6).

Who hath His eyes like unto a flame of fire, and His feet are like fine brass. These two attributes confirm the unique sovereignty of the One who will judge with equity and righteousness. His eyes, being as flames of fire, confirm His moral intolerance to the sight of all evil. He will search out with fiery pursuit all that man seeks to hide from His eye. His feet like fine brass implies that He will stamp out with unyielding fiery justice every element of evil His eyes bring to light. Fire in Scripture is always a symbol of judgment, as seen in the Old Testament Offerings by fire, and the destiny of the unsaved (Revelation 21:8).

> **v. 19.** *I know thy works, and charity* (love), *and service, and faith, and thy patience* (endurance), *and thy works; and the last to be more than the first.*

When an occasion demands a censure or judgment, our Lord, in His role as Judge of all the earth, will always first highlight those divine features and achievements worthy of praise which He sees in the saints. What a lesson for us today when commenting on the qualities and service of another servant of God.

I know thy works, and love, and service, and faith, and thy patience. The saints toiled tirelessly, everything they did was motivated by their love for the Lord. Their service confirmed the spiritual gifts which they selflessly exercised for the blessing of the saints, whom they served with love and faith, knowing that all which was of God would be for His glory and a blessing for the saints. The labours of the saints were noted for their endurance in spite of apparent opposition from an ungodly element in the church.

And the last (works) *to be more than the first.* It was the faithful element in the church at Thyatira which was commended for its devotion to service, and for its faith, endurance, and love. One may be sure that they sustained great trial and persecution as they stood firm for: *the truth as it is in Jesus* (Ephesians 4:21). The more the dear saints were tried and tested for their faith, the sweeter and more precious to God was their love and service; hence, their last works yielded more for the glory of God than their first. It is a proven fact that when the saints of God are severely tried and tested for their faith, a greater and deeper commitment to the Lord in testimony, service, and worship ensues. Oh, that such a high level of devotion to God were constant with us; alas, to our shame we know it is not so.

> **v. 20.** *Notwithstanding I have* a few things *against thee, because thou sufferest that woman Jezebel, which calleth herself a prophetess, to teach and seduce My servants to commit fornication, and to eat things sacrificed unto idols.*

The words: *a few things,* do not appear in the original text; being inserted in the A.V. they lessen the seriousness of what the Lord had against the church. The primary fault of the church was that they had suffered the presence of the woman Jezebel, and allowed her corrupting influences to defile the saints, so damaging the testimony. In Smyrna, Satan was outside the church as a roaring lion persecuting and devouring the saints; but in Thyatira, Satan is very much in the church, not in a spirit of subtlety, but with open boldness misleading the saints. The Lord had a very serious charge against the angel (*responsible brothers*) of the church, for they were allowing evil practices and doctrines to dominate the testimony. It is an accepted fact in Scripture that when a woman is introduced as a type, she is expressive of the state of things, but when a man is brought to the forefront, he more often than not indicates the activity and conduct of the state. According to 1 Kings 16:30-33, it was Jezebel's wickedness before God which represented the state of the nation of Israel; whereas Ahab represented the idolatrous activities of the nation. The Lord parallels the evil and idolatrous activities of the kingdom under Ahab, with the spiritual and moral state of the church at Thyatira.

The wickedness of the church at Thyatira was compounded by the election of the first Pope, Gregory I, in the 6th Century. But it was not until about the 7th Century that the then Pope was appointed head of Christendom with its headquarters in Rome. It was then that the dark ages began with most severe persecutions against any who did not accept and follow the church's teachings (*dogmas*).

The dominance of the church continued to the 16th Century, the time of the Reformation when Martin Luther nailed his '95 Theses' to the door of the cathedral in Wittenberg, Germany, in 1517. The theses condemned, among many other false beliefs, the teaching that the Salvation of a soul was by works alone. The church totally ignored the truth in Ephesians 2:8-9; which declares that it is: B*y grace are ye saved through faith; and that not of yourselves: it is the gift of God: not of works, lest any man should boast.* Furthermore, Paul tells us that the believer is: *justified by faith* alone (Romans 5:1). Clearly, the Reformation was of God, but Protestantism which sprang out of the Reformation, was of Satan; for it preserved many of the rites, ceremonies, and teachings of the Roman church, which continue to this day.

v. 21. *And I gave her space to repent of her fornication; and she repented not.*

The Lord in His love and mercy has no desire to judge any who profess to be the children of God through faith and repentance. Clearly, in the history of the Roman church, now over 1400 years since its inception, every opportunity to repent has been given to those who follow the teachings of Thyatira. Sadly, in the spirit of rebellion they have not and will not repent. Hence, the spirit of corruption and evil in the church continues to increase, even to this day. Accordingly, a fearful day of judgment awaits her (Revelation 18:8).

> **v. 22.** *Behold, I will cast her into a bed, and them that commit adultery with her into great tribulation, except they repent of their deeds.*

Those who practise the corrupting influences of Jezebel in the church will be cast into a bed of affliction (*not a bed of pleasure, comfort, and rest*), together with all who adhere to her evil teachings and practices, and commit adultery with her. The destiny of those born and brought up in the evil environment, who have imbibed and practise Jezebel's teachings, will be the same as for Jezebel herself, i.e., hell, the lake of fire, Gehenna. Spiritual adultery refers to those who have illicit commerce with the world, also those who wilfully meddled with evil things, who by their actions defiled themselves. But God, as ever, is merciful, and while such souls live, He gives them the opportunity to repent, otherwise they will experience great tribulation, and their destiny will be Gehenna.

> **v. 23.** *And I will kill her children with death; and all the churches shall know that I am He which searches the reins and hearts: and I will give unto every one of you according to your works.*

The Lord warned the church of Thyatira that all their converts and adherents to evil practices will suffer eternal death, unless they repent.

The noun *reins*, in Greek means *kidneys*, but its use here: *searches the reins*, implies that the Lord would have us to be aware of the fact that He knows our innermost mind, thoughts, and feelings, which He will test from time to time. *I will give unto every one of you according to your works.* This clause implies that all will appear for judgment before Christ (2 Corinthians 5:10). For the Christian, it will be the seat of manifestation (*Gk. bema*), to receive awards according our works and deeds done in the body, and then to enjoy eternal bliss in heaven with our precious Lord and Saviour, Jesus Christ. But for the unsaved, it will be to appear (*stand*) before the Great White Throne to be judged and condemned for their unbelief and ungodly works, and then be cast into Gehenna for ever, (Revelation 20:11-15).

> **v. 24.** *But unto you I say, and unto the rest in Thyatira, as many as have not this doctrine, and which have not known the depths of Satan, as they speak; I will put upon you none other burden.*

For the first time our attention is drawn to a faithful remnant, albeit small, but very faithful in refusing the current teaching of the day. They would not hold nor teach the evil doctrine which sanctions committing fornication and eating things offered to idols etc. etc.; rather, they were prepared to suffer the consequence of standing apart from the worldliness and corruption of the church. Thus, a remnant had been preserved from knowing the depths of Satan by a manifest purpose to walk the path of Truth and Holiness (Psalm 1:1-3). The Lord honoured their faithfulness and preserved them from further stress and anxiety.

> **v. 25.** *But that which ye have already hold fast till I come.*

With the forces of evil around them, not only from the world, but more particularly from the professing church, they require every bit of encouragement to hold fast. The saints had the precious truths of Christ and His church; they had the sure and certain hope of their salvation; they had the indwelling of God's Holy Spirit; above all, they treasured their union as one with Christ their risen Head; these are the things they were to hold fast. They had a little strength, as did the church of Philadelphia, and the acknowledgement of this fact would encourage them to lean more heavily on the strength of the Lord from day to day, and to hold fast until the Lord comes. Here, the expression: *till I come*, refers to His coming with power and great glory with His saints.

vv. 26–29. The order of the injunctions given at the end of this letter and to the following three is different from what we have in the first three. The final appeal given in the letters to the first three churches was: *He that hath an ear, let him hear what the Spirit saith unto the churches*, and comes before the promised blessings. The blessings differ from each other, but are commensurate with the prime subject of the respective letters. However, in the last four letters we notice that the promised blessings are given before the call to: *hear what the Spirit saith unto the churches*. The reason for the different format is this; in the letters to the first three churches, the call to hear was addressed to all in the church, whereas in the last four letters, the call: *He that hath an ear, let him hear what the Spirit saith unto the churches*, was addressed to the overcomer only, for none is expected to hear what the Spirit saith, save the overcomer.

> **v. 26.** *And he that overcometh, and keepeth My works unto the end, to him will I give power over the nations.*

This verse assures us that the redeemed saints who overcome the power and influences of Satan will, together with Christ, exercise authority over the nations throughout the Millennial reign of Christ. The reason for this promise of God being made to the overcomer in the church of

Thyatira is that from the coming-in of Christendom in the 7th Century, the church has sought to have dominion over the nations of the world. The Lord has purposed that the influence and power of the church will disappear into oblivion. The works of the Lord relate to all that the saints do in their path of service for the Master. These are in stark contrast to the works of Jezebel, as detailed in verse 20. Persevering in the Lord's work to the end refers either to the end of one's Christian's life on earth, or to the time of the coming of the Lord for His own.

v. 27. *And he shall rule them with a rod of iron; as the vessels of a potter shall they be broken to shivers* (pieces)*; even as I received of My Father.*

Here we are told that it will be Christ, together with the overcomer, who will, with divine authority and supremacy, shepherd the nations with a rod of iron. Like a clay pot broken into shivers (pieces), so will the nations be void of unified strength (Psalm 2:9); for none will rise up against the Lord of Glory.

v. 28. *And I will give him the morning star.*

The brightest celestial body which may be seen in the sky after sunset is Venus. Venus is also the brightest star in the sky before sunrise. Accordingly, Venus is known by expert astronomers as the evening and morning star. However, it is not Venus which is referred to here by John and also by Peter in his second epistle, chapter 1:19. Indeed, the Lord Jesus rightly refers to Himself as: *the Bright and Morning Star*, in chapter 22:16.

There was a profound and divine reason why the Spirit of God drew the attention of the saints of this church to, *the Morning Star*. They had already venerated and elevated in their hearts and minds the corrupt woman Jezebel, so displacing Christ as their guiding light. All who had not imbibed the evil doctrine, to them alone would be given, *the Morning Star;* Christ Himself. For the Christian, we are awaiting the coming of the Bright and Morning Star, the Lord Jesus who, when He comes will rapture us to heaven to begin the eternal day of glory; glory which shall envelop us throughout the golden ages of eternity. The Morning Star will be unseen by the unregenerate world, which will be asleep in the moral and spiritual darkness of sin.

The poet wrote:

> *The night is far spent, the day is at hand,*
> *No sign to be looked for, the Star's in the sky.*
> *Rejoice then, ye saints, 'tis your Lord's own command;*
> *Rejoice, for the coming of Jesus draws nigh.*
>
> T. Kelly

Verse 29 is addressed to the individual hearer alone. It is important to have the assurance that what one hears is of the Spirit of God, and to act accordingly.

Chapter 3

Letter to **Sardis** 1-6

> **v. 1.** *And unto the angel of the church in Sardis write; These things saith He that hath the seven Spirits of God, and the seven stars; I know thy works, that thou hast a name that thou livest, and art dead.*

Sardis means a remnant, incomplete, of the flesh, and represents the church from the period of the Reformation to the present time and beyond. A mixture of the true and false church. If Thyatira represented the harshness of Popery in the dark ages, Sardis represents Protestantism and complacency, which followed the Reformation in the 16th Century.

He that hath the seven spirits; is a statement already made in chapter 1 verse 4. It occurs again in chapters 4:5 and 5:6. However, we know there are not seven Spirits of God, but One, as we read in Ephesians 4:4. The statement is a confirmation of the complete and diversified attributes and actions of the Holy Spirit. A definition of this statement is found in Isaiah 11:2, where we read of the seven attributes of the Spirit of God. The attributes will continue to be exercised by the Lord whenever the occasion demands, confirming that we have the assurance of the Lord's intercession for every situation which may arise in our walk and service for Him.

The seven stars. We have already noted that the seven stars are the seven angels of the seven churches (chapter 1:20). Here in the letter to Sardis we observe that the stars are not in His right hand as they are in chapter 1:16, indicating strength, honour, and security; nor are they on (not 'in' as in the KJV) His right hand as in chapter 1:20, for the purpose of testimony and service; but He simply has them as His possession, to guide, employ, and control as He wills.

I know thy works, that thou hast a name that thou livest, and art dead. The Lord knew full well the kind of works of which the church at Sardis was so proud; for which they were known by name. But they were not the works of the Holy Spirit, rather of the flesh and in the spirit of Protestantism. As mentioned earlier, the Reformation was the result of the energy and movement of the Spirit of God in the hearts of men such as Martin Luther *et al.*; but Protestantism, of which Sardis was a protagonist, was the work of Satan, designed to destroy a unique work of God.

Sadly, Sardis, coupled with the trappings of the Roman church, was now under the control of the world. With government aid they built material churches, rather than establishing assemblies of God's people and spreading the Gospel of the Grace of God. In Christendom as a whole, the spirit of Sardis is seen in practice with the appointment by man, of bishops, deacons, clergy, etc., some of whom are appointed by the government of the day, a government which is Godless. Yes, the church had a name of which it was proud (*full of moral vanity*), it existed, but it was spiritually cold and void of divine life, dead.

> **v. 2.** *Be watchful, and strengthen the things which remain, that are ready to die: for I have not found thy works perfect before God.*

It was because the church at Sardis had not been watchful, that false teachers, with their close alliance with the Roman Catholic church, had come in and set aside the former godly works and divine teachings which sprang from the Reformation. The works of Martin Luther, *et al.* were for the glory of God. They were therefore exhorted to strengthen, apply, teach, and cherish the truths of Holy Scripture which they had learnt, and not allow them to be forgotten and die *(disappear from their hearts, minds and vocabulary)*.

I have not found thy works perfect (complete) *before God.* The inference here is that the church at Sardis clung to the Satanic trappings of the Roman church, when the Reformation movement had insisted on a complete separation from its false teachings and practices. Sadly, the church at Sardis did not sever its links with the Roman church, so any work done in Sardis would not have been complete or acceptable to God. Such work would have been done under the control of the Roman church.

v. 3. *Remember therefore how thou hast received and heard, and hold fast, and repent. If therefore thou shalt not watch, I will come on thee as a thief, and thou shalt not know what hour I will come upon thee.*

The saints at Sardis were to remember the Truths of Scripture which were brought to light by faithful servants of the Lord at the Reformation. Such truths as the gospel of the Grace of God; the salvation of souls; that a person is saved by faith alone; that a saved soul cannot ever be lost; the hope of the church; these truths and many others should have been cherished and promulgated by the church. Sadly, they had let such precious truths slip out of their hearts, vocabulary, ministry, and practice. They were now to call such truths to mind, repent of their failure, and daily be ready for when the Lord comes. But if they did not repent and watch, it would be a confirmation that such individuals were not Christians, and therefore have no reason to watch. Instead, the day of the Lord will come upon them as a thief in the night, unexpectedly (1 Thessalonians 5:2-3).

> **v. 4.** *Thou hast a few names even in Sardis which have not defiled their garments: and they shall walk with Me in white: for they are worthy.*

The statement, *a few names*, implies that there was a remnant in Sardis who were faithful to their heavenly calling. Such were quite separate from the majority who had defiled their garments (had proved to be unsaved) with regard to their walk and testimony, thereby confirming they were outside the family of God. The few, on the other hand, were those who desired no standing in the world, they gladly would remain unknown, even as out-casts of society; but they were known personally by the Shepherd who calleth His own sheep by name. The Lord said that the faithful few shall walk with Him in white in the coming day of glory, in garments made white in the blood of the Lamb. The Lord will declare them worthy to appear with Him in white because of their righteous works and faithfulness in service and testimony on earth.

> **v. 5.** *He that overcometh, the same shall be clothed in white raiment; and I will not blot out his name out of the Book of Life, but I will confess his name before My Father, and before His angels.*

An overcomer is a Christian believer who has not been defiled by the corrupting influences of the world; who has kept himself clean by the daily washing of the Water of the Word; such will be clothed in white raiment. There are four distinct occasions in this book where we have mentioned, white clothes/raiment. Here in chapter 3, verse five. Then again in chapter 6:11, where white robes were given to the martyred, faithful remnant of the Jews. In chapter 7, verses 9, 13 and 14; we have a company of all nations, kindreds, people, and tongues, which had come through: *great tribulation;* this company is not the church, nor is it the faithful Jewish remnant, but a mixed multitude faithful to the Lord, who have washed their robes and made them white in the blood of the Lamb. The last mention of white robes is found chapter 19, verses 8 and 14. The occasion referred to in verse 8 is the marriage of the Lamb to the Bride of Christ, the church. But in verse 14 the company is comprised of Old and New Testament saints – previously raptured to heaven – coming with the Lord in power and great glory; being the fulfilment of Enoch's prophecy which was made nearly 4,000 years earlier, but wondrously recorded by the Spirit of God in Jude's epistle, verse 14. The Holy Spirit's interpretation of the statements, fine linen, clean and white, white raiment is: *the righteousnesses of the saints.*

So, the Lord confirms He will not blot out the names of the overcomers from the Book of Life, which is the record of Christian profession to be made known personally to each believer before the Judgment Seat *(Gk. Bema)* of Christ. All whose names are in the Book of Life will be commended to His Father, and made known to His angels. We must never under-estimate the great honour which the Lord will bestow upon all who have fought a good fight, finished the path of testimony, and kept the faith.

The references to the *Book of Life,* in Psalm 69:28; and to *the Book,* in Psalm 139:16; also, to the *Book of Life,* here in Revelation 3:5; all relate to the record of one's service Godward, for which one will be answerable to God and rewarded accordingly (2 Corinthians 5:10). The first Biblical reference we have of a Book of Life *(names)* held by God, is in Exodus 32:32. Such was the commitment, devotion, confidence, honour and reverence Moses had toward both Almighty God and for Israel as a nation that he was prepared to sacrifice the record of his life, by having his name erased from God's Book of Life, and thereby ensure that by the mercy of God Israel would be saved.

All who complete their path of faith for the glory and honour of God, the Lord will delight to confess their names before His Father and the angelic host of heaven; confirming their unassailable right to: *an inheritance incorruptible, and undefiled, and that fadeth not away, reserved in heaven* (1 Peter 1:4).

> **v. 6.** *He that hath an ear, let him hear what the Spirit saith unto the churches.*

This injunction is directed to the overcomer. All who continue indifferent to the Spirit's call are not expected to hear His voice.

Letter to **Philadelphia** 7-13

> **v. 7.** *To the angel of the church in Philadelphia write; These things saith He that is Holy, He that is true, He that hath the key of David, He that openeth, and no man shutteth; and shutteth, and no man openeth.*

Philadelphia means brotherly love. The seeds of this church were sown during the first century, the results of which have continued to the present day and will continue until the Lord comes to call His Bride away to glory. Following the Reformation in the 16th Century when Martin Luther and others promulgated the truth of God's order for man's salvation, there was a further spiritual awakening in the 18th Century, when true evangelical, missionary movements occurred throughout the world, and continue to this day.

This is the only church of the seven, to which the Lord addresses Himself as the: *Holy and the True*. These divine titles are unique to the

Lord Himself. The Lord Jesus was Holy in His person, His character, His words, His thoughts, His actions, and His purposes. He was also the Truth. In John 14:6, the Lord Jesus says of Himself: *I am the way, the truth, and the life;* and in John 15:1; He says: *I am the true vine.* Divine perfection marked that blessed Person in every step of His pathway on earth.

Philadelphia is the second of only two of the seven churches, Smyrna being the other, against which the Lord had no complaints of impropriety or unfaithfulness; there was just commendation and promised blessings. Smyrna suffered severe persecution, but Philadelphia had little strength; both were faithful to their holy calling of God (2 Timothy 1:9).

He that hath the key of David. David was the first divinely appointed king of the kingdom of Israel, and was a type of the future and final King of the nation, the Lord Jesus Christ, the Messiah. The Lord, at His first coming as the promised Messiah, was rejected and cast out, but when He comes again, with power and great glory as King of kings and Lord of lords, He will be acknowledged and accepted by the nation, which will turn to God in a day (Romans 11:26). As David exercised power and authority, opening and shutting at will, so our Lord does more perfectly today. This is why here He calls attention to His administrative power and authority. The statement: *key of David,* comes from the figure we have in Isaiah 22:22, relating to Shebna, who misappropriated the treasures of the House of the Lord for his own aggrandisement, having hewn out for himself an ornate sepulchre and siting it in a prominent rock, presumably as an egotistic monument. But God destroyed Shebna and his achievements and appointed in his place, Eliakim (type of the Lord Jesus) who governed the land with justice and equity. The key of the house of David was laid upon his shoulder *(full responsibility),* so when he opened, no one shut, and when he shut, no man opened. Thus, the Lord uses the key of David today according to His sovereign will.

> **v. 8.** *I know thy works: behold, I have set before thee an open door, and no man can shut it; for thou hast a little strength, and hast kept My word, and hast not denied My name.*

The Lord was cognisant of, and treasured the integrity of their labours of love in His name. The door in the type is the entry to works *(divine service),* which the Lord directs under His sovereign authority. It is only as the Lord opens doors in any part of the world that a servant will be divinely exercised, and led to take up a service in His name. No man on earth is able to open doors for the Lord's service; it is the divine prerogative of the Lord Himself. If the Lord has not opened a door in a given area, any presumed service there will prove fruitless. Furthermore, only the Lord in the exercise of His sovereign authority can shut a door which He had previously opened for His service.

The church was marked by three divine features. They had a little strength *(power)*; they had kept sacred His Word *(testimony)*, and had not denied His name *(faithfulness).* The Philadelphian church knew the importance of recognising their littleness and weakness. They were unknown in the world, and had no part in it, and as the Lord Jesus said of His disciples in His unique, high priestly prayer: *they are not of the world, even as I am not of the world* (John 17:14). As with the apostle Paul, their spiritual strength lay in the acknowledgement of their weakness and littleness. Paul said that it was when he owned his personal, spiritual weakness, that he became strong in the Lord (2 Corinthians 12:10). Thus, we should understand that any attempt to serve the Lord in our own strength will come to naught.

The saints had faithfully kept alive and treasured in their hearts, the inviolable preciousness of God's Word, it was daily meat and drink to their souls. They clearly believed that: *All Scripture is given by inspiration of God, and is profitable for doctrine, for reproof, for correction, for instruction in righteousness: that the man of God may be perfect, thoroughly furnished unto all good works* (2 Timothy 3:16-17). What a wonderful example these Philadelphian saints set before us!

Furthermore, the saints had not denied the Lord's Name, for they knew something of its uniqueness and power. They knew and believed that the salvation of a soul can be in no other Name than the: *Lord Jesus Christ*. God's Word declares that: *there is none other Name under heaven given among men, whereby we must be saved* (Acts 4:12).

The power of the Name of Jesus was seen in the healing of the man who was born a cripple (Acts 3:3-9). Every day he sat at the gate of the Temple which is called Beautiful and asked for alms, which he did of Peter and John when they were about to go into the Temple. But Peter and John did not want to contribute to the continuance of the man's crippled state, but rather do something to bring about a glorious revolution in his life. Peter and John said to the man: *Look on us*, then Peter said: *Silver and gold, have I none; but such as I have give I unto thee: In the Name of Jesus Christ of Nazareth rise up and walk*. The man was immediately healed, rising up, walking, and leaping, and praising God.

A day is coming, when: *At the Name of Jesus every knee should bow, of things in heaven, and things in earth, and things under the earth; and ... every tongue should confess that Jesus Christ is Lord, to the glory of God the Father* (Philippians 2:10-11).

> **v. 9.** *Behold, I will make them of the synagogue of Satan, which say they are Jews, and are not, but do lie; behold, I will make them to come and worship before thy feet, and to know that I have loved thee.*

CHAPTER 3

The synagogue of Satan is the gathering place of all deceivers who falsely say they are Jews, and claim entitlement to a part of Israel's inheritance. It is clear the Philadelphian saints did not accommodate them, nor give them opportunity to poison the hearts and consciences of the saints; their presence rightly occasioned deep exercise of heart and spiritual judgment. The Lord Jesus was a Jew, and all believing Jews now acknowledge the Lord Jesus Christ, not only as the rejected Messiah of Israel, but also as the Saviour of the world, the: *King of kings, and Lord of lords. Behold, I will make them to come and worship before thy feet, and to know that I have loved thee.* In a coming day, the Lord is going to ensure that the enemies of the Lord and of His saints are made to acknowledge their error in rejecting Christ as Saviour; as recorded in Isaiah 60:14: *The sons also of them that afflicted thee shall come bending unto thee; and all they that despised thee shall bow themselves down at the soles of thy feet; and they shall call thee, The city of the Lord, the Zion of the Holy One of Israel.* This statement is confirmed in Philippians 2:10-11. The enemies of the Lord will realise they have missed out on being beneficiaries of the love of God and of the Lord Jesus Christ, and of having the assurance of eternal life in heaven, which is for all who repent of their sins and believe the Lord Jesus to be the Saviour of the world.

> **v. 10.** *Because thou hast kept the word of My patience I also will keep thee from the hour of temptation* (trial), *which shall come upon all the world, to try them that dwell upon the earth.*

The word of My patience; has reference to the Lord's yearning to come to the clouds, and call to Himself all the redeemed to be with Him in heaven. Our Lord will then continue to patiently wait for the word from His Father to come with ten thousand times ten thousands, and thousands of thousands of His saints, with power and great glory (Jude

14) to reign over the earth in righteousness for 1,000 years (Revelation 20:6). This will be the time when His enemies will be made His footstool (Psalm 110:1; and Hebrews 1:13).

I also will keep thee from the hour of trial, which shall come upon all the world, to try them that dwell upon the earth. This statement is the clearest assurance we have in Scripture that the Church will not be on earth during the hour of trial which will affect the entire world, as detailed in chapters 6–18 of this book. So, while the hour of trial will impact on all nations of the earth for the seven-year period, it will be more severe for the land of Israel. The last 3.5 years of the seven-year period (Daniel 9:27), are defined by the Lord Jesus as a time of: *great tribulation* (Matthew 24:21. Such is spoken of by Jeremiah the prophet as: *the time of Jacob's trouble* (Jeremiah 30:7); and in Daniel 12:1: *a time of trouble.* The hour of such trials will see the governmental judgments of Almighty God on all earth dwellers, Jew and Gentile alike. Our heavenly calling makes us strangers and pilgrims on earth, not earth dwellers, for our citizenship is in heaven (Philippians 3:20; JND. N.T.). The hymn writer shares his thoughts:

> *We have a home above, from sin and sorrow free;*
> *A mansion which eternal love, prepared our rest to be.*
>
> Henry Bennett

For us to fully grasp the significance and sequence of events referred to above, we need to understand the meaning of the message the angel Gabriel gave to Daniel (Daniel 9). Gabriel's message was: *Seventy weeks* (of years) *are determined upon thy people and upon thy holy city, to finish the transgression, and to make an end of sins, and to make reconciliation for iniquity, and to bring in everlasting righteousness, and to seal up the vision and prophecy, and to anoint the most Holy (Daniel 9:24).* Before proceeding further, do please read Daniel 9:24-27.

CHAPTER 3

The 70 weeks of years = 490 years which are divided into 3 periods. The first period of seven weeks of years = 49 years, as detailed in Daniel 9:25, began with the rebuilding of Jerusalem, the Temple and the wall of the city; carried out in troublesome times and completed in the times of Ezra and Nehemiah. Then began the second period of 62 weeks of years = 434 years, which continued to the time of the cutting off of the Messiah, i.e. the rejection of the Lord Jesus by the nation of Israel and the world.

We may justly ask ourselves, when was the moment the Lord Jesus was cut off? (Daniel 9:26). Let us remember that when He was arrested in the garden of Gethsemane (Matthew 26:57), He retained His power and right to heal the ear of Malchus, a servant of the high priest. He had right to appeal to His Father to forgive all involved in His crucifixion; He also could assure the penitent thief on the cross of a place in the paradise of God. And while our Lord was alive on the Cross, He still had the right to appeal to His Father for more than twelve legions of angels to deliver Him; but He would not, for His yearning was that the Scriptures might be fulfilled (Matthew 26:53-54). At the end of the three hours of darkness, when He committed His spirit into the hands of His Father (Luke 23:46), He ended His life of testimony on earth. Then, was the actual moment of His, *cutting off* from the world. The next time the unregenerate world sees the Lord Jesus will be when He comes with power and great glory (Matthew 24:30).

The hymn writer has put it so beautifully:

> *Then, finished all, in meekness;*
> *Thou, to Thy Father's hand;*
> *Perfect Thy strength in weakness;*
> *Thy spirit didst commend.*
>
> J. N. Darby

To finish the transgression, and to make an end of sins, and to make reconciliation for iniquity, and to bring in everlasting righteousness, and to seal up the vision and prophecy, and to anoint the most Holy (Daniel 9:24). The fulfilment of this part of the prophecy of Daniel will coincide with the second coming of the Lord Jesus to this earth. His coming will be with power and great glory, and with tens of thousands of His saints. All this, in accord with the prophecy of Enoch, which is recorded in Jude, verse 14. He will come to establish His kingdom and reign for a thousand years (Revelation 20:6). The Lord Jesus will then establish His people, the entire nation of Israel, in their Promised Land.

From the moment the Lord Jesus was cut off, there is an unspecified period of time before the beginning of the last week of years. This unspecified period is the present day of God's Grace to the world, when the Gospel of the Grace of God is daily preached that souls may repent and believe in the Lord Jesus Christ as the Saviour of the world. This day of God's Grace will end with the rapture of the saints of God to heaven (1 Thessalonians 4:16-17). Then, the Gospel of the Grace of God will cease to be preached; instead, the Gospel of the Kingdom (Millennial Kingdom) will be preached in all the world (Matthew 24:14). The period of time between the rapture of the church to heaven and the beginning of the hour of trial lasting seven years is neither given nor implied. Albeit, spiritual intuition tells one that there will be an unspecified lapse of time before the beginning of the tribulation period.

Thus, at a moment in God's time, for the time is not revealed, the last week of Daniel's 70 weeks of years will begin. A specific period of 7 years when the world at large will experience cataclysmic events as God pours out His governmental judgments upon the nations. The 7-year period, being the last in Gabriel's message to Daniel, will be divided into two periods of 3.5 years. The Lord Jesus Himself called the last period of 3.5 years, a time of: *great tribulation* (Matthew 24:21), which will have a particular and intensive impact on the land of Israel; albeit, the entire world will continue to suffer until the Lord God's just judgments are exhausted. So horrendous will the governmental judgments of God be, that Scripture records: A*nd except those days should be shortened, there should no flesh be saved: but for the elect's sake* (faithful remnant of Israel) *those days shall be shortened* (Matthew 24:22).

v. 11. *I come quickly: hold that fast which thou hast, that no man take thy crown.*

I come quickly. A more accurate translation from the Greek text is: *I am coming quickly*, implying that as Christians we should daily live our lives in the expectation of the Lord coming to the clouds to call us to glory at any moment. We understand the statement: *I am coming quickly,* is in relation to God's time, not man's time which is measured by the 24-hour day. God's time is eternity where time does not exist. Peter wrote about heaven in his second epistle: *Beloved, be not ignorant of this one thing, that one day is with the Lord as a thousand years, and a thousand years as one day (2 Peter 3:8).*

However, when the Scriptures speak of specific events occurring on earth – not heaven – and the lapse of time is given, we should understand the time to be earth's time, either literal or figurative. So, when the Lord says: *I am coming quickly,* we understand it to mean at any time.

Hold that fast which thou hast. What exactly was it the saints were exhorted to hold fast? Among the many things they were to hold fast was the truth of their salvation; that they have eternal life and shall not come into condemnation; that they have passed from death unto life. They were to hold fast to the hope of the Lord's coming to rapture them away home to glory; for they were already partakers of the divine nature. They were to treasure and testify to their standing in Christ; that they have an inheritance which fadeth not away, reserved in heaven; and to freely acknowledge they are beneficiaries of all the spiritual blessings in the heavenlies in Christ, which is the highest of blessings God vouchsafes (Ephesians 1:3).

It is the constant endeavour of Satan to rob the saints of the joy of these, and so many other blessings; they are, therefore, exhorted to value and hold fast all the heavenly treasures.

That no man take thy crown. The crown referred to here is not a physical article but an award of honour which God will bestow upon individual saints, being a divine approbation in respect of one's walk, work, service, testimony, and faithfulness in their particular calling of God. However, visions John had of events in the heavens would confirm that actual crowns will be seen on the heads of many, and some of the crowns will be golden, a sign of royal dignity and the divine righteousness of the Lord Jesus Himself (Revelation 14:14). In chapter 4:4; the twenty and four elders have on their heads, crowns of gold, and in verse 10 we read that they: *cast their crowns before the Throne, saying: Thou art worthy, O Lord, to receive glory and honour, and power: for Thou hast created all things, and for Thy pleasure they are and were created.* The elders lay down their given glory (golden crowns), and render to the Lord of all creation appropriate and supreme glory in praise, worship, and thanksgiving.

> **v. 12.** *Him that overcometh will I make a pillar in the Temple of My God, and he shall go no more out: and I will write upon him the name of My God, and the name of the city of My God, which is new Jerusalem, which cometh down out of heaven from My God: and I will write upon him My new name.*

The overcomer, although marked by weakness in this church, is one who adheres to the truth, as it is in Jesus, and in spite of difficulties, holds fast and perseveres in the path of faith, treasuring in his heart the precious Name of Jesus. Notwithstanding the church's weakness, and in answer to their faithfulness, the Lord says: *Him that overcometh will I make a pillar in the Temple of My God* (verse 12). Their weakness on earth will become pillars of strength in heaven, being the holy sanctuary of God from which they will no more go out, for everything in heaven is marked by permanency, nothing is transient. The use of the term: *Temple of My God*, implies we shall be worshippers of God throughout eternity.

And I will write upon him the name of My God, and the name of the city of My God, which is new Jerusalem, which cometh down out of heaven from My God: and I will write upon him My new name. All the redeemed in heaven will bear the name of our Saviour God as his possession, and be secure for all eternity. Being marked by the name of the city of God will be a confirmation of our citizenship, and the right to be in heaven. Furthermore, we shall be marked by the new name of our blessed Saviour, a testimony of our indissoluble union with Him.

v. 13. *He that hath an ear, let him hear what the Spirit saith unto the churches.*

Again, the call to hear what the Spirit saith to the churches is to redeemed souls.

Letter to **Laodicea** 14 - 22

v. 14. *And unto the angel of the church of the Laodiceans write; These things saith the Amen, the faithful and true witness, the beginning of the creation of God.*

Laodicea means the opinion and rights of the people shall rule. In the church, the authority of the Word of God was disregarded, coupled with a lukewarmness toward God and the Lord Jesus Christ. The letter is not a history of what had been accomplished, but a warning of what will be the testimony of a worldly, unfaithful church. The letter is clearly prophetic, relating what the church will become, i.e., lukewarm.

Although the roots of the failure of this church lay in Ephesus, which had lost her first love for Christ, the church's total, spiritual breakdown was observed by the all-seeing eyes of One who, as a flame of fire, was walking in the midst of the seven candlesticks *(churches)*. Although there have been features of the Laodicean church down through the centuries, the final corrupt state has yet to be reached. When that time comes, the church's testimony will be so distasteful to the Lord Jesus, He will spue it out of His mouth.

These things saith the Amen. The Lord would vindicate His Own Name by addressing Himself as the Amen. One meaning of this title is to be found in 2 Corinthians 1:20: *For all the promises of God in Him* (Christ), *are yea, and in Him Amen, unto the glory of God by us.* In other words, the Lord Jesus Christ rules out any need to furnish evidence to ratify His origin and deity; for He is the beginning and ending of all things; and it is by Him alone that all things subsist and have their being. *Amen,* means faithful and true witness; it is a positive statement, a confirmation of the veracity of all God has both said and done through Christ.

The faithful and true witness. The accolade is unique to the Lord Jesus. It could not be said nor will it be said of any other person from Adam down to the present day. From the manger to the Cross, every thought, word, and step of the Lord Jesus was in full alignment with the mind and will of God. The unimpeachable evidence that our Lord was and is the faithful and true witness is that He is in heaven, having been raised from among the dead by the glory of the Father, and exalted to the right hand of the greatness on high. When all else failed, He was the faithful witness of God's love, mercy, and grace, and of the counsels of God regarding the destiny of man.

The beginning of the creation of God. Not only was our Lord present at the very beginning of this creation, for He said: *Let us make man* (Genesis 1:26), He is also the beginning of all that God has done and will yet do. He is also the beginning and first-fruit of the New Creation of man: *If any man be in Christ, he is a new creation: old things are passed away; behold, all things are become new* (2 Corinthians 5:17).

We conclude, therefore, that Christ being the beginning of the creation of God, all that follows must take character from Him. Certainly, in the new heaven and earth, nothing will appear that does not reflect the glorious, divine attributes of Christ (Revelation 21:23).

> **vv. 15-16.** *I know thy works, that thou art neither cold nor hot: I would that thou wert cold or hot. So then because thou art lukewarm, and neither cold nor hot, I will spue thee out of My mouth.*

Lukewarmness in every sphere of life on earth is naturally distasteful and unpleasant to man, but more especially so to the Lord Jesus when it is a matter of our love and commitment to Him in our faith, walk and service. The Lord was acutely aware of the insincerity of the works of the Laodicean church because it left a bitter taste in His mouth. The general testimony of the Laodicean church was that they were half-hearted and lukewarm in whatever they supposedly did for the Lord. If their service had been defined as hot, it would have indicated faithfulness, commitment, and truth. And if their disposition Godward had been classified as cold, it would have confirmed they were not fellow-workers in the service of God, and in all probability unsaved; in which case the mercy and grace of God would have continued to reach out to them that they might be saved. However, the church's commitment to the Lord was neither hot nor cold (neither one thing nor the other). Therefore, the Lord confirms that in His time He will spue it out of His mouth, and disown it as a testimony of God's love and grace to the world.

v. 17. *Because thou sayest, I am rich, and increased with goods, and have need of nothing; and knowest not that thou art wretched, and miserable, and poor, and blind, and naked.*

Without a sincere conviction of their sin, they unashamedly boasted about their material possessions. Being absorbed with the passions of the flesh, they were carnal; confirming they were void of spiritual wealth. The apostle Paul wrote: *to be carnally minded is death; but to be spiritually minded is life and peace. Because the carnal mind is enmity against God: for it is not subject to the law of God, neither indeed can be* (Romans 8:6-7). Notwithstanding the church's boasting of material prosperity, it was, in fact, spiritually poverty-stricken. John's use of five powerful negative adjectives defined their state as: *wretched, miserable, poor, blind, and naked.* This is the divine estimate of all who, like the Laodiceans, put their faith and trust in the wealth and hope of this world. The apostle Peter wrote, referring to the destiny of this present creation, together with all man's achievements: *The heavens shall pass away with a great noise, and the elements shall melt with fervent heat, the earth also and the works that are therein shall be burned up* (2 Peter 3:10). May our gracious Lord preserve us from putting our faith, hope, and confidence in things material, but rather to search out and treasure from the Scriptures the things: *God hath prepared for them that love Him … yea, the deep things of God* (1 Corinthians 2:9-10).

v. 18. *I counsel thee to buy of Me gold* (divine righteousness) *tried in the fire, that thou mayest be rich* (spiritually); *and white raiment* (practical righteousness), *that thou mayest be clothed* (adorned), *and that the shame of thy nakedness* (spiritual), *does not appear; and anoint thine eyes with eyesalve* (spiritual discernment), *that thou mayest see* (things by faith).

Divine righteousness had altogether slipped from their hearts and minds. The Laodicean saints neither appreciated the righteousness of God, which a Christian is made in Christ, nor practical righteousness, which should have been evident in them before the world. They were lovingly advised to commit themselves to works of righteousness which would require self-sacrifice and lowly submission to the chastening hand of the Lord (Hebrews 12:11). They would soon learn that the Lord alone has all the spiritual resources they require, and that He has fixed the terms on which He sells.

The prophet Isaiah wrote of God's free grace to the nations: *Ho, every one that thirsteth, come ye to the waters, and he that hath no money; come ye, buy, and eat; yea, come, buy wine and milk without money and without price* (Isaiah 55:1). Although the prophet's initial concern was for Israel, the broad scope of his language would imply that the nations of the world were included in his appeal.

With regard to the saints in Philadelphia, they found and secured all their spiritual resources in Christ, whereas the Laodiceans manifested a spirit of complacency, indifference, and self-sufficiency, hence the earnest appeal for them to come, buy, eat, and drink. In other words, they were to come to Christ in the spirit of repentance, dependence, and faith; surrender their wills to Him, feed upon the heavenly manna (Christ), and freely drink in the water of life (John 4:14).

The Lord yearned for the Laodicean saints to be spiritually rich in God. The apostle Paul writing to the saints at Corinth, wrote: *for ye know the grace of our Lord Jesus Christ, that, though He was rich, yet for your sakes He became poor, that ye through His poverty might be rich* (2 Corinthians 8:9). The abundance of the riches God has bestowed upon us is summed up in Paul's letter to the Ephesian saints: *the God and Father of our Lord Jesus Christ, who hath blessed us with all spiritual blessings in heavenly places in Christ* (Eph. 1:3).

We, being a new creation in Christ; born again as a child of God; adopted as a son of God; and indwelt by the Holy Spirit of God, have the possession and assurance of eternal life with Christ in heaven. We have an inheritance in Christ; we know we are going to be translated into His likeness, and being a member of the heavenly kingdom of priests will one day reign with Christ in His Millennial kingdom. These are just a few of the spiritual blessings which God, in His infinite love, has bestowed upon us. The saints of God are richer than the wealthiest man on earth; earthly riches are perishable, but ours are heavenly, spiritual, eternal, and divine.

Practical righteousness refers to daily walking, doing, speaking, and thinking all things in the spirit of humility; being in full alignment with the mind and will of God. Such features were lacking in the testimony of the Laodicean church. Accordingly, the Lord pronounces upon their nakedness, as being destitute of divine righteousness, and exhorts them to purchase white garments to cover their moral and spiritual nakedness. We know from Scripture that reference to white garments in Revelation 19:8 relates uniquely to the practical righteousnesses of saints, exercised in their path of testimony on earth.

Alas, there were members in the church not clothed with the righteousness of Christ, which must surely imply that such were not of the family of God.

Their spiritual condition was that they were poor, subjects of absolute penury, void of any vision of the Lord's glory, and lacking the capacity to spiritually discern Scripture truth. They were also destitute of divine riches, and blind as to the way of Salvation, in other words, unregenerate. However, they were exhorted: *anoint thine eyes with eyesalve, that thou mayest see.* Certainly, if they had put their faith and trust in the Lord Jesus, they would have received an unction from the Holy One (the indwelling of the Holy Spirit), which is the only way by which they could acquire eternal life, spiritual perception, and divine intelligence.

> **v. 19.** *As many as I love, I rebuke and chasten: be zealous therefore, and repent.*

The Lord's rebuke and chastening of those He loves confirms that the words were directed to the responsible element *(the angel)* of the Laodicean church. The faithful in that church who desired to be partakers of God's holiness would learn that: *no chastening for the present seemeth to be joyous, but grievous: nevertheless afterward it yieldeth the peaceable fruit of righteousness unto them which are exercised thereby* (Hebrews 12:11).

The Lord, as always in this day of grace, is merciful, giving opportunity for souls to repent. The Lord loves the souls of all, but not their sin, for sin must be cancelled out through repentance and faith in the Lord Jesus Christ who shed His precious blood to atone for their sins and the sin of the world. The chastening hand of the Lord is testimony to His great love for us and His desire to have us with Him: *Holy and without blame before Him in love* (Ephesians 1:4).

> **v. 20.** *Behold, I stand at the door, and knock: if any man hear My voice, and open the door; I will come in to him, and will sup with him, and he with Me.*

To the church of Philadelphia, the Lord had set before them an open door that they, like the Colossian saints, might freely speak of the mystery of Christ (Colossians 4:3), engaging their hearts with all that our blessed Saviour has done, having glorified His Father and opened the door of eternal Salvation to all who repent and believe. Sadly, the door of the church of Laodicea was closed; the Lord was outside knocking to come in. Laodicea was open to the world and all its vices, but closed to the Lord of glory. However, there were in the church those who belonged to the family of God, and it was to these saints, the Lord addressed His words. If they came out of the system, the Lord would come in unto them, and sup (commune) with them.

Godly and highly esteemed expositors of the Holy Scripture, the faithful fathers of yesteryear, taught that the time periods of the first three of the seven churches; Ephesus, Smyrna, and Pergamos, have long passed. Notwithstanding, it would be correct to say that features and characteristics which marked the first three churches are certainly found in the last four, Thyatira, Sardis, Philadelphia, and Laodicea. The spirit and character of Thyatira, Sardis, and Laodicea will continue to the great day of the Lord, when He will come with power and great glory with His saints to establish His Kingdom (Jude 14).

A special dispensation applies to the church of Philadelphia because, long before that great day, God will signal the end of this current day of His grace to the world by sending His Son, the Lord Jesus, to call and rapture away to glory all the redeemed (1 Thessalonians 4:16-17). Meanwhile, the error of Thyatira, with the Pope of Rome being recognised as the Universal bishop of the church, will continue unabated. Likewise, the character of the church of Sardis, being responsible for the spirit of Protestantism, which corrupted the work of the Reformation, together with the Laodicean church with its lukewarmness, will continue to the end of this age, which ends when the Lord Jesus comes with His saints to establish His millennial kingdom.

Today, the faithful saints of God see all around in Christendom the sad demise of a faithful church of God. The precious Scriptures are mis-interpreted, mis-applied, mis-used, and scurrilously amended to suit modern-day parlance. Furthermore, there is a manifest lack of reverence in many church gatherings. Such is the current character of the Laodicean church, which will continue to the end of this age; at a given point in time, the Lord will spue it out of His mouth.

I will come in to him, and will sup with him, and he with Me. It has ever been the yearning of the Lord Jesus to be in the company of His people and to spiritually feast with them (Matthew 18:20 & Luke 24:41-43). Today, we understand, experience, and treasure, the spiritual significance of these Scriptures when we: *continue steadfastly in the apostles' doctrine and fellowship, and in Breaking of Bread, and in prayers* (Acts 2:42).

> **v. 21.** *To him that overcometh will I grant to sit with Me in My throne, even as I also overcame, and am set down with My Father in His throne.*

The promise to the overcomer in Laodicea is distinct and significant. Instead of sitting down and having fellowship with the world, as did Lot when he sat in the gate of Sodom (Genesis 19:1), they were to overcome the forces of evil in their walk by taking their example from the Lord Jesus who overcame the powers of Satan and is now sat down in His Father's throne. Only then would they be reckoned overcomers and granted (in a coming day in heaven) to sit down with the Lord Jesus in His throne.

The overcomer is one who: *walketh not in the counsel of the ungodly, nor standeth in the way of sinners, nor sitteth in the seat of the scornful. But his delight is in the law of the Lord; and in His law doth he meditate day and night* (Psalm 1:1-2).

My throne, of which the Lord Jesus speaks, is His by right as King, to exercise royal dominion and power over all creation. The Lord Jesus is currently sitting patiently in His Father's throne, awaiting the command of His Father to come to the clouds, and call all the redeemed to Himself, to be with Him in heaven. The Lord will then continue His patient wait for the time when He will come again, and this time with all His saints with power and great glory to establish His Millennial kingdom. It will be then that we shall reign with Him; as Paul wrote to Timothy: *If we suffer, we shall also reign with Him* (2 Timothy 2:12), sitting with Him in His throne.

v. 22. *He that hath an ear, let him hear what the Spirit saith unto the churches.*

The voice of Satan has been heard over and over again down through the centuries; sadly, many have heeded his advice with hideous consequences. To each of the seven churches, the divine counsel given is to hear and respond to what the Holy Spirit says. The command to those who hear implies positive action to be taken which accords with the mind and will of God. Such will occasion the fulfilment of all God's promises through the Lord Jesus. The Lord Jesus has prepared a place for us in heaven, and has promised He will come to receive us unto Himself, that where He is (in heaven), there we may be also for all eternity. When that glorious moment comes, heaven will echo with the sound of praise from all the redeemed. (Revelation 1:5-6).

CHAPTER 3

Unto Him that loved (loves J.N.D.) *us, and washed us from our sins in His own blood, and hath made us kings* (a kingdom J.N.D.) *priests unto God and His Father; to Him be glory and dominion for ever and ever. Amen.*

Chapter 4

v. 1. *After this I looked, and, behold, a door was opened in heaven: and the first voice which I heard was as it were of a trumpet talking with me; which said, Come up hither, and I will shew thee things which must be hereafter.*

Chapters 4 & 5 introduce us to the preparation of events which shall be hereafter, in other words, what is still prophecy. John, having been caught up from earth to heaven, is to be regarded as representative of the church relative to all which follows in this book. The day of God's Grace to the world will have closed, and the saints will have been raptured to heaven and translated into the likeness of their glorified Lord (Philippians 3:20-21). It will be from heaven that the saints will observe the providential judgments of Almighty God upon the world at large. The mass of false Christian profession will continue until finally being rejected and spued out of the Lord's mouth. All that has been prophesied about God's judgments of the world and its inhabitants is about to be fulfilled.

After this I looked. John has been shown the history of the church from its inception *(Pentecost)*, to the conclusion of the Day of God's grace to the world. He is now shown the things which must be hereafter; that is, the time from the rapture of the saints to heaven to the coming of the Lord Jesus to establish His millennial kingdom.

CHAPTER 4

And, behold, a door was opened in heaven. The opened door will reveal that the saints are safe and secure in heaven. It will be through the open door that God will pour out His judgments upon the world. *And the first voice which I heard was as it were of a trumpet talking with me.* The voice John heard was the voice he first heard when on earth (chapter 1:10), but when he is caught up to heaven he hears and understands things from heaven's point of view.

Today, the saints of God should ever live in the spirit of being seated spiritually with Christ in heaven (Ephesians 2:6), that in all things we might have the mind of heaven. When the trumpet sounded in the camp of Israel throughout their wilderness journeys (Exodus 19:19 *et al.*), it would have been heard above all the sounds of the camp. Today, our ear should be tuned to hear what the Lord has to say to us, above the cacophony of this world's activities.

Which said, Come up hither, and I will shew thee things which must be hereafter. John, being in heaven, was to look at things as from heaven, and that is how the saints of God today should view all things spiritual, to ensure they will arrive at a divine understanding of God's purpose and counsel. *The things which must be hereafter,* have reference to the time following the rapture of the church to heaven, when the judgments of Almighty God will be expended upon the nations of the earth (Chapters 6-20).

> **v. 2.** *And immediately I was in the spirit: and, behold, a throne was set in heaven, and one sat on the throne.*

At this point, John was wholly taken over by the Spirit of God, and in this disposition of soul was receptive to all he sees and hears from the throne of God. For the saints of God today to have the certainty of the mind of God on any matter, it is absolutely essential for them to be wholly taken over by the Spirit of God. *A throne was set in heaven, and one sat on the throne.* The throne will symbolise the universal government of Almighty God, confirming that judgments issuing from it will be final and not questioned, amended, or rescinded.

v. 3. *And He that sat was to look upon like a jasper and a sardine stone: and there was a rainbow round about the throne, in sight like unto an emerald.*

The One sitting upon the throne is not named nor seen as a person, but He is described as being like a jasper and a sardius stone. It is indeed God Himself who cannot be looked upon (Exodus 33:20), but permits His glory to be seen by faith in heaven. So, His unique, all-various glories are seen in the distinctive effulgence which emanates from the jasper and sardius stones. Jasper is a form of quartz, a variety of chalcedony; the purest and finest form of diamond. When its light is passed through a prism, its composition reveals all the colours of the rainbow, symbolising the multi-various attributes of God in Christ. Jasper was the last precious stone in the breastplate, signifying that all the glorious attributes of Jehovah were exercised to bring the nation of Israel safely into the promised Land (Exodus 3:8). While the nation has not yet taken possession of the Land, the promise of Jehovah will be fulfilled throughout the Millennial reign of Christ, when: *every man shall sit under his vine and under his fig tree* (Micah 4:4).

Sardius, also known as Ruby, was the first gem-stone in the first row of the breastplate (Exodus 28:17). Thus, whenever Aaron wore the breastplate over his garments of glory and beauty, Israel were reminded that they were redeemed by blood, the blood of an innocent lamb. Today, we can say, we have been redeemed to God by the precious blood of Christ.

CHAPTER 4

And there was a rainbow round about the throne. The rainbow has ever been a symbol of the promises of God, as in the case of God's promise to Noah following the flood (Genesis 8:21-22). The rainbows which we occasionally see in the sky are in arc-form with their ends touching the earth or sea. The rainbow John sees is a complete circle enveloping the throne of God, thereby confirming that God's promises are eternal. All the activity which the saints will see around the throne in heaven will have eternal consequences, and be for the glory of God and His Son, Jesus Christ, with the saints who will forever rest complacent in His love.

In sight like unto an emerald. Emerald is a clear green colour. Of all the colours in God's creation; green is the most restful to the eye. Green is also the colour which, in Scripture, symbolises health, prosperity and rest. When we walk with the Lord in accord with His Word He will lead us to lie down in green pastures, beside still waters (Psalm 23:2), an environment of rest and tranquillity. Before the Lord Jesus fed the 5,000, He directed the disciples to get the people to sit down on the green grass, that they might be at rest while the Lord fed them (Mark 6:39).

> **v. 4.** *And round about the throne were four and twenty seats: and upon the seats I saw four and twenty elders sitting, clothed in white raiment; and they had on their heads crowns of gold.*

The plural noun *seats,* does not convey the divine dignity of the surroundings in heaven; the noun *thrones,* is a more accurate translation and agrees with the context; for those sitting upon them will be enveloped in majestic glory. Monarchs today, when holding audiences with the public, will sit upon the throne of their realm, while the people will sit upon chairs. The scene which is set before us in this verse is illustrative of the royal dignity with which the saints of God will be clothed.

David, on behalf of all the children of Israel, divided the sons of Aaron for appointment to the twenty-four courses of the priesthood in the house of the Lord, (1 Chronicles 24). Thus, the four and twenty elders of our verse would be representative of all the saints in glory. Being dressed in white raiment signifies the priestly character of the redeemed, while being crowned with golden crowns would be confirmation of the royal dignity bestowed upon them.

v. 5. *And out of the throne proceeded lightnings and thunderings and voices: and there were seven lamps of fire burning before the throne, which are the seven Spirits of God.*

The throne which John saw speaks of the unassailable authority and incontrovertible supremacy of the Godhead. It is not the throne of Grace to which the saints on earth have unimpeded access at all times; it is the throne from which God will pour out His unmitigated judgments upon the world during the Tribulation period of seven years (Daniel 9:27). The lightnings, thunderings, and voices are symbolic of the character of God's fearful judgments. The lightnings, typical of the Holy Spirit's power which, within a flash, will bring to light on the minds of individuals, their personal history of an ungodly life, and be made aware of the fiery consequences. The thunderings, symbolic of the earth-shattering sound of God's judgments which will be of such magnitude as to fill men with fear. The voices speak of the all-various attributes of the Holy Spirit arresting the consciences of men, and denying them settled peace of mind. The seven lamps of fire confirm that everything which is of man, the evil, the corruptness and impurity of the world will be burnt up to achieve a perfect and lasting cleansing and renewal of the world (2 Peter 3:10 and Revelation 21:5). It is worthy of note, that the Holy Spirit of God never employs the symbol, *lamps of fire,* when speaking of His Grace to the Church.

The seven Spirits of God. We already know from our consideration of chapter 1:4 that there are not seven spirits of God, but seven attributes of Jehovah which fully define the character of the Spirit of God in Grace, as recorded in Isaiah 11:2. Furthermore, the: *seven lamps of fire*, do not refer to the seven churches, nor to the all-various attributes of God's Grace, but to the seven-fold qualities of God's Holy Spirit which will be active in the perfect execution of His judgments on all that is contrary to His holiness.

> **v. 6.** *And before the throne there was a sea of glass like unto crystal: and in the midst of the throne, and round about the throne, were four beasts* (living creatures) *full of eyes before and behind. The sea of glass like unto crystal.*

Here, we have the antitype of the water-filled laver at which the priests were directed to wash before they could proceed in holy service. The procedure which applies to us today is that we should daily be washed with the washing of water by the Word (Ephesians 5:26), and only then shall we be spiritually fit to serve and worship the Lord.

When we are in glory, we shall see ourselves as having been eternally cleansed, with every glorious feature of the Lord Jesus shining through us like crystal. We shall rest with undisturbed complacency in the love of our blessed Saviour. Our path of trial on earth eternally ended and the victory over sin and death won by the Lord Jesus will be ours to enjoy, seated around God's throne for all eternity.

Four beasts (living creatures) full of eyes before and behind. That the living creatures were in the midst and round about the throne, confirms that their intuitive attributes will fully reflect the perfect and righteous judgments of Almighty God. Being *full of eyes before and behind*, signifies that not only were they cognizant of what was required before the holy throne of God, but also that nothing will escape the all-seeing eye of Him who is Judge of all the earth.

v. 7. *The first living creature was like a lion, and the second living creature like a calf, and the third living creature had a face as a man, and the fourth living creature was like a flying eagle.*

The living creatures symbolise the heads of God's creation on earth. The lion, being head of wild beasts, speaks of the majestic power and unassailable authority of the throne. The calf (*ox*), is the head of the domestic animal kingdom, and has reference to enduring patience and faithfulness in service. The face of a man tells us of the divine wisdom, intelligence, and righteous judgments of the throne, while in the flying eagle we have the allusion of the swiftness of the all-seeing eye to detect and execute judgment from above on all which is evil. The divine attributes of all creation will be brought into line with the mind of heaven.

v. 8. *And the four living creatures had each of them six wings about him; and they were full of eyes within: and they rest not day and night, saying, Holy, holy, holy, Lord God Almighty, which was, and is, and is to come.*

Each of them had six wings. In Isaiah 6:2 we have Seraphim in attendance above the throne, and each of them had six wings. *With twain he covered his face*, being the display of reverence; *with twain he covered his feet*, in an act of humility; *and with twain he did fly*, confirming committed activity in the service of the Lord. There is little doubt the living creatures here would have employed their wings in the same way as the Seraphim, resting not day and night saying: Holy, holy, holy, Lord God Almighty. Thus, the living creatures symbolise the time when all creation will honour the One sitting upon the throne, who liveth for ever and ever.

They were full of eyes within. Within, implies they were divinely motivated to perceive all that was essential to maintain the holiness of the throne of God, and of Him that was, is, and is to come, even the Lord of Glory. Then, all the redeemed in heaven, whose praise and worship will echo throughout the courts of heaven for all eternity, will exalt the One who was before time and all things, as detailed in Proverbs 8:22-31. The Lord speaks of Himself in Proverbs 8:30-31. *Then I was by Him* (God, His Father), *as one brought up with Him: and I was daily His delight, rejoicing always before Him; rejoicing in the habitable part of His earth; and My delights were with the sons of men.*

> **vv. 9-11.** *And when those living creatures give glory and honour and thanks to Him that sat on the throne, who liveth for ever and ever, the four and twenty elders fall down before Him that sat on the throne, and worship Him that liveth for ever and ever, and cast their crowns before the throne, saying, Thou art worthy, O Lord, to receive glory and honour and power: for Thou hast created all things, and for Thy pleasure they are and were created.*

In response to the worship of the living creatures, the four and twenty elders – representatives of all the saints of God in heaven – fall prostrate before the Lord of glory, and render worship and thanksgiving to Him who alone is worthy to receive glory, honour, and power. In confirmation of their sincerity of heart, the four and twenty elders lay down their given glory by casting their crowns of honour and dignity before the throne; so that, as on earth so in heaven, He might have the pre-eminence (Colossians 1:18). In the judgment of Almighty God, the Lord Jesus was alone worthy to receive glory, honour and power. He has already been, and will be clothed with the Shekinah (*dwelling*) glory (Matthew 17:2). But the glory which has been bestowed upon Him, and to which our verse refers, is that of a glorified Man in heaven. So, in the Lord's high-priestly prayer in John 17:24, He appeals to His Father that His disciples and all the saints of God should behold the glory His Father has given Him, even the glory of the Son of Man; such will continue to shine throughout eternity.

Finally, our Lord is worthy to receive power. In resurrection glory, the Lord Jesus told His disciples that: *All Power is given unto Me in heaven and in earth* (Matthew 28:18). God has: *set Him* (His Son) *at His own right hand in the heavenly places, far above all principality, and power, and might, and dominion, and every name that is named, not only in this world, but also in that which is to come* (Ephesians 1:20-21). Such power now resides in the Lord Jesus, for God: *hath put all things under His feet* (Ephesians 1:22). The Lord Jesus will have the power to execute all God's governmental judgments on the world and its inhabitants during the Tribulation period.

Thou hast created all things, and for Thy pleasure they are and were created. Nothing could have been more pleasing to God, apart from the sacrificial death of the Lord Jesus to atone for the sin of the world, than His perfect creation (Genesis 1:31). A creation that brought order out of chaos, light instead of darkness, life out of death, fruitfulness in place of barrenness, calm instead of storm, peace instead of conflict, beauty instead of ugliness, and harmony instead of discord; and finally, man after His own image.

The last clause of verse 11 is key to the divine objective set out in this book. God has determined that all creation will be thoroughly cleansed of all that sin has ruined and polluted, that all which God created will once again minister eternal pleasure to Him and His Beloved Son.

Chapter 5

> **v. 1.** *And I saw in the right hand of Him that sat on the Throne a book written within and on the backside, sealed with seven seals.*

The book was in the right hand of Him that sat upon the Throne to signified the distinguished honour bestowed upon the Lord of Glory (Psalm 110:1 & Ephesians 1:20). That the book was written within and on the back confirmed that the entire counsel of God respecting His dealing with this world was about to be unveiled. No further revelation of God's purposes was to be vouchsafed. The book was a scroll, sealed with seven seals.

> **vv. 2-5.** *And I saw a strong angel proclaiming with a loud voice, Who is worthy to open the book, and to loose the seals thereof? And no man in heaven, nor in earth, neither under the earth, was able to open the book, neither to look thereon. And I wept much, because no man was found worthy to open and to read the book, neither to look thereon. And one of the elders said unto me, Weep not: behold, the Lion of the tribe of Judah, the Root of David, hath prevailed to open the book, and to loose the seven seals thereof.*

While the angels of God excel in strength (Ps.103:20), their might is exercised only in obedience to the will of their Creator. There are, of course, prominent angels such as Gabriel and Michael. However, as Scripture is silent as to which angel was proclaiming, we likewise should remain silent, save to say that no one in God's creation was worthy or able to open, look, or read the detail of the seven seals.

And I wept much. John was so deeply saddened that no created being was worthy to open and to read the book that it occasioned an outpouring of tears from his heart, but John is consoled by one of the elders who assures him there is one who is worthy to open the book. Some have thought the tears of John were a sign of the weakness of the creature, but if *'wept much'*, is sometimes the expression of weakness, it is equally the expression of a right and godly exercise. It has been said, that without tears, *The Revelation of Jesus Christ* was not written; and that without tears it cannot be understood.

It is one of the 24 elders (12 representatives of Old Testament saints and 12 representatives of New Testament saints) who is led to console John by directing his attention to the One who alone is qualified to carry out the task. Who is He? None other than the Lion of the Tribe of Judah, the Lord Jesus. The dying patriarch, Jacob, could not have dreamed that his glorious prediction (Genesis 49:9-10) pointed to the advent of the Messiah over 2000 years later. In His lion-like character, the Lord crushes every opposing force, and establishes His universal kingdom on the ruin of all opposition.

The Root of David. We may ask, why not Abraham or Moses? Well, Abraham was the depository of the Promise of God (Genesis 12:3); and Moses was the expression of the Law, in contradistinction to Grace which came by Jesus Christ (John 1:17). David, on the other hand, is representative of Royalty, the first king, and in type a figure of the eventual and only King of kings, and Lord of lords (1 Timothy 6:15 & Revelation 19:16).

CHAPTER 5

v. 6. *And I beheld, and, lo, in the midst of the Throne and of the four beasts* (living creatures), *and in the midst of the elders, stood a Lamb as it had been slain, having seven horns and seven eyes, which are the seven Spirits of God, sent forth into all the earth.*

The four living creatures were symbols taken from the heads of God's creation here below. The Lion speaks of majesty; the Ox (calf) of patience and endurance; the Man, of intelligence, and the Eagle for rapidity of action and whose domain is the heavens; they all represent the different attributes of God's power and judgment. They were cherubic figures, angels who, when they give glory, honour, and thanks to Him that sat upon the Throne, occasion the worship of the four and twenty elders who cast their crowns before Him that liveth for ever and for ever.

The living creatures will be full of eyes before and behind, implying intuitive intelligence and fulness of spiritual discernment. Moreover, each creature had six wings which denoted supernatural rapidity in the exercise of God's judgments. Finally, they were representative or heads of the animal creation, including man. The attributes of the living creatures were beautifully and perfectly seen in the Lord Jesus as Son of Man on earth. Furthermore, such unique qualities will feature in God's judicious government which will be exercised throughout the world, via human and/or angelic instruments according to His sovereign will.

When John looked, he beheld a Lamb, not a Lion; he perceives weakness, not majesty; *a Lamb as it had been slain*. The prints of His wounds which were seen by His disciples (John 20:20-27) are now seen by John in the glorified Man. We too, when in glory, will gaze upon those wounds, ever to be reminded in our hearts of all our Blessed Saviour endured in order to redeem us back to God.

A Lamb standing. Our Lord is about to take to Himself His great power and reign. For the present, He sits on the right side of His Father's Throne (Revelation 3:21 & Psalm 110:1). But here, the session of our Lord's patience is at an end, He vacates the Throne and stands ready to act. *N.B.* Sitting refers to a state of quiescence, while standing intimates a readiness for action.

Having seven horns and seven eyes. Seven denotes perfection in divine matters, while the horns speak of divine strength, the eyes speak of discernment, perception and intelligence. Thus, the fullness of administration by the Holy Spirit is seen in government by the seven Spirits of God.

> **v. 7.** *And He came and took the book out of the right hand of Him that sat upon the Throne.*

In Luke 4:14-21 we have the record of the Lord Jesus in a synagogue in Nazareth. He was given the book of Isaiah to read. What our Lord read was a message of hope, peace, healing, and life; in other words: *The Gospel of the Kingdom of Jesus Christ.* But the book the Lord Jesus will take up in a coming day, as recorded here in verse 7, will be the book, full of the judgments of almighty God to be executed upon a sin-stricken world and its inhabitants.

> **v. 8.** *And when He had taken the book, the four living creatures and four and twenty elders fell down before the Lamb, having every one of them harps, and golden vials full of odours, which are the prayers of saints.*

The book contains all the details (Revelation 6–20) of the apocalyptic judgments God is about to exercise upon all the dwellers on earth. What saith the Scripture? *Vengeance is Mine; I will repay, saith the Lord*

(Romans 12:19). It is at this point we shall see the transference of the reins of government to the slain Lamb. The divine sceptre of authority will be wielded by the Lord in association with His heavenly saints, here represented by the elders. The elders have Harps. Throughout the millennium, earthly praise will be with all manner of instruments as detailed in Psalms 149 & 150. The Harp appears to be the instrument of heavenly praise in a new song. Song and Harp are generally named together. Psalm 33:2; *et al.*

Golden Vials (bowls) *full of odours* (incense), *which are the prayers of saints* (Psalm 141:2). During the course of the apocalyptic judgments, there will be on earth a company saved from among the Jews and Gentiles (ref. Revelation 11:3; 12:17; 13:7-10). The saints being prayed for are those who will suffer mercilessly under the tyrannical civil power of the Beast, and under the religious apostate power of the Antichrist, see 1 John 4:3. Many will be martyred, but will have a heavenly place and portion assigned to them, while others who survive will form the nucleus of the inhabitants on earth throughout the Millennium. It will be the saints, who survive the persecution, whose prayers for the suffering saints ascend to heaven as sweet incense; they will rejoice in the advent of the righteous reign of Christ for 1,000 years, see Revelation 20:3.

vv. 9-10. *And they* (the elders) *sung a new song, saying, Thou art worthy to take the book, and to open the seals thereof: for Thou wast slain, and hast redeemed us to God by Thy blood out of every kindred, and tongue, and people, and nation. And hast made us* (them) *unto our God kings and priests: and we* (they) *shall reign over the earth.* N.B. According to the original Greek text; the personal pronouns *us,* and *we,* should be third person pronouns, because John, in the opening of verse 9, is speaking of the elders.

The song will be about the triumphs of the Lord Jesus as a result of His death on the cross; He triumphed over sin, death, and the devil, and secured for Himself a company, redeemed back to God by His precious blood. The new song will have as its theme the conquering Lamb of God, a song embracing the past and the future, the cross and the kingdom.

Thou art worthy to take the book, and to open the seals thereof. It was in the Spirit of a Lamb that our Lord glorified God on earth; as a Lamb that He died to atone for the sins of the world; and it will be as a Lamb that was dead that all created intelligences will acknowledge and praise. It will be on the ground of the Lamb's worthiness that all the purposes of God will be carried out to a glorious conclusion.

For Thou wast slain, and hast redeemed us to God by Thy blood out of every kindred, and tongue, and people, and nation. As the Lion of the Tribe of Judah He acts in power, but as the Lamb of God's providing, He will act with authority. *Redeemed* us, refers exclusively to all believers in the Lord Jesus Christ, throughout all nations of the world, Jew and Gentile, who have repented of their sins and put their faith and trust in the Lord Jesus Christ.

We note that the elders do not sing of their own redemption, but all the redeemed now in glory will, as will all on earth who come triumphantly through: *great tribulation.* The priestly service of the elders was on behalf of others. The saints, now in heaven, will reign over, not on, the earth for 1,000 years in blessed association with their Saviour and Lord, Jesus Christ. ref. Revelation 20:4, last clause.

> **v. 11.** *And I beheld, and I heard the voice of many angels round about the Throne and the living creatures and the elders: and the number of them was ten thousand times ten thousand, and thousands of thousands.*

In the Revelation, John confirms what he saw 44 times, and what he heard 27 times. Now there may not be any significance in the actual numbers, but the recurring testimony of the apostle to the fact that the visions were actually seen and the various voices and sounds heard is clearly personal and decisive, and therefore unimpeachable.

The highest numerical number which can be expressed in the original Greek language is 10,000. The sum of 10,000 x 10,000 = 100,000,000. The hosts John saw in heaven was thousands and thousands of 100,000,000s, a company it will not be possible to number for multitude.

> **v. 12.** *Saying with a loud voice, Worthy is the Lamb that was slain to receive power, and riches, and wisdom, and strength, and honour, and glory, and blessing.*

In this verse we have the seven glorious and unique attributes which perfectly reflect the dignity and authority the Lord will exercise throughout His millennial reign. What a glorious prospect lies before us, to know that we shall have part in the unending anthem of praise that will echo throughout the courts of heaven for all eternity. Power is ascribed to Him, the first of the attributes because circumstances call for its immediate exercise.

Riches refers to the wealth of the universe which He has bought with His blood. Wisdom as seen in Him of all the ways and works of God. Strength is that quality which enables Him to execute what God has determined should be done. Honour implies that every mark of public distinction is worthy to be conferred on the Lamb. Glory refers to the public and moral display of the Lamb in heaven and on earth. Blessing has reference to every form and character of blessedness and happiness being ascribed to the Lamb.

v. 13. *And every creature which is in heaven, and on the earth, and under the earth, and such as are in the sea, and all that are in them, heard I saying, Blessing, and honour, and glory, and power, be unto Him that sitteth upon the Throne, and unto the Lamb for ever and ever.*

The full tide of praise is not yet exhausted. It will continue to roll on, gathering force and volume till the entire universe is embraced. Every created being in the vast universe of bliss will praise our blessed Saviour. The fourfold ascription of praise is significant: blessing, honour, glory and power, signifies the spontaneous, universal outburst of worship and praise unto the Lamb, for ever and ever.

v. 14. And the four living creatures said, Amen. And the four and twenty elders fell down and worshipped. N.B. The words: *Him that liveth for ever and ever,* are not in the original text.

The four and twenty elders represent all the redeemed; they, together with the four living creatures who represent the attributes of Christ, fall down and worship the Lord of Glory. Amen.

The opening clause of chapter four implies that the church age has ended. The detail of what John saw in heaven, as given in chapters four and five, confirms that all the saints of God have been raptured to heaven. Although we are not explicitly told about the rapture, unless we grasp the reality of the fact that it has taken place, we shall not be able to understand all that now follows in this book. The assurance given in chapter 3:10 confirms that the raptured saints will be observers in heaven of all the providential judgments of Almighty God, which He will pour out upon the world and its inhabitants; the time is known as the Tribulation period, the details of which begin here in chapter 6.

CHAPTER 5

The judgments of Almighty God come under three headings. There are seven Seal judgments; seven Trumpet judgments; and seven Vial (*Bowl*) judgments. As each judgment is executed, beginning with the opening of the first Seal judgment, the severity of successive judgments increases through to the last Vial judgment. It is important to note that from first to last, the judgments are not concurrent, but consecutive.

The titles of the three groups of judgments are significant. The *Seal judgments* are so called because they cannot be enforced until the Lord breaks the seal which bears the signet of Almighty God. The title: *Trumpet judgments,* implies that the world as a whole will clearly hear the warnings, and will experience the gravity and impact of God's judgments upon the kingdoms of this world. *The Vial* (*Bowl*) judgments are the severest of all the judgments, and are so called because they contain the seven last plagues which will be poured out upon the remaining inhabitants of the world, particularly upon the nation of Israel, expressing the unmitigated wrath of Almighty God. However, as the Lord Jesus said in His Olivet discourse, and with specific reference to the period of: *great tribulation,* i.e., the last half of Daniel's 70th week (Daniel 9:27): *except those days be shortened, there should no flesh be saved: but for the elect's sake those days shall be shortened* (Matthew 24:22).

Chapter 6

v. 1. *And I saw when the Lamb opened one of the seals, and I heard, as it were the noise of thunder, one of the four living creatures saying, Come (and see).*

A more accurate translation of this verse from the original Greek is: *And I saw when the Lamb opened one of the seven seals, and I heard one of the four living creatures saying, as a voice of thunder, Come.* (The words, *and see*, do not appear in the original Greek text).

So, it is the Lord who will be in control of the administration of the judgments, for He alone is worthy to open the seals (Chapter 5:5). Likewise, in the final judgment of this world, it is the Lord who will sit upon the Great White Throne and pass judgment on all whose names are not found written in the Lamb's Book of Life (Revelation 20:15).

As John observes the Lamb opening the first seal, he hears the thunderous voice of one of the living creatures, a voice which will be heard throughout the world. The living creature, being an executive of the throne of God, calls to the rider on a white horse to Come. The force of the verb *Come*, implies, spring into action. The command will be from heaven, and cannot be disregarded, for the time is the beginning of the 70th week of Daniel's prophecy (Daniel 9:27). Thus, the individual or the power addressed by the living creature will be a latent force in the world, ready to spring into action. It will be a time of great trial for the entire world.

> **v. 2.** *And I saw, and behold a white horse: and he that sat on him had a bow; and a crown was given unto him: and he went forth conquering, and to conquer.*

A horse in these Scriptures is not a literal horse, but a symbol of a national power able to subdue other nations speedily in one way or another. The riders on each of the four horses symbolise the authority of each national power exercising their respective powers. The white horse in this instance symbolises swiftness, power, and peaceful victories. The rider has a bow, but no mention of a quiver with arrows. The laurel crown given to the rider on the horse would signify, not only authority to exercise power, but also the recognition of accomplished victories. So, we get a picture of bloodless warfare, conducted from a distance, with a world-wide impact, and triumphant. The world will be subjugated to a dominant force, achieved without struggle or carnage. Opposition to the God of creation and to the Lord Jesus Christ will deepen as the trials become more intense. Being the first tribulation judgment, it is the least tortuous of all the judgments which will follow.

It will be a time of uneasy peace. One is reminded of the words of the apostle Paul in his letter to the saints of Thessalonica: *For when they shall say, Peace and safety; then sudden destruction cometh upon them, as travail upon a woman with child; and they shall not escape* (1 Thessalonians 5:3). So, we come to the second seal judgment.

> **vv. 3-4** *And when He had opened the second seal, I heard the second living creature say, Come (and see). And there went out another horse*

that was red: and power was given to him that sat thereon to take peace from the earth, and that they should kill one another; and there was given unto him a great (mighty) *sword.*

The commands of all the living creatures will be instantly obeyed to ensure that the exercise of God's judgments is not hindered. Accordingly, the rider comes forth on a red horse. The red horse is a symbol of power through death and bloodshed. We should note that the riders on all four horses will not be angels or theophanies, but actual unregenerate authorities whom God will use for His divine purpose. However, because the horseman will be engaged in the slaughter of mankind, the taking of life can only be on the authority of God; therefore, the rider will be given specific power for that purpose. This will also be the case with the rider on the fourth horse (verse 8), who will have divine authority to kill with the sword. The rider on the red horse generates a general, fractious upheaval among mankind, resulting in the removal of peace from the earth, and initiating world-wide internecine homicide. The Lord Jesus spoke about this particular, prophetic event, as recorded in Matthew 24:7, *For nation shall rise up against nation, and kingdom against kingdom.*

The one on the horse is given a great sword in order to slay many. This is significant because in the Scriptures the sword is the principal weapon of warfare and death. Death will be the primary outcome of the opening of the second seal. When the Lord God drove Adam and Eve out of the Garden of Eden, He placed at the East of the Garden, Cherubims with a flaming sword to guard the way to the Tree of Life. 4,000 years later, that flaming sword was sheathed in the Lord Jesus who answered to God for our sins and the sin of the world by His death on the Cross. But with our Lord's resurrection, the Cherubims and flaming sword no longer bar the way to the Tree of Life. The way is now open to all who will go in via repentance before God and faith in the Lord Jesus Christ. Thus, the Lord Jesus: *Through death, destroyed him that had the power of death, that is, the devil* (Hebrews 2:14). Alas, in the early stages of the Tribulation period, many souls will be slain as a result of the judgments of Almighty God.

> **vv. 5-6.** *And when He had opened the third seal, I heard the third living creature say, Come (and see). And I beheld, and lo a black horse; and he that sat on him had a pair of balances in his hand. And I heard a voice in the midst of the four living creatures say, A measure of wheat for a penny, and three measures of barley for a penny; and see thou hurt not the oil and the wine.*

The black horse, being a symbol of death and mourning, will have a devastating impact on life in the world. There will be a world-wide famine, the like of which will not have been known before. The rider upon the black horse will have a pair of balances in his hand to ensure that everything which happens is carefully weighed and measured in accord with the will of God. The rider will seek to control the meagre food supply at the time of great famine. The suffering and shortage of food will be uniform throughout the world; hence, the balances in the hand of the rider on the horse.

However, it will be the poor who will suffer most, with many dying. At this time, the rich by their wealth will escape the physical suffering, but only for a short interval of time.

> **vv. 7-8.** *And when He had opened the fourth seal, I heard the voice of the fourth living creature say, Come (and see). And I looked, and behold a pale horse: and his name that sat on him was Death, and Hell* (Hades)

followed with him. And power was given unto them over the fourth part of the earth, to kill with sword, and with hunger, and with death, and with (by) *the beasts of the earth.*

The opening of the fourth seal reveals a horse with the colour of a corpse, which suggest severe forebodings, for here we have the portents of what God has called: *My four sore judgments* (Ezekiel 14:21), i.e., the sword, famine, evil beasts, and pestilence, which will impact upon a fourth part of the earth. There is little doubt that the fourth part of the earth refers to the area of the world which had for some time been under the influence of Christendom during the past 2,000 years.

Although the opening of this seal reveals the severest of the first four seal judgments, we read in Matthew 24:6-8 that such are only: *The beginning of sorrows*. The fulfilment of the seal judgments, and all that follows in this book, remain in the realm of prophecy. We should note that, unlike the riders of the three previous horses, the rider of this horse is named Death, and Hades which follows with him. The rider is so called because he will be the very embodiment of Satan who brought death into God's sinless creation. On this occasion Satan will require the authority of God to take life from the earth. This Scripture confirms that Death and Hades are inseparably linked. While Death takes care of the body, Hades receives the immortal soul for safe keeping until such time when it surrenders the unregenerate souls to appear before the Great White Throne for judgment. It is then that both Death and Hades will be cast into Gehenna, the lake of fire (Revelation 20:14).

And power was given to him (not *them*, but the rider on the horse) *over the fourth part of the earth, to kill with sword, and with hunger, and with death, and by* (not *with*) *the beasts of the earth*. The sword is the instrument of war and death; and as with the man on the red horse who slew

CHAPTER 6

millions, so with the fourth seal open, the sword will continue to slay throughout the fourth part of the world. Plough-shears will be turned into instruments of war, the earth will not be tilled, famine will rage and millions will die. All who survive the first three plagues, beasts of the earth will kill and devour.

Today, it is difficult for a child of God, living in a peaceful environment to conceive the consequence such devastating judgments will have, but, make no mistake, such judgments there will be. However, we know that when these prophecies come to pass, all the redeemed will be at home in heaven as observers of the working-out of God's plans.

> **v. 9.** *And when He had opened the fifth seal, I saw under the altar the souls of them that were slain for the Word of God, and for the testimony which they held.*

Chapters 24 and 25 of Matthew's Gospel detail events of the last days (*the period we are currently considering*), prior to the coming of the Lord with all His saints to reign over the earth for 1,000 years. This particular vision of John corresponds with what the Lord said in Matthew 24:8.

Following the rapture of the church to Heaven, the Gospel of the Kingdom will have been preached, a gospel message relating to the Millennial reign of Christ (Revelation 20:6). The souls John sees under the altar are of those who had accepted the truth of the Gospel of the Kingdom, and had suffered death for the testimony of their faith. That the souls of those who cry out are seen under the altar in the ashes, confirms they had offered themselves as a burnt-offering to God, a sweet savour sacrifice.

The preaching of the Gospel of the Grace of God began to be preached on the Day of Pentecost, and has continued throughout this day of God's grace to the world, but will cease the moment the church of God is raptured to heaven. Before the day of God's grace began, and before the Lord Jesus was crucified, the Gospel of the Kingdom was preached, as for example by John the Baptist. Sadly, the nation, for whom the Lord came as the long-promised Messiah/King, rejected God's unique gift, crying out: *Away with Him, we will not have this man to reign over us* (John 19:15 and Luke 19:14). There then followed this present day of God's grace to the world which has lasted two thousand years. From the moment the Lord Jesus calls all the redeemed home to glory, the Gospel of the Kingdom will again be preached throughout the habitable earth. The message will relate to the Millennial Kingdom of our Lord Jesus Christ, when He will reign in righteousness throughout the world.

v. 10. *And they cried with a loud voice, saying, How long, O Lord, holy and true, dost Thou not judge and avenge our blood on them that dwell on the earth?*

The language of the souls of the Jewish saints who have suffered death is most definitely not the language of a Christian today who is saved by Grace; for he/she is exhorted to: *Be ye kind one to another, tenderhearted, forgiving one another, even as God for Christ's sake hath forgiven you* (Ephesians 4:32). Furthermore, should the occasion ever arise when our suffering for righteousness is likely to end in death, we should have on our lips, words from our heart akin to the words of Stephen when he was stoned to death for his testimony of the love and grace of God: *Lord: Lay not this sin to their charge* (Acts 7:60). Although the souls under the altar will have sacrificed their lives in defence of the Gospel of the Kingdom, they will nevertheless be anxious for divine retribution to be exercised against the persecutors who were responsible for their death. However, the occasion for such retribution will be in God's time.

v. 11. *And white robes were given unto every one of them; and it was said unto them, that they should rest yet for a little season, until their fellowservants also and their brethren, that should be killed as they were, should be fulfilled.*

Each of the souls receives a white robe, being testimony to their faithfulness and the recognition of their service Godward. Whenever white robes are referred to it invariably, as here, relates to the righteousnesses of the saints (Revelation 19:8).

In response to their call: *How long?*, it is made plain to them that they must rest for a little season until others of their brethren, who likewise will be persecuted unto death for testimony sake, join them.

v. 12. *And I beheld when He had opened the sixth seal, and, lo, there was a great earthquake; and the sun became black as sackcloth of hair, and the moon became as blood.*

The opening of this sixth seal is further confirmation of Old Testament prophecies such as Isaiah 13:6-11, and the entire chapter 34. The *great earthquake* is symbolic, and relates to the universal upheaval and subversion of the natural order of things of life on earth, *i.e.*, political, social and ecclesiastical. The overthrow of rule and authority, of national governments and established institutions, will occasion total chaos on the earth.

And the sun became black as sackcloth of hair, and the moon became as blood. That the sun becomes black as sackcloth of hair signifies that a supreme ruler in the world at the time will be dethroned, humbled, and reduced to wearing the garment of a beggar. The moon, a subordinate light, relates to secondary authorities who will no longer guide the people safely in a sphere of moral darkness and physical chaos, but will occasion their death as signified by the colour of the moon appearing as blood.

> **v. 13.** *And the stars of heaven fell unto the earth, even as a fig tree casteth her untimely figs, when she is shaken of a mighty wind.*

We are still in the realm of symbolic language. The stars relate to heads of government and to those who rule and exercise authority, civil and ecclesiastical. By the mighty power of the Spirit of God, they will fall from their pedestals of dignity, honour, and power, just when they are about to reach the pinnacle of their ambitions; they will be brought down to earth like the fall of unripe figs, powerless, discarded, and useless.

> **v. 14.** *And the heaven departed as a scroll when it is rolled together; and every mountain and island were moved out of their places.*

The heaven referred to in this verse does not refer to the atmospheric heavens, which is Satan's domain and who is known as: *The prince of the power of the air, the spirit that now worketh in the children of disobedience* (Ephesians 2:2). Neither does it refer to the starry heaven (Genesis 15:5), nor to the heaven of heavens where God dwells in light unapproachable (1 Timothy 6:16). Rather, the term *heaven* here relates to the highest echelons of the ecclesiastical and political power and influence, the civil establishments which will control every aspect of life on earth; these will disappear being rolled up like a parchment scroll and set aside. Such will have no part in God's plans for a new heaven and a new earth (Chapter 21:1).

And every mountain and island were moved out of their places. The mountains are symbolic of prominent and dominant land powers overshadowing dependencies. The islands were, according to Scripture, sources of wealth (Isaiah 23:2 and Ezekiel 27:3-15) to sustain industry and the lust of mankind; all of which will be changed and resituated to coincide with God's plan for a new earth.

> **v. 15.** *And the kings of the earth, and the great men, and the rich men, and the chief captains, and the mighty men, and every bondman, and every freeman, hid themselves in the dens and in the rocks of the mountains.*

This verse marks a change in the definition of the characters mentioned; they are not symbols but actual individuals making up every strata of civilisation from the kings of the earth to the beggars in the streets. All will seek to escape and hide themselves from the impact and consequences of the devastating judgments of the: *Wrath of the Lamb*. Furthermore, no matter where they hide, be it dens or caves in the mountains, they will not be able to insulate themselves from the physical pain of the judgments, nor conceal themselves from the all-seeing eye of the Judge of all the earth.

> **v. 16.** *And said to the mountains and rocks, Fall on us, and hide us from the face of Him that sitteth on the throne, and from the wrath of the Lamb.*

This verse confirms that hiding in the dens and mountain caves will be no security from the physical inflictions occasioned by the judgments of God. So, knowing they cannot escape from coming face to face with Him that sitteth on the Throne, they will want to die and be buried from falling rock, believing they will then escape appearing before the Great White Throne for final judgment. At that time, and later as recorded in chapter 9:6, God will not permit them to die.

v. 17. *For the great day of His wrath is come; and who shall be able to stand?*

What the unregenerate world will have experienced from the opening of the first six seals is: *the wrath of the Lamb*. But as the Lord Jesus said: *All these are* only *the beginning of sorrows* (Matthew 24:8). It will be clear to the prayerful reader that Chapter 7 is a parenthesis between the opening of the sixth and seventh seals. This Chapter makes plain that God, for His pleasure, has determined the security for eternal blessing of vast numbers of saints. They will be souls from Israel and from the Gentiles who will have accepted the preaching of the Gospel of the Kingdom, which commenced immediately following the rapture of the Church to heaven.

As we proceed through: *The Revelation of Jesus Christ*, we shall see that the salvation of the two vast groups, referred to here, does not take place between the opening of the sixth and seventh seals, but during the period of: *great tribulation*. We shall also notice that the actual scene of blessing during the Millennial age is not heaven but earth, applying to the saved of Israel and of the Gentiles.

Chapter 7

v. 1. *And after these things I saw four angels standing on the four corners of the earth, holding the four winds of the earth, that the wind should not blow on the earth, nor on the sea, nor on any tree.*

And after these things, tells us clearly that John is recording the vision in the order in which it was revealed to him, and not in the order in which the events will occur. The angels will be appointed of God to temporarily restrain the out-pouring of the severe judgments about to fall upon the whole earth. The winds speak of the divine power to apply the judgments, while the earth has reference to whatever settled government will still exist upon earth. The sea represents the nations in turmoil, and the trees are symbolic of the pride, persistent loftiness, and arrogance of man's heart, in spite of the stormy trials the world has already experienced.

vv. 2-3. *And I saw another angel ascending from the east, having the seal of the living God: and he cried with a loud voice to the four angels, to whom it was given to hurt the earth and the sea, saying, Hurt not the earth, neither the sea, nor the trees, till we have sealed the servants of our God in their foreheads.*

The angel from the sun-rising may well be an arch-angel having authority to command the four angels holding the four winds to delay pouring out their specific judgments upon the world. Here we have confirmation that the angelic host is at all times subject to the will of God, their creator. Scripture is silent as to the exact nature of the seal God's servants will receive in their foreheads, but clearly it will be distinctive, their minds being filled with the will of God. We may recall that when Stephen stood before the Council and faithfully witnessed about his faith, the Council: *Looking steadfastly upon Stephen, saw his face as it had been the face of an angel* (Acts 6:15). Likewise, the sealing of the saints will be a supernatural attestation that they belong to God.

v. 4. *And I heard the number of them which were sealed: and there were sealed an hundred and forty and four thousand of all the tribes of the children of Israel.*

Verses 5-8 state that 12,000 from each of the twelve tribes of Israel were sealed. Total = 144,000. This is further confirmation that God has purposed to secure for His pleasure a representative company from the twelve tribes of Israel for their eternal blessing. However, we should understand that 144,000 is a symbolic figure, albeit, being a multiple of 12, it is the number which represents perfection in administration which will exist throughout the Millennial age. While this company will be secured and set apart for future blessing, it is worthy of note that in the detailed list neither the family of Dan nor Ephraim is mentioned. The reason is clear, for both families turned to idolatry. Regarding Dan, it is recorded in Judges 18:30: *and the children of Dan set up the graven image;* and in Hosea 4:17, we read: *Ephraim is joined to idols; let him alone.* Before more severe judgments fall upon the world, an innumerable company of all nations will be secured for God's glory.

v. 9. *And after this I beheld, and, lo, a great multitude, which no man* *could number, of all nations, and kindreds, and people, and tongues, stood before the throne, and before the Lamb, clothed with white robes, and palms in their hands.*

It is a precious thing to acknowledge that God, in His sovereign love and mercy, will be calling from out of the Gentile nations, a vast, innumerable company of saints who will have come through the time of *tribulation,* having washed their robes and made them white in the blood of the Lamb. The company will not be part of the church of God, but a part of the vast multitude of Israeli and Gentile saints who will occupy the world during the Millennial age.

We note that they stand before the throne as worshippers, not around the throne like the four and twenty elders who are sitting on thrones in heaven having cast their crowns before the throne of God and worship Him who liveth for ever and ever. This saved Gentile company will be standing on earth, having branches of palm trees in their hands which they will undoubtedly wave to signal joy, peace, and victory over death.

> **vv. 10-12.** *And cried with a loud voice, saying, Salvation to our God which sitteth upon the throne, and unto the Lamb. And all the angels stood round about the throne, and about the elders and the four living creatures, and fell before the throne on their faces, and worshipped God, saying, Amen: Blessing, and glory, and wisdom, and thanksgiving, and honour, and power, and might, be unto our God for ever and ever. Amen.*

The day is coming when all creation and all created intelligences will hear the divine doxology echoing throughout the courts of heaven and throughout the world: *Salvation to our God which sitteth upon the throne, and unto the Lamb.* Such heavenly praise will continue throughout the golden ages of eternity. The great call, *Salvation to our God,* is the recognition that Salvation has its source in God and the Lamb. God is shewing mercy to the Gentile nations who hitherto had not heard the *Gospel of the Grace of God* but on hearing the Gospel of the Kingdom have responded to the message, and through God's sovereign mercy have been saved. They thankfully own their salvation to God, knowing that their destiny and blessing will be on earth throughout the Millennial age.

vv. 11 & 12. It is not the four and twenty elders and living creatures who are the worshipers here, for their worship is detailed in chapters 4 & 5. Here we have the redeemed of the Gentiles together with the angelic host engaged in an eternal peon of praise, worship, and thanksgiving, embracing all the glorious attributes of Almighty God and the Lamb. How wonderful that their doxology ends with *Amen (so be it)*, thus confirming that nothing will ever interrupt or countermand the praise of the redeemed.

> **v. 13.** And *one of the elders answered, saying unto me, What* (who) *are these which are arrayed in white robes? And whence came they?*

One of the four and twenty elders poses a question for John. The elders, being representatives of the church, were redeemed back to God through repentance before God and faith in the Lord Jesus Christ during the day of God's Grace to the world. The elders knew that the day of God's Grace ended long ago, so they ask, Where did these Gentile saints come from?; and how, they wondered, did they become eligible to wear white robes of righteousness, and render thanksgiving and praise acceptable to God?

> **v. 14.** *And I (John) said unto him, Sir, thou knowest. And he said to me (John), These are they which came out of great tribulation, and have washed their robes, and made them white in the blood of the Lamb.*

CHAPTER 7

In the vision, John recognises the honoured position of the elders and the divine counsel vouchsafed to them; accordingly, he says: *Sir (My lord), thou knowest*. The multitude, arrayed in white robes had come out of, not just tribulation but: *great tribulation*. Scripture does not say that on their death they were taken to heaven; the simple reason being, they do not form part of the church of God; their destiny is to be inhabitants on the new earth along with the faithful remnant of Israel which will occupy the entire Promised Land, with every man sitting under his own vine and fig tree (Micah 4:4).

They *have washed their robes, and made them white in the blood of the Lamb.* In the Scriptures, a man's clothes were a symbol of his status and way of life. The washing of one's clothes, figuratively speaking, signifies the moral cleansing of a person's way of life. Being made white in the blood of the Lamb would be accomplished by an individual's repentance before God, their belief and faith in the death and atoning work of the Lord Jesus Christ on the Cross, and the acknowledgment of His resurrection and glorification to the right hand of the throne of God.

> **v. 15.** *Therefore are they before the throne of God, and serve Him day and night in His temple; and He that sitteth on the throne shall dwell among them.*

That this company is seen before the throne signifies they are before God morally; it is as God sees them on earth, morally suited to be before Him in spirit. Serving Him day and night, signifies the continuity of their service. The Temple here is not Ezekiel's Temple as detailed in Ezekiel 40-46, but in spirit they are privileged to draw near to God where He is. It is how John beholds them in the mind of God,

The Mighty God upon His throne will in spirit overshadow them. The words: *Shall dwell among them,* convey the wrong message. According to the original Greek text, the statement should read: *Shall spread his tabernacle over them*. In other words, they will for all eternity be beneficiaries of His provision, protection, and care. In a moral sense, they will be in priestly service, worshippers in His Temple, the moral environment of godliness.

> **v. 16.** *They shall hunger no more, neither thirst anymore; neither shall the sun light on them, nor any heat.*

The environment on earth during the Millennium will parallel that which existed before sin came into the world, i.e., paradise on earth. Pangs of hunger will never be known, yearning to quench one's thirst will never occur; and, as in the time before the Flood, the sun will shine through water-laden clouds to protect man from the aging influence of the sun. Sunburn will never be known.

> **v. 17.** *For the Lamb which is in the midst of the throne shall feed them, and shall lead them unto living fountains of water: and God shall wipe away all tears from their eyes.*

It is worthy of note that it is the Lamb which shall feed, lead, refresh, and protect the Gentile saints who will have come through: *great tribulation*. However, it is God who shall wipe away all tears, for it is God against whom all mankind have sinned and occasioned tears of sorrow. In the days when our Lord was on earth, His disciples never wanted for food, drink, and protection, for He met all their physical and material needs and was their constant shield and defender. Thus, will it be throughout the Millennial age, the Lord will reign in righteousness, and be the sole provider and protector over the earth, leading the saints unto fountains of living water. When God made man, He gave him eyes to behold the glory of His creation and to therein rest complacent in an environment of beauty, peace, and joy; not eyes for the purpose of shedding tears of sorrow occasioned by sin. There was that unique occasion in the life of the Lord Jesus when He was confronted with the death of Lazarus; He wept. The verb, *wept,* in Greek is *dakruo,* which literally means: *to cry silently, to shed tears*; the verb occurs nowhere else in the Scriptures. The Lord was so deeply moved on coming face to face with the consequence sin that tear-drops trickled down His lovely face. No man had ever wept or could weep with such profound depths of holy feeling as did our blessed Lord on that occasion. In the eternal state it is God who will wipe away all tears; there will be no more crying (Revelation 21:4).

Chapter 8

v. 1. *And when He had opened the seventh seal, there was silence in heaven about the space of half an hour.*

The opening of the seventh seal will mark the beginning of the last half of Daniel's seventieth week, the period the Lord Jesus termed as a time of: *great tribulation*. The silence in heaven was an ominous sign, being the precursor of events more horrendous than anything which had gone before in respect of God's judgments falling upon the world. We know from the Scriptures that judgment is God's strange work (Isaiah 28:21); for it is not in the nature of God to want to judge with devastating consequences for: *God is love* (1 John 4:8). It is as though God will be delaying actions which are foreign to His holy nature. We know from our experience of nature in general that immediately prior to a threatening atmospheric storm a deathly silence occurs in the animal kingdom, e.g., not a bird will be heard or seen in the sky. We should understand that the: *half an hour,* to be earth's time, a literal period.

v. 2. *And I saw the seven angels which stood before God; and to them were given seven trumpets.*

The definite article, *the,* before *seven angels,* does not imply that the angels had already been referred to, rather that they are a God-appointed group to herald in the seven trumpet judgments. Seven, being the perfect number, confirms that the judgments of Almighty God are perfect and complete. An earlier judgment fell upon Jericho, as recorded in Joshua 6:20. When the seven priests blew their trumpets in unison, the walls of Jericho sunk into the ground, enabling the children of Israel to march in and take the city unhindered. Here in this verse, each of the seven angels blows their trumpets in succession, signalling God's preparation for the moral and spiritual cleansing of the world in readiness for the Millennial Kingdom. The sound of the trumpets will leave none in doubt about God's plans.

> **v. 3.** *And another angel came and stood at the altar, having a golden censer; and there was given unto him much incense, that he should offer it with the prayers of all saints upon the golden altar which was before the throne.*

Clearly, the angel referred to here is not a created angel, for nowhere do we read in Scripture of angels offering incense at the golden altar. The angelic being here is undoubtedly the Lord Jesus Christ. There are three occasions in this book where the expression: A*nother angel,* is used, and on each occasion it refers to the Lord Jesus Christ (8:3; 10:1 and 18:1). The angel stands at the altar (*brazen*) to take burning coals to put in the golden censer. Much incense is given Him that He might give efficacy to the prayers of all saints at the golden altar. The saints referred to in this verse are all those who are then suffering for the testimony of their faith and belief in the Gospel of the Kingdom.

> *Much incense is ascending*
> *Before the eternal Throne;*
> *God graciously is bending,*
> *To hear each feeble one.*

> *To all our prayers and praises,*
> *Christ adds His sweet perfume,*
> *And He the censer raises,*
> *These odours to consume.*
>
> M. Bowly.

v 4. *And the smoke of the incense, which came with the prayers of the saints, ascended up before God out of the angel's hand.*

Today, when trials befall the saints of God, they do not call for vengeance on those who afflict them, but their prayers at the throne of grace are that God's mercy might touch and move in unregenerate hearts, to convict such individuals of sin and bring them in the spirit of repentance to the throne of grace. In the coming day of great trial for the faithful remnant of Israel, their prayers will call for vengeance on their oppressors. Nevertheless, such prayers will ascend as incense to the throne of God. The sweet psalmist of Israel spoke of his prayers being as incense (Psalm 141:2). God will hear the prayers of the saints during the: *great tribulation* period and will answer accordingly, as confirmed in the following verse.

v. 5. *And the angel took the censer, and filled it with fire of the altar, and cast it into the earth: and there were voices, and thunderings, and lightnings, and an earthquake.*

The action of the angel (*Lord Jesus Christ*) here will be the answer to the prayers of the saints on earth. His censer without incense, being filled with fire off the brazen altar, is cast into the earth. Such an event will symbolise the outpourings of the judgments of God. Thus, the reprobate world will be made ready to experience devastating judgments. For an explanation of the: *voices, thunderings, and lightnings;* refer to notes on

Chapter four, verse five. The earthquake referred to here is an added feature of God's judgment, and signifies that the counsels of earthly government will be reduced to a state of chaos, be dysfunctional, and irreparably disturbed.

> **v. 6.** *And the seven angels which had the seven trumpets prepared themselves to sound.*

With reference to the seal judgments, it was the Lamb who opened the seals to release the judgments of God. Here, the seven chosen angels will stand ready to act on the command of God who will direct and control the out-pouring of His judgments on the world. The sounding of the first trumpet will signal the start of seven horrendous trials / plagues.

> **v. 7.** *The first angel sounded, and there followed hail and fire mingled with blood, and they were cast upon the earth: and the third part of trees was burnt up, and all green grass was burnt up.*

Hail and fire mingled with blood. To understand the mind of the Spirit, we must accept that in these judgments it is still symbolic language which is being used. We know something of the destructive force of hail from the record we have of the seventh plague upon Egypt (Exodus 9:22-25). The hail was accompanied with fire to ensure the plague would be most grievous and without parallel for suffering and loss. Here, the symbols of hail and fire mingled with blood were cast upon the earth, confirming that specific judgments will be from heaven with deadly effect on all mankind. In the original Greek Text, following the words: *And they were cast upon the earth,* we have the words: *And the third part of the earth was burnt up* (*ref. Interlinear Greek-English New Testament, Nestle Marshall*); for some inexplicable reason such words do not appear in the Authorised Version.

However, the statement implies that the third part of the earth will be uninhabitable and of no use for the cultivation of crops; there will be barrenness, sterility, and famine. The judgment of God will bring about the loss of a third part of the trees and all green grass. From time to time the Scriptures refer to the trees of the forest as symbols of man's arrogance, loftiness, and pride. Nebuchadnezzar, in Daniel 4:20-23, is likened unto a great strong tree, but God brought him down to earth, and for seven years he was as the beasts of the field, eating grass with the dew of heaven upon his back each morning. One third of the higher, governing echelons of society will be destroyed or rendered impotent.

And all green grass was burnt up. According to the Scriptures, man is as grass, and his glory as the flower of grass (1 Peter 1:24). Green grass speaks of the material prosperity of man. Thus, all man's godless wealth, his prosperity, and livelihood will cease to exist as essential elements for life world-wide, for such will disappear under the judgments of God. The flower of the grass plant is the most insignificant and ephemeral of all flowering plants; being the measure of man's natural glory, it likewise will be burnt up.

> **v. 8.** *And the second angel sounded, and as it were a great mountain burning with fire was cast into the sea: and the third part of the sea became blood.*

We are still in the realm of symbols; for the *great mountain* here has reference to an influential power on earth which is godless. We read in Jeremiah 51:25: *Behold, I am against thee, O destroying mountain* (Babylon), *saith the Lord, which destroyest all the earth: and I will stretch out Mine hand upon thee, and roll thee down from the rocks, and will make thee a burnt mountain.* The fate of Babylon, a great Chaldean kingdom, answers to what we have here in our verse. A mountain in Scripture frequently speaks of an established, dominant, influential power; our verse refers to just such a power, i.e., the Roman Empire: *A great mountain burning with fire;* conveys the thought of an extremely oppressive regime on fire to enforce its dogmas, and burning with fury because of the judgment of Almighty God upon it. Such a regime is cast into the sea; in other words, it is broken up and scattered throughout the nations of the world, a world in a disturbed state by reason of what has already taken place, occasioned by the judgments of God.

We should understand that all references to: *the third part,* in these judgments of God relate to that part of the world dominated by the restored Roman Empire. The mountain being cast into the sea of nations initiates the incandescent fury of the Roman power, and results in the death of a third part of mankind in the region.

> **v. 9.** *And the third part of the creatures which were in the sea, and had life, died; and the third part of the ships were destroyed.*

The living creatures that were in the sea may well refer to the indigenous peoples of the lands into which the great mountain (*Roman power and influence*) will be cast. Civil unrest amongst the unrelated peoples will occasion the death of a third of the natural inhabitants. A third part of the ships being destroyed will signify the destruction, in part, of communications, international trading, and travel. In that part of the world there will be domestic, political, and commercial chaos.

> **v. 10.** *And the third angel sounded, and there fell a great star from heaven, burning as it were a lamp, and it fell upon the third part of the rivers, and upon the fountains of water.*

If we for a moment stop to review the significance of a few of the symbols employed by the Spirit of God in this book, we shall better understand the Scriptures before us. The *great star* of this verse will undoubtedly be a prominent, powerful, and influential religious figure with overall authority in Christendom under the power of Satan. A star is a symbol of a highly respected individual and a guide. The sea is a symbol of disturbed nations. A river is the channel men use to convey what is necessary to sustain life: *A great star from heaven, burning as it were a lamp,* signifies that the figure falls with shame and ignominy from an elevated and exalted position in the world. In his fall, he will exhaust all his Satanic energies by pouring them out on the rivers, i.e., interrupting the movement of international commerce. The reference to the fountains of water implies that influential sources of what is essential for life will be seriously disrupted, while he himself is burnt out under the judgment of Almighty God, just as a shooting star disappears in the heavens.

v. 11. *And the name of the star is called Wormwood: and the third part of the waters became wormwood; and many men died of the waters, because they were made bitter.*

The star is called *Wormwood* (*Artemisia absinthium*), a plant which is highly poisonous, a symbol of the deadly effect of Satanic powers quenching the thirst of men with morally corrupting influences. The star will be an apostate individual with high authority in the revived Roman empire, falling suddenly from his exalted position. A third part of the source of water, the fountain, (*influential heads*) is poisoned (*as a dunghill, cesspool*); therefore, all that the apostate says and does will have deadly consequences. And the medium (rivers) employed to supply the water will likewise be poisonous, and a third of men will die morally. Dying morally is far more grievous than to die physically. To die morally, one will continue to live a corrupted life with the painful consequences and consciousness of sin.

> **v. 12.** *And the fourth angel sounded, and the third part of the sun was smitten, and the third part of the moon, and the third part of the stars; so, as the third part of them was darkened, and the day shone not for the third part of it, and the night likewise.*

The sounding of the fourth angel's trumpet signals the partial collapse of one third of men with supreme or intermediate authority (*sun, moon*) over the Roman Empire and over the lives of mankind generally (*stars*). They are deposed from their positions of power, influence, and light; and thereby rendered totally non-effective, lacking any authoritative power for a total of 8 hours every day.

There seems to be little doubt that the area affected will be the western part of the Roman empire where Christendom is about to be spued out of the mouth of the Lord Jesus, its testimony having become so abhorrently distasteful.

So, the various levels of authority will not only fail to give the light, essential to life for 8 hours of every day; they will also lose the capacity and ability to direct, control, and advise, thereby adding to the chaos of life already dysfunctional by reason of earlier judgments. There will be no escape from the outcome of these Trumpet judgments. Mankind will suffer greatly both physically and mentally from the solemn judgments of Almighty God.

> **v. 13.** *And I beheld, and heard an angel* (eagle) *flying through the midst of heaven, saying with a loud voice, Woe, woe, woe, to the inhabiters of the earth by reason of the other voices of the trumpet of the three angels, which are yet to sound!*

It is clear that this verse marks a division between the two groups of trumpets. The last three trumpets, when sounded, will herald in judgments more severe than the first four. The flying eagle says with a loud voice, Woe, woe, woe, being the precursors of fearful happenings about to occur with the sounding of the last three trumpets. That the eagle is flying in the mid heaven (*atmospheric heavens*) is significant, for that is the realm of Satan, who currently is the prince of the power of the air (Ephesians 2:2). While the lion is the king of the forest beasts, so the eagle is king of the birds of the air, for no other bird flies higher in the air than the eagle. Thus, the eagle flying in the heavens will give warning for all to hear and know that the woe judgments will not be the acts of Satan, but of God. The message of the eagle is to the earth dwellers throughout the world, signalling that fearful judgments are about to afflict all.

Chapter 9

v. 1. *And the fifth angel sounded, and I saw a star fall from heaven unto the earth: and to him was given the key of the bottomless pit.*

According to the Greek text, the correct rendering of the words: *I saw a star fall from heaven unto the earth,* is: *I saw a star out of the heaven fallen to the earth.* We remain in the realm of symbols, for the star which has fallen to the earth will be none other than a Jewish dignitary, an extreme apostate to whom will be given the key of the bottomless pit. The bottomless pit is not Gehenna, the lake of fire and destiny of all unregenerate souls, but the den and source of Satanic evil, distress, and despair.

v. 2. *And he opened the bottomless pit* (abyss); *and there arose a smoke out of the pit, as the smoke of a great furnace; and the sun and the air were darkened by reason of the smoke of the pit.*

The bottomless pit is the place where everything evil originates and is imprisoned; it is not where evil will be punished, that will be Gehenna, the lake that burneth with fire which can never go out. Smoke out of the pit has reference to the power of spiritual darkness. Its influence will afflict, darken, and torment the minds and consciences of apostate Jews and ungodly men, and so isolates them from the source of divine light. That the *sun and the air were darkened,* implies that man will be spiritually blinded and unable to discern between light and darkness, between right and wrong, and be totally under the control of Satan.

The bottomless pit is the domain of Satan, and where he will be bound for one thousand years during the Millennial Age; but he will eventually be cast into Gehenna, the lake of fire, where he will be tormented for ever and ever.

> **v. 3.** *And there came out of the smoke locust upon the earth: and unto them was given power, as the scorpions of the earth have power.*

The locusts upon the earth in their unparalleled masses effect enormous devastation to vegetation. That is why they symbolise the masses of evil, unregenerate men who have their origin from the abyss and act as scorpions to poison the minds and hearts of men. Happily, such evil will not affect all who are sealed for God.

> **v. 4.** *And it was commanded them that they should not hurt the grass of the earth, neither any green thing, neither any tree; but only those men which have not the seal of God in their foreheads.*

This verse is evidence enough, if evidence were needed, that the locusts referred to here are symbolic. The only food of the locust is green vegetation which was not to be injured. However, the locust, being unregenerate men, will inflict pain on all who have not the seal of God in their foreheads. As referred to earlier, grass, green plants, and trees, are symbolic of mankind in various stations of life, from the highest to the lowest, and here refer to all who will have the seal of God in their foreheads, which will include a faithful remnant of Israel. Satanic forces, i.e., as locust, will be at work under the control of God Himself, being the executor of all the judgments.

CHAPTER 9

v. 5. And *to them it was given that they should not kill them, but that they should be tormented five months: and their torment was as the torment of a scorpion, when he striketh a man.*

The human forces, likened unto swarms of locusts, were forbidden to kill any man, but to torment them for a period of five months. The torment here relates to pernicious teachings from evil men (*locust*), who so profoundly disturb the mind and conscience of mankind generally, particularly of the nation of Israel, to leave them greatly afflicted and desperately pained in their souls; yet they turned not to God. We may ask, why did the period for tormenting man have to be five months? The period is surely not without significance, for nothing in God's Word is unimportant, seeing all was divinely inspired by the Holy Spirit of God through His faithful servants. The statement, five months, occurs again in verse 10 of our chapter. The only other reference we have in the Scriptures of a five-month period is in Luke 1:24, when Elisabeth, on conception, hid herself for five months; not out of shame, but to rejoice and spend time privately in praise, worship, and thanksgiving to God.

However, the five-month period of torment equates with the average life span of a species of the locust insect. Thus, God will fix the duration of time man will suffer the torment of locust, stinging like scorpions; not to kill man but to break down man's spirit of rebellion against God. When God made Adam, he was a complete person, richly blessed with every faculty necessary for a full and rich life on earth as God's representative. So, five is man's number, signifying completeness, being blessed with five senses; feeling, hearing, seeing, smelling, and tasting, that he might be wholly committed to the will of God. Man is also blessed with five digits on each hand that he might faithfully serve God; and with five toes on each foot that he might obey the holy injunction given to Abraham:

Walk before Me, and be thou perfect (Genesis 17:1). Throughout the five-month period of torment, every faculty of mankind will be tested to the full, all with a view to bringing them to repentance. Furthermore, God's judgments will afflict men in their circumstances, and then torment them in their minds and bodies.

v. 6. *And in those days shall men seek death, and shall not find it; and shall desire to die, and death shall flee from them.*

Alas, rather than repent, man will seek a way of escape from the sufferings of the judgments of God. They will hope that by dying they will escape God's judgments, but God will not let them die; rather, they will experience a painful agony of conscience, a living death without dying. Man will also learn that no torture can equate with spiritual torture.

vv. 7-10. *And the shapes of the locusts were like unto horses prepared unto battle; and on their heads were as it were crowns like gold, and their faces were as the faces of men. And they had hair as the hair of women, and their teeth were as the teeth of lions. And they had breastplates, as it were breastplates of iron; and the sound of their wings was as the sound of chariots of many horses running to battle. And they had tails like unto scorpions, and there were stings in their tails: and their power was to hurt men five months.*

We have in these verses a picture revealing the full character of the evil forces ascending from out of the abyss to torment men. We have speed, and power, as in the horses preparing for battle; they usurped royal dignity by wearing crowns of gold; they bear images of deception as in the faces of men; they set snares of entrapment as in the hair of women; their devastating aggression is with teeth as of a lion; they exercise impregnable resistance in their conscience as typified in the breastplates of iron; they make a fearful sound in their movement and activity as an ongoing battle; and finally, the painful scorpion-like sting of their mission will be in their tails. Isaiah tells us that: *The prophet that teacheth lies, he is the tail* (Isaiah 9:15). The venomous substance of the scorpion sting is like pernicious false doctrine, designed to destroy the truth of the Godhead, and of the eternal efficacy and worth of the atoning work of Christ. Notwithstanding the devastating impact the activity of the locust-like creatures will have on mankind, their power to hurt will be limited literally to five months. These forces will attack the mind and consciences of men, particularly of the Jewish nation, but also the Gentile nations of the old Roman empire. However, they will not touch nor affect any who are sealed by God.

vv. 11-12. *And they had a king over them, which is the angel of the bottomless pit, whose name in the Hebrew tongue is Abaddon, but in the Greek tongue hath his name Apollyon. One woe is past; and, behold, there come two woes more hereafter.*

The king here will be the one who has the key to the bottomless pit. Satan is the king and it is he who will release all the forces of evil onto the world. His name is Abaddon (*Hebrew*) which means: *a destroying angel*; while Apollyon (*Greek*) means: *a destroyer*. Ever since man's fall in Eden's garden it has been the mission of Satan to sear and destroy the consciences of mankind, and that is exactly what his purpose will be in using the key to open the bottomless pit to release a multitude of evil forces upon the Jewish nation and the western part of the old Roman empire. That will conclude the impact on mankind of the first woe judgment. The two remaining woes will be unmitigated torment, grief, and death.

v. 13. *And the sixth angel sounded, and I heard a voice from the four horns of the golden altar which is before God.*

The trumpet sound of the sixth angel will be a portent of ominous consequences arising from the second woe judgment. The essential feature marking the second woe as distinct from the first is that it does not torment peoples, but will result in the slaughter of one third of mankind.

vv.14-16. *Saying to the sixth angel which had the trumpet, Loose the four angels which are bound in (at) the great river Euphrates. And the four angels were loosed, which were prepared for an hour, and a day, and a month, and a year, for to slay a third part of men. And the number of the army of the horsemen were two hundred thousand thousand: and I heard the number of them.*

Accordingly, this second woe judgment will be far more widespread in that it will embrace the entire, reformed Roman empire. Ref. Daniel 7:23-27.

It is clear that the four angels referred to by the voice (*the Lord Jehovah*) from the golden altar, *the altar of intercession*, are distinct from the four angels mentioned in chapter 7:1, where the angels are seen standing upon the four corners of the earth to restrain the four winds – forces of evil - from blowing upon earth, sea, and trees, and so stay the disturbance of a temporary equilibrium; furthermore, the angels there are seen as far apart as possible. But here in verse 14 of our chapter, the four angels are bound in the same spot by the river Euphrates; they are loosed, being fully prepared for the fixed time. Note, the angels will not have been prepared over a period of time, for they will have ever been ready for when the specified time arrives to carry out the judgment of God in the slaughter of a third part of mankind.

CHAPTER 9

And the number of the army of the horsemen were two hundred thousand thousand: and I heard the number of them.

The great force of evil, viewed as horsemen numbering two hundred million, is figurative of an innumerable host of Satanic forces which, symbolically speaking, will arise from the bottomless pit to carry out their deadly work. The deafening and fearful noise of such advancing armies will be heard throughout the lands of Asia and Europe.

> **vv. 17-19.** *And thus I saw the horses in the vision, and them that sat on them, having breastplates of fire, and of jacinth, and brimstone: and the heads of the horses were as the heads of lions; and out of their mouths issued fire and smoke and brimstone. By these three was the third part of men killed, by the fire, and by the smoke, and by the brimstone, which issued out of their mouths. For their power is in their mouth, and in their tails: for their tails were like unto serpents, and had heads, and with them they do hurt.*

The horses referred to here are symbolic of the dominant authorities existing in the lands affected by the judgments of God, who by their very appearance instil fear and foreboding in the hearts of the people who remain defiant to God's demands. Such authorities will be used by God to action His judgments, resulting in the death of millions of souls. The breastplates of fire with jacinth and brimstone worn by the Satanic forces indicate that such will have their consciences seared and hardened, being rebellious and totally indifferent to the laws of the God of creation. Jacinth is a stone of the deepest blue; the blue colour in the flame of a fire is the hottest part of the flame, signifying the intense ferocity of the horsemen. Burning brimstone (*sulphur*) is long-lasting and gives a vivid yellow/orange colour flame, leaving one in no doubt that the objective of the horsemen is the destruction of the consciences of men.

The heads of the horses, being as the heads of lions, confirms that the ferocity of all the fiery and deadly rhetoric issuing from their mouths will occasion death by apostacy of one third of the men throughout Asia and Europe. It is said their tails will be like serpents with heads, confirming that not only what goes before them will be deadly, but also what follows; for their purpose to hurt, lame, and kill; their actions will be intelligently exercised. The prophecy of Joel 2:1-11 refers to this very day of great trial.

> **vv. 20-21.** *And the rest of the men which were not killed by these plagues yet repented not of the works of their hands, that they should not worship devils, and idols of gold, and silver, and brass, and stone, and of wood: which neither can see, nor hear, nor walk: Neither repented they of their murders, nor of their sorceries, nor of their fornication, nor of their thefts.*

Notwithstanding the judgments (*plagues*) already inflicted upon Israel and the so-called christianised world, resulting in the death of millions of souls, all the ungodly who survived the plagues will continue to live in the spirit of rebellion against God, and repent not of their evil works. They will continue defiantly in their idolatry and Satanic sedition against God and His Son. Instead of such judgments rendering their consciences pliable and amenable to the will of God in the spirit of repentance, their will and resistance will be hardened against God's Son. The apostle Paul, in his letter to the Roman Christians, catalogues the Satanic characteristics of all who do not honour God or know His Son Jesus Christ, as their own personal Saviour and Lord (Romans 1:21-32).

Chapter 10

v. 1. *And I saw another mighty angel come down from* (out of) *heaven, clothed with a cloud: and a rainbow was upon his head, and his face was as it were the sun, and his feet as pillars of fire.*

Following the events from the sounding of the sixth trumpet, we have a long parenthesis from chapter 10:1 to chapter 11:14. The parenthesis will begin with the appearance of another mighty (*strong*) angel coming down from heaven. The angel here is undoubtedly the Lord Jesus, for He comes clothed with the dignity of divine glory which is ever a token of His faithfulness, power, and authority. The children of Israel were both led and protected throughout their wilderness journeys by a pillar of cloud by day and a pillar of fire by night, symbols of the Lord Jehovah's presence with them day and night (Exodus 13:21-22 and 40:36-38).

A rainbow upon His head will be a reassuring reminder of His covenant promise to Noah regarding this creation (Genesis 8:21-22). His face (countenance) was as the sun, manifesting the excellencies of the unparalleled glories of His person, and His supreme authority over all creation which will never be eclipsed or superseded (Matthew 17:2). His feet as pillars of fire signify that in a coming day the Lord Jesus will tread down all His enemies under His feet with unyielding ferocity and red-hot judgment, stamping out for ever everything that is unholy.

vv. 2-4. *And he had in his hand a little book open: and he set his right foot upon the sea, and his left foot on the earth, and cried with a loud voice, as when a lion roareth: and when he had cried, seven thunders uttered their voices. And when the seven thunders had uttered their voices, I was about to write: and I heard a voice from heaven saying unto me, Seal up those things which the seven thunders uttered, and write them not.*

The little book which the Lord Jesus will be holding is distinct from the book referred to in chapter 5:1, which was sealed with seven seals. Here the book is open, for nothing will be concealed of all that has yet to occur in the execution of the judgments of God. More will be said about the little book when we come to verses 9 and 10.

Having set His right foot upon the sea and His left foot upon the earth, He proclaims with a loud and fearful voice, as that of a lion, His rightful possession of the entire world which He purchased with His own blood. Not only are all things given unto Him (Matthew 11:27), but also, all power is given unto Him (Matthew 28:18). *A loud voice, as when a lion roareth,* implies that the world at large will hear a voice of supreme authority which should fill the hearts of mankind with fear. When Jehovah occasioned His voice to be heard in Old Testament times, it sounded like thunder, but it was to announce His authority and judgment, e.g., 1 Samuel 2:10. Here, the seven thunders confirm the complete authority, perfection, and righteousness of the terrifying judgments yet to fall upon mankind, particularly upon the land of Israel. John heard the detail of the judgments, but was directed to seal them up and not to write them down. So devastating and horrendous will be the judgments that John is spared the task of speaking about them and recording the detail; thus, such judgments remain a mystery today.

vv. 5-7. *And the angel which I saw stand upon the sea and upon the earth, lifted up his* (right) *hand to heaven, and sware* (swore JND) *by Him that liveth for ever and ever, who created heaven, and the things that therein are, and the earth, and the things that therein are, and the sea, and the things which are therein, that there should be time no longer* (that there should be no longer delay JND): *But in the days of the voice of the seventh angel, when he shall begin to sound, the mystery of God should be finished, as He hath declared to His servants the prophets.*

The angel, who is the Lord, lifts up His right hand to heaven, signifying His authority, power, and right, as invested in Him (Matthew 28:18). The right to swear by Him (*God the Creator of all things*) that there should be no longer a delay to bringing an end to the seven vial judgments, and the coming-in of His Millennial Kingdom.

The words: *In the days of the voice of the seventh angel,* have reference to the sound of the seventh trumpet which heralds the beginning of the seven vial judgments, and the completion of the mystery of God. The vial judgments will be the severest of all God's judgments expended upon the peoples of the world, but affecting more particularly the Jewish nation. Daniel speaks of this time when he says: *And there shall be a time of trouble, such as never was since there was a nation even to that same time* (Daniel 12:1). So distressing and over-whelming will be Israel's unspeakable suffering, torment, and death during the last half of the seventieth week of Daniel's prophecy (Daniel 9:27) that, as the Lord Jesus said: *Except those days should be shortened, there should no flesh be saved: but for the elect's sake those days shall be shortened* (Matthew 24:22).

The mystery of God should be completed. The significance of these words becomes clear when we understand that God, in the exercise of His patience, mercy, and grace, will have allowed man to continue in his wicked ways for 6,000 years. Whilst we acknowledge that God's ways are past finding out, and His judgments unsearchable, He has not remained indifferent to man's disobedience for, in a coming day, everyone will be made to give an account of their life before the One who gave His own life, and shed His blood to atone for the sin of the world. When all God's judgments relating to man and the universe are complete, the mystery of the ways of God will have been fully revealed.

> **vv. 8-10.** *And the voice which I heard from heaven spake unto me again, and said; Go and take the little book which is open in the hand of the angel which standeth upon the sea and upon the earth. And I went unto the angel, and said unto him, Give me the little book. And he said unto me, Take it, and eat it up; and it shall make thy belly bitter, but it shall be in thy mouth sweet as honey. And I took the little book out of the angel's hand, and ate it up; and it was in my mouth sweet as honey: and as soon as I had eaten it, my belly was bitter.*

Here, the Lord Jesus is again the key person giving instruction to John about the little book which is open. John will know that the little book contains the details of the seven vial judgments which are about to be poured out and, therefore, requests it from the hand of the Lord Jesus. John is commanded to eat it up; having done so, it will be sweet as honey in his mouth, but bitter in his belly. It is clear that the revelation John receives from the hand of God will be sweet to his heart because by faith he will be looking beyond the present time of trial to the day of glory when every child of Israel will, with peace and joy, sit under his own vine or fig tree (Micah 4:4). But as he meditates upon the judgments yet to fall upon the nation of Israel in particular, all becomes bitterness of sorrow to his soul. In this little scenario, there is an important lesson for the child of God today. Before we can be of service to our Lord among the saints of God, we must read, mark, learn, and inwardly digest the truths of Holy Scripture, for in them we shall find everything necessary to build us up spiritually and prepare us for His service. Bearing in mind we are still in the realm of symbols, the act of eating the Word of God is to allow its precious truth to form part of us, so that the truth of the Word becomes evident in our walk and testimony. It would be most dishonouring to the Lord for one to display one's knowledge of the truths of Holy Scripture, if such truths are in no way reflected in our walk and ways. Reading the Word may be sweet to our taste, but digesting the truth can be a bitter and painful process. Applying the truths of Holy Scripture to our day to day lives may occasion sacrificial action which might be hurtful to our natural being, but they will surely be beneficial for our spiritual growth and new life in Christ. The words of Jeremiah are apposite: *Thy words were found, and I did eat them; and Thy word was unto me the joy and rejoicing of mine heart* (Jeremiah 15:16). Furthermore, in the Psalms, we read: *How sweet are Thy words unto my taste! yea, sweeter than honey to my mouth!* (Psalm 119:103). Oh, that we had a greater hunger for the truths of Holy Scripture!

v. 11. *And he said unto me, Thou must prophesy again before many peoples, and nations, and tongues, and kings.*

Because John had eaten the little book, figuratively speaking, he was fully qualified to continue as a recipient and recorder of all associated with: *The Revelation of Jesus Christ*. All John's prophecies to date have been about peoples, Jews and Gentiles of all nations, high and low-born, kings and princes. Now, He is directed to continue with his record of all that he hears and what is revealed to him.

Chapter 11

v. 1. *And there was given me a reed like unto a rod: and the angel stood, saying, Rise, and measure the temple of God, and the altar, and them that worship therein.*

We continue in the realm of symbolic language. The Spirit of God will help us in our understanding where figures are given in this chapter as to whether they are symbolic or literal. John, with divine authority (*the rod*), was to gain a spiritual apprehension of what belongs to God. The act of measuring signifies a rightful claim to ownership. Measuring the temple was to identify true worshippers who belong to God through our Lord Jesus Christ; it will be they who comprise the temple of God. The altar to be measured was the brazen altar, and would remind us of the One who suffered in our stead to bring us to God. So, the altar here speaks of the saints suffering for righteousness. John would gain a divine impression of the depths of suffering the Jewish saints will be going through. The measuring of those who worship would be the act of identifying all who belong to God through Christ.

v. 2. *But the court which is without the temple leave out, and measure it not; for it is given unto the Gentiles: and the holy city shall they tread under foot forty and two months.*

This verse is in stark contrast to the previous verse where we have John exhorted to measure all that was holy. In this verse, the unregenerate Gentile nations are going to tread underfoot the outer court and profane all that is holy in it for forty and two months (*3.5 years*). It will become an unholy place. So, we see there will be a clear separation between what is holy and what is unholy. For this reason alone, God will not have the outer court of the temple measured, for He will not lay claim to what is defiled and polluted with evil. However, in His time, all that is unclean will be consumed in the fire of His judgments. Luke 21:24 refers to the part the Gentile nations will play during the forty and two months when Jerusalem shall be trodden down of the Gentiles until the: *times of the Gentiles be fulfilled* (Luke 21:24). The dominance and times of the Gentile nations over the Jews began when the two tribes (*Judah and Benjamin*) went into captivity under Nebuchadnezzar (*Book of Daniel*). The dominance and oppression of the Gentiles on the beloved city (*Jerusalem*) and the nation (*Israel*), which remains the apple of God's eye (Zechariah 2:8), will become more severe and intense until: *the times of the Gentiles* concludes with the appearing of the Lord with power and great glory to set up His Millennial Kingdom. Meanwhile, we who are of the family of God should take account of what is unholy in the whole of Christendom and in the world today, and separate ourselves from all such by not measuring/laying claim to anything of the world.

> **vv. 3-4.** *And I will give power unto My two witnesses, and they shall prophesy a thousand two hundred and three score days, clothed in sackcloth. These are the two olive trees, and the two candlesticks standing before the God of the earth.*

The two witnesses will be divinely accredited and inspired to preach the Gospel of the Kingdom (*the coming Millennial age*) for 3.5 years. During that time, they will serve the Lord in the spirit of humility and integrity, possessing nothing of this world's goods, and clothed in sackcloth; but they will be rich in God (2 Corinthians 8:9).

John defines the two witnesses as two Olive trees and two Candlesticks. It is generally accepted by learned, biblical scholars that here the cardinal number, *two*, is a symbolic number, confirming that in line with Scripture (Matthew 18:16 and 2 Corinthians 13:1) there will be an adequate and true witness of all that will be said and done by a faithful remnant of Jews in the land over the period of forty and two months, the last 3.5 years of Daniel's 70th week. It will be a time of the most severe persecution the Jewish nation will have ever experienced; hence the words of the Lord Jesus in Matthew 24:22. The two witnesses are termed *Olive trees*, because not only is the Olive tree the source of Holy anointing oil, a symbol of the Holy Spirit, it is also the tree of promise (see Genesis 8:11), for God has promised He will bring His people into their inheritance (Leviticus 20:24). The two witnesses are referred to in Zechariah 4:11-14 as *Candlesticks* (*lamps*) because they will be the only source of divine light radiating from them as they stand to witness for the Lord God of all the earth. Accordingly, their message has reference to the Lord's right to land and sea (chapter 10:5).

The saints of God on earth today are likewise indwelt with the Holy Spirit of God, that they too might be spiritual and moral lights in the world of moral darkness, and so fulfil the injunction of the Lord Jesus: *Let your light so shine before men, that they may see your good works, and glorify your Father which is in heaven* (Matthew 5:16).

> **vv. 5-6.** *And if any man will hurt them, fire proceedeth out of their mouth, and devoureth their enemies: and if any man will hurt them, he must in this manner be killed. These have power to shut heaven, that*

it rain not in the days of their prophecy: and have power over waters to turn them to blood, and to smite the earth with all plagues, as often as they will.

The divine power of the message from the two witnesses will be such that if any attempt to frustrate or injure them, their words of divine truth will be as flaming fire which will convict and consume them with a profound sense of guilt, shame, and sin; and such will weigh so heavily on their consciences, it will kill them. Furthermore, the witnesses will be invested with the same divine powers as exercised by Elijah and Moses. Power to destroy their enemies with fire (2 Kings 1:12); power to shut heaven that it rains not (1 Kings 17:1); power to turn water into blood (Exodus 7:20); power to smite the earth with plagues (Exodus, chapters 7-11), and to exercise these powers as often as they will.

vv. 7-8. *And when they shall have finished their testimony, the beast that ascendeth out of the bottomless pit shall make war against them, and shall overcome them, and kill them. And their dead bodies shall lie in the street of the great city, which spiritually is called Sodom and Egypt, where also our* (their) *Lord was crucified.*

The prophecy of the two witnesses will undoubtedly be about the coming Millennial Kingdom; and God has fixed a time limit for the promulgation of the message. The beast which ascendeth out of the bottomless pit is without doubt the revived Roman empire, which will flex its Satanic muscle with a view to killing the two witnesses, but God will not allow it to pursue its malevolent objective, until the time set by God for the proclamation of the prophecy is finished. There is an interesting parallel in the time span for the preaching by the two witnesses, with our Lord's open testimony to the world which was also three and a half years. Although Satan, via his emissaries, sought many times to take the life of the Lord Jesus, he failed because the Lord was in complete control of His own life as recorded in John 10:17-18.

The dead bodies of the two witnesses will lie unburied in the street of the great city (*Jerusalem*) which spiritually is called Sodom and Egypt for three and a half days, during which time the entire world, via current media networks, will see them. The city is called Sodom because it parallels the historical wickedness of the city (Genesis 13:13); and Egypt, because it reflects the gross corruption and idolatry of the world (Ezekiel 20:7-8).

> **vv. 9-10.** *And they of the people and kindreds and tongues and nations shall see their dead bodies three days and an half, and shall not suffer their dead bodies to be put in graves. And that dwell upon the earth shall rejoice over them, and make merry, and shall send gifts one to another; because these two prophets tormented them that dwell upon the earth.*

The action of the unregenerate Jew and Gentile dwellers on earth, being under the Satanic influence of the beast in not allowing the bodies of the faithful witnesses to be buried, will be palpable evidence of their hostility toward the witnesses and total rejection of the message they preach. That they rejoiced over the dead bodies and sent gifts one to another, will be a vain attempt to cancel out the conscious pain and spiritual torment they will experience from the message of the witnesses.

> **vv. 11-12.** *And after three days and an half the Spirit of life from God entered into them, and they stood upon their feet; and great fear fell upon them which saw them. And they heard a great voice from heaven saying unto them, Come up hither. And they ascended up to heaven in a cloud; and their enemies beheld them.*

The three and a half days that the bodies lay unburied for all the world to see must be understood as literal days. In spite of the devastating judgments which will have resulted in the death of millions of souls, the reprobates will remain unmoved. After the three and a half days, the spirit (breath) of life from God will come into the witnesses, and they will stand upon their feet. The fact that the witnesses stand upon their feet will be the unimpeachable evidence that God has raised them from the dead. When those who dwell upon the earth see the witnesses raised from the dead, and hear the call: *Come up hither*, and see them ascend to heaven in a cloud, they will be filled with great fear and foreboding, for sore dread will overtake them. Such was not the reaction of Mary Magdalene when eventually she knew it was the Lord Jesus standing before her; she was filled with great joy. It was all the evidence she needed to go and tell the disciples she had seen the Lord Jesus in resurrection (John 20:11-18).

When the church is raptured to glory, the world will not hear the voice of the trump of God which will summon all the redeemed to glory; neither will they see the dead resurrected, nor see the saints who are alive, caught up to heaven and changed into bodies of glory. However, the world will quickly wake up to realise that the day of God's grace to the world is over. The world may for a short time be disturbed by the chaos which will follow in governmental rule, commerce, education, travel, and life in general, but it will continue its rebellion against God while attempting to adjust to normality, which will be short lived.

> **v. 13.** *And the same hour was there a great earthquake, and the tenth part of the city fell, and in the earthquake were slain of men seven thousand: and the remnant were affrighted, and gave glory to the God of heaven.*

The sounding of the fifth trumpet signals the coming in of the first woe which occasions the plague of locust, being like scorpions they stung and tormented the people for five months (Chapter 9:1-11). The sixth trumpet sounded for the second woe which saw a Satanic army of two hundred million slaughter a third of mankind (Chapter 9:13-19). A further element of the second woe will be a great earthquake, with a tenth part of the city falling, and seven thousand men being killed.

What is detailed in this verse is not symbolic, but literal. Coincident with the resurrection of the witnesses will be a great earthquake to occasion the destruction of a tenth part of the city (*Jerusalem*). The number ten is a perfect number in the Scriptures, signifying perfection, completeness, and satisfaction; anything short, when ten is required, implies weakness. So, this was the measure of God's blessing to the children of Israel. According to Deuteronomy 14:22 & 27-29, one tenth (a tithe) of all Israel's blessings: the fruit of the land, the increase of their herds, and business profits, was to be given as a tithe to the Lord year on year. Alas, this divine requirement soon lapsed and was forgotten, so now God punishes them by disturbing their self-satisfied smugness with the destruction of a tenth part of their city, coupled with the death of a perfect yet substantial number of men, i.e., seven thousand. Such will be the impact of God's judgment on the hugely decimated city that the remnant will greatly fear and wonder about what may happen next, and in desperation will give glory to the God of heaven. This reaction of the remnant will not be the result of conviction of sin and repentance, but rather a vain attempt to escape the judgments of God. They should have accepted the title rights of the Lord Jesus as Lord of all the earth; a title the rebellious remnant will not accept. Today, for an individual to know the full salvation God offers to mankind, it is not sufficient to simply say: *I believe*; there must be sincere repentance of sin, and a declaration of one's faith in the Lord Jesus, accepting His atoning work on the cross of Calvary. Verse **14** tells us the second woe is past, and, behold, the third woe comes quickly.

> **v. 15.** *And the seventh angel sounded; and there were great voices in heaven, saying, The kingdoms of this world are become the kingdoms of our Lord, and of His Christ; and He shall reign for ever and ever.*

The middle part of this verse should more correctly read: *the kingdom of the world of our Lord and His Christ is come*; not that the setting up of the kingdom will have actually come, but it will be so joyously anticipated as to occasion rejoicing in heaven by the angels and the redeemed. The third woe and its pending judgments is signalled by the seventh angel sounding the seventh trumpet. However, as we have already seen in chapter 10:6-7, there should no longer be any delay for the coming in of the kingdom of the world of our Lord and of His Christ, for that moment is near. With the sounding of the seventh trumpet we note that there are no immediate judgments mentioned, but there is rejoicing in heaven among the angels and the redeemed, because they will be observers of the judgmental acts of Almighty God upon the reprobate nations of the world, knowing that, following the conclusion of all God's judgments, the Lord will reign for ever and ever.

> **vv. 16-17.** *And the four and twenty elders, which sat before God on their seats* (thrones), *fell upon their faces, and worshipped God, saying, We give Thee thanks, O Lord God Almighty, which art, and wast,* (and art to come), *because Thou hast taken to Thee Thy great power, and hast reigned.*

The words 'and art to come' are an unwarranted interpolation.

All the redeemed in heaven will be engaged in an eternal burst of praise, in blest anticipation of the kingdoms of this world becoming the kingdom of the Lord Jesus Christ. Such is the disposition of the redeemed in heaven that they act as though our Lord had already taken His great power and begun His eternal reign. But we know from the Scriptures which follow that the severest of all the judgments of Almighty God are yet to fall upon the nations of the world, more particularly upon the nation of Israel. The example of the four and twenty elders is a valuable, spiritual lesson for the saints of God today.

When the Lord Jesus spoke of Abraham rejoicing to see His day (John 8:56), He was referring to the day when He will come to this world with His saints, with power and great glory, to establish His world-wide Millennial kingdom and reign in righteousness for a thousand years. It will be the occasion when all Israel is saved in a day (Romans 11:26). Our Lord longs to see every member of the nation which ever was and still is *the apple of His eye* (Deuteronomy 32:10 & Zechariah 2:8), sitting under his own vine and under his own fig tree (Micah 4:4).

The apostle Paul wrote about a *crown of righteousness* being given to all who love His appearing (2 Timothy 4:8); when our blessed Lord will exercise total control of the world, with all His enemies under His feet (Hebrews 2:8). We too should love and rejoice in the glorious prospect of such day; a day referred to in Hebrews 12:2; and speaking of the Lord Jesus: *Who for the joy that was set before Him endured the cross, despising the shame, and is set down at the right hand of the throne of God.* Furthermore, it will be a day when: *At the name of Jesus every knee should bow, of things in heaven, and things in earth, and things under the earth; and that every tongue should confess that Jesus Christ is Lord, to the glory of God the Father* (Philippians 2:10-11).

> **v. 18.** *And the nations were angry, and Thy wrath is come, and the time of the dead, that they should be judged, and that Thou shouldest give*

reward unto Thy servants the prophets, and to the saints, and them that fear Thy name, small and great; and shouldest destroy them which destroy the earth.

There are four distinct segments in this verse which are not sequential. The first: *And the nations were angry, and Thy wrath is come.* What we have here was prophetically uttered in Psalm 2, the first Messianic Psalm: W*hy do the heathen rage, and the people imagine a vain thing? The kings of the earth set themselves, and the rulers take counsel together, against the Lord, and against His anointed.* The nations will be angry (*full of wrath*) because of how the devastating judgments of Almighty God had painfully ransacked their consciences. They could neither escape nor hide from the all-searching eye of God, yet they remain indifferent and unrepentant before Him. The judgment of the nations takes place before the coming-in of the Millennial reign of Christ. The second segment is: *And Thy wrath is come, and the time of the dead, that they should be judged.* This takes us to the end of the Millennium, when all the unregenerate from the time of Adam to the time referred to in Revelation 20:7-9 will be judged by that One whom God has already appointed (Acts 17:31). The procedural details of the judgments are given in Revelation 20:11-15. Some expositors believe the judgment applies to saints who died being martyred because of their testimony of faith, but this interpretation flies in the face of what is declared in John 5:24, that the believer will not come into condemnation (judgment), but is passed from death unto life. The term: *judgment seat*, in Romans 14:10 and 2 Corinthians 5:10, is better translated *the bema*, being the seat of manifestation when the record of the path of service on earth of the Lord's disciples will be privately manifested before them, and then rewarded accordingly. All this takes place before the commencement of the Millennial reign of Christ. A more trustworthy interpretation regarding the first part of verse 18 before us is detailed in Revelation 20:11-15.

The third segment: A*nd that Thou shouldest give reward unto Thy servants the prophets, and to the saints, and them that fear Thy name, small and great;* takes us back to the moment following the rapture of the saints to heaven, but also includes those who will have come out of: *great tribulation, and washed their robes, and have made them white in the blood of the Lamb.* ref. Revelation 7:14. All will be rewarded according to their works in the path of divine service.

The final segment: *and shouldest destroy them which destroy the earth;* clearly has reference to the great destroyer of the earth, Satan. His emissaries will occasion the spoiling of the physical creation. Their fate is recorded in Revelation 20:10-15.

> **v. 19.** *And the temple of God was opened in heaven, and there was seen in His temple the ark of His testament* (covenant)*: and there were lightnings, and voices, and thunderings, and an earthquake, and great hail.*

Starting with this verse, we have another parenthesis up to chapter 14:20. What is brought before us in chapters 12–14 are accounts of the dramatic events which took place from the time of the expected birth of Christ to the moment when He, the Lord Jesus, treads out the winepress of the wrath of God just prior to Him coming with power and great glory to establish His Kingdom.

The vision John had of the temple and the Ark in heaven was a confirmation of the eternal covenant God has with His ancient people, that a faithful remnant would truly be brought into blessing in the land of promise. Although there was no actual temple in heaven as confirmed by John in chapter 21:22, the vision symbolises the spiritual meeting place of the faithful remnant together with the assurance of blessing on earth. Mention of the Ark is significant in that it would contain the tables of the law, the law which was perfectly and eternally ratified for the glory and honour of God in the Person of the Lord Jesus Christ as Man. For an explanation of the lightnings, voices, and thunderings, see notes on chapter 4, verse 5. And for an interpretation of the earthquake, see note on chapter 8, verse 5. But here we have another element of God's judgment, *great hail;* signifying that the judgment will not be a short, sharp blow, but a continuous out-pouring of the wrath of God of unparalleled intensity, inflicting much pain.

Chapter 12

v. 1. *And there appeared a great wonder* (sign) *in heaven; a woman clothed with the sun, and the moon under her feet, and upon her head a crown of twelve stars.*

The noun *wonder* is incorrect, for a *wonder* signifies something unexpected, whereas a *sign* has a specific objective and message in view. The woman clothed with the sun is clearly a figure of Israel as prophesied in Isaiah 9:6. The sun is the supreme light of the heavens, signifying that Israel will be the paramount nation in the new earth, with lesser nations (*the moon*) under her control. The woman has on her head a crown with twelve stars. The number twelve in Scripture has reference to perfect administration, and that is exactly what the twelve tribes of the nation of Israel will exercise during the Millennial age.

v. 2. *And she being with child cried, travailing in birth, and pained to be delivered.*

The nation of Israel had been under the oppressive control of the Roman empire for many hundreds of years, and yearned to be free of the burden which shackled it. Yet, when that moment came, they rejected the One whom God had sent to be their Messiah, King, Redeemer, and Deliverer (Luke 23:18). Nevertheless, Israel was the mother of Christ as confirmed by Micah 5:2. The nation will again suffer greatly during the: *great tribulation*, period, the last half of Daniel's 70th week, before the Lord, their Messiah, comes to deliver them and set up His Kingdom.

v. 3. *And there appeared another wonder* (sign) *in heaven; and behold a great red dragon, having seven heads and ten horns, and seven crowns upon his heads.*

The dragon is one of several titles of Satan (Revelation 20:2); and being red, indicates he is the purveyor of death through bloodshed. The title also implies that he symbolises cruelty and violence which have ever been his trademark. The seven crowned heads do not refer to the seven hills upon which Rome is built, but rather to the seven world kingdoms (nations) which, in their time, have overwhelmed Israel. The time span covering the world kingdoms is from when the nation was enslaved in Egypt under the Pharaohs to a time yet future. Such nations have and will continue their hostility against Israel. It will be the time when the revived Roman empire, comprising ten nations (kingdoms) in unison, represented by the ten crowned horns, will cruelly dominate and control the religious, political, and business world. Satan, as the dragon, will continue to harass and persecute with increasing ferocity the nation of Israel, which will ever remain the apple of God's eye (Deuteronomy 32:10).

v. 4. *And his tail drew* (draws) *the third part of the stars of heaven, and did cast them to the earth: and the dragon stood before the woman which was ready to be delivered, for to devour her child as soon as it was born.*

The tail of the dragon represents its demonic power, as the prophet that teacheth lies (Isaiah 9:15), to draw away a third of the religious heads *(stars of heaven)* of the christianised world. By exercising an evilly moral influence upon them and casting them to the earth, the dragon renders them null and void. Satan, being the prince of the power of the air (Ephesians 2:2), saw the incarnation of the Son of God as a threat to his power over death in the world and over mankind. As the dragon, Satan knew all too well the veracity and power of the words of Jehovah in Genesis 3:15 which would be fulfilled by the coming into this world of the Son of God who, through His own death, would destroy him that had the power of death, that is the devil; ref. Hebrews 2:14.

So, the dragon stands over the woman (*Israel*) who is about to be delivered of the child (*Lord Jesus*), with the sole purpose of slaying the child on birth. But God now intervenes, and although: *in Ramah* (places in Israel), *was there a voice heard, lamentation, and weeping, and great mourning, Rachel weeping for her children, and would not be comforted, because they are not* (Matthew 2:18), the child Jesus was safe. Herod, who epitomised the dragon, by the cruellest act of infanticide failed to achieve his satanic objective.

v. 5. *And she brought forth a man child, who was to rule all nations with a rod of iron: and her child was caught up unto God, and to His throne.*

This verse confirms that what we have here is not a historical record of the Lord's incarnation and life on earth, but rather a detail of what God has planned for His Son and the nation He loves throughout the millennial age. The man child who will rule all nations with a rod of iron has reference to the Lord Jesus when He will reign in righteousness with His saints throughout the Millennial age; a time when absolutely everything in creation will be subject to Him (Psalm 2:8-9). The child, when born, will be caught up to God and to His throne, signifying that everything occurring on earth and in heaven will be under the control of the Lord Jesus.

CHAPTER 12

> **v. 6.** *And the woman fled into the wilderness, where she hath a place prepared of God, that they should feed her there a thousand two hundred and threescore days.*

The woman's flight into the wilderness marks the beginning of the last half of Daniel's 70th week, a period the Lord Jesus referred to as a time of: *great tribulation*. The woman is so precious to God that her time in the wilderness where God will protect, sustain, and nourish her is detailed in days rather than, *a time, and times, and half a time*. However, we should note that the first six verses of this chapter stand alone in presenting to us a complete picture of events which shall take place. Accordingly, the verses of the chapter are not consecutive; it is clear that when the dragon is cast out of heaven into the earth (verse 9), it is then that the woman (*faithful remnant of Israel*) will take her flight into the barren wilderness.

> **vv. 7-9.** *And there was war in heaven: Michael and his angels fought against the dragon; and the dragon fought and his angels, and prevailed not; neither was their place found any more in heaven. And the great dragon was cast out, that old serpent, called the Devil, and Satan, which deceiveth the whole world: he was cast out into the earth, and his angels were cast out with him.*

From verse 7 we return to the chronological order of events as they will occur from verse 19 of chapter 11. The statement: *and there was war in heaven*, is the only reference in Scripture of such a war. In Isaiah 14:12-15, we have details of the fall of Satan from his renowned position as an angel of God which occurred way back before the present creation, but there was not a war in heaven at that time. However, there was the occasion, as recorded in Genesis 6, when some of the angels which fell with Satan did not keep their first estate and mingled with the daughters of men; these are reserved in everlasting chains, in darkness, awaiting the judgment of the great day (Genesis 6:2 and Jude 6). The war in heaven will not occur in the heaven of heavens where God dwelleth in eternal light, a realm into which no man can enter, but in the atmospheric and starry heavens, and in the heavenly realm where Satan appears as an accuser of the brethren; verse 10.

The war in the heavens brought about a cleansing of the heavens, when the archangel Michael and his angels triumphed over the dragon and his angels and cast them out into the earth. Notwithstanding the fact that at this time the church of God will have been raptured away to heaven and translated into the likeness of our blessed Saviour (Philippians 3:21), we are ever mindful that in this present day of God's grace to the world, the Christian warfare is: *Not against flesh and blood, but against principalities, against powers, against the rulers of the darkness of this world, against spiritual wickedness in high places* (Ephesians 6:12). These are the very forces, i.e., the dragon and his angels, which Michael and his angels will triumph over and cast out into the earth. In verse 9, we have a four-fold title of Satan. The dragon, because of his unspeakable cruelty. The old serpent, because of his subtlety and lies. The Devil, because he is a diabolical traducer of the truth, and a slanderer. Finally, Satan, because he is a liar, an accuser of the brethren, and the archenemy of God. When cast out of heaven, Satan will no longer be an accuser of the brethren before God.

> **v. 10.** *And I heard a loud voice saying in heaven, Now is come salvation, and strength, and the kingdom of our God, and the power of His Christ: for the accuser of our brethren is cast down, which accused them before our God day and night.*

There is little doubt that the loud voice John heard in heaven was that of the redeemed, rejoicing because Satan and his hosts had been cast out of the heavens. Rebellion in the realms of heaven forever ended; never again will the heavens be invaded and defiled by Satan; all cleansing having been accomplished through the efficacy of the blood of the Lamb. Well might a chorus echo throughout the courts of heaven, of the One who alone triumphed over sin, death, and the grave (1 Corinthians 15:55)

> *Hark! those loud triumphant chords.*
>   *Jesus takes the highest station.*
> *Oh, what joy the sight affords.*
>   *Crown Him! Crown Him!*
> *King of kings, and Lord of lords.*
>
>   T. Kelly

Now is come salvation, does not refer to the church, but to the expectation of the faithful witness on earth during the tribulation period; the church has already been raptured to heaven, away beyond the range of Satan's activities on earth. So, we should understand that at that time: *the salvation, the strength* (power), and *the kingdom,* relate to what will still be future. *The salvation,* is in anticipation of the moment when the Lord will come with power and great glory to establish His own Millennial kingdom. *The strength* (power), relates to the fulfilment of the Lord's own words: *All power is given unto Me in heaven and in earth* (Matthew 28:18). *The kingdom,* speaks of the time when God will be supreme over all (1 Corinthians 15:24). The expression, *our brethren,* refers to the saints still on earth who were passing through sore trial and tribulation. Such redeemed ones had been falsely accused before God, day and night by Satan, but no longer.

v.11. *And they overcame him by the blood of the Lamb, and by the word of their testimony; and they loved not their lives unto the death.*

Because of their sincere acceptance of the call to repentance through the preaching of the Gospel of the Kingdom, and having been cleansed by the blood of the Lamb, they will have a clear conscience before God. Furthermore, they will be able, by the power of the Spirit of God, to resist and overcome the evil influences of Satan. In longing to be with their Lord, they will be prepared to lay down their lives in defence of their faith, confirming that their love for God is greater than their love for life on earth.

> **v. 12.** *Therefore rejoice, ye heavens, and ye that dwell in them. Woe to the inhabiters of the earth and of the sea! For the devil is come down unto you, having great wrath, because he knoweth that he hath but a short time.*

The angelic hosts of heaven, together with the saints already in heaven, are exhorted to rejoice because the archenemy and destroyer of souls is cast out of the heavens. Satan will never again defile the courts of heaven. The words, *the inhabiters of,* are an unfortunate interpolation and sadly spoil the correct meaning of the verse. The *earth* and *sea*, upon which a woe is pronounced, are symbolic realms. The *earth* has reference to governments of the world whose peoples appear to be settled and content, while the *sea* speaks of those parts of the world which will be in a state of political and social upheaval. Thus, no part of the inhabited world will escape the rage and great wrath Satan will pour out. His actions will be cruel and expeditious because he will know that his time is quickly coming to an end before he is cast into the bottomless pit for a thousand years (Revelation 20:1-3). N.B. The thousand years are literal; see last clause of chapter 20 verse 3.

> **v. 13.** *And when the dragon saw that he was cast unto the earth, he persecuted the woman which brought forth the man child.*

Satan's enmity against the woman (*tribe of Judah*) will be tantamount to unleashing his profound hatred, anger, and intense wrath upon her. So severe will Satan's rage be against the Jews that, as the Lord Jesus said: *Except those days should be shortened, there should no flesh be saved: but for the elect's sake those days shall be shortened* (Matthew 24:22). Satan knows full well that it was via the tribe of Judah that the Lord Jesus, as the Messiah, came into manhood for the express purpose of destroying him and his works (1 John 3:8). Satan's destruction will be the fulfilment of the Scripture which says that the seed of the woman (*the Lord Jesus*) shall bruise (*crush*) his head (Genesis 3:15); in other words, destroy him and cast him into Hell, Gehenna, the Lake of Fire (Revelation 20:10).

> **v. 14.** *And to the woman were given two wings of a great eagle, that she might fly into the wilderness, into her place, where she is nourished for a time, and times, and half a time, from the face of the serpent.*

As the lion is the king of the beasts of the field, so the eagle is the king of the birds which fly in the heavens. The eagle soars higher than any other bird and in its flight is not molested by any. Thus, it was with Israel when God brought them up out of Egypt, and notwithstanding their combat with, and their defeat of Amalek in the Vale of Rephidim, He bore them on eagles' wings to the mountainous region of Sinai (Exodus 19:4). The eagles' wings given to the woman (*Judah*) are symbolic of the miraculous way the Lord will guide and shield the faithful remnant from subtle and venomous assaults of the serpent at this time. *That she might fly into the wilderness,* implies that the faithful remnant will be isolated from the rest of the world and although denied the natural necessities of life will be nourished and sustained by the Lord throughout the last three and a half years of Daniel's 70th week; away from the face of the serpent.

v. 15. *And the serpent cast out of his mouth water as a flood (river) after the woman, that he might cause her to be carried away of the flood (river).*

The, *water as a flood (river)*, out of the mouth of the serpent is not literal water, but, like a river in flood, the nations opposed to the woman will pour out evil and pernicious sayings, designed to deceive, distress and confuse her that she might be carried away on a flood (river) of false hopes. However, the serpent's ultimate objective will be to fully expose the woman to the murderous assaults of the hostile nations of the world, and thereby terminate her existence as a people who remain the: *apple of God's eye* (Deuteronomy 32:9-10 and Zechariah 2:8).

v. 16. *And the earth helped the woman, and the earth opened her mouth, and swallowed up the flood which the dragon cast out of his mouth.*

The earth in this verse refers to nations which are stable in government and fully sympathetic with the woman in her plight. There is no doubt that, when God's people are under serious threat, providential intervention will intervene to ensure God's purpose is not frustrated. In this case, the nations in sympathy with the woman will do all they can to mitigate her sufferings at the hand of Satan, by neutralising his flood of abuse. This will be accomplished by broadcasting world-wide the truth regarding God's plans which are to ensure that Israel, the nation He loves, will, in due course, take full possession of the Land of Promise, Israel, which He has already given to them.

v. 17. *And the dragon was wroth with the woman, and went to make war with the remnant of her seed, which keep the commandments of God, and have the testimony of Jesus Christ.*

The dragon becomes extremely angry with all Israel because his efforts to dispose of the nation fail; this has ever been Satan's objective right from the beginning. We see this in the spiritual significance of the burning bush in Exodus 3:2. The thorn bush, a symbol of Israel; the fire, speaking of the cruel persecution inflicted on the nation in captivity in Egypt. That the bush was not consumed confirmed that no matter how severe the trials inflicted upon the children of Israel they could not be destroyed because the Lord Jehovah was in the midst of them, in the fire. Thus, it will ever be with the faithful remnant, up to the time and beyond, when in Israel every man sits under his vine and under his fig tree (Micah 4:4).

Being the period of: *great tribulation,* the dragon will turn his ferocious attention to the faithful remnant of the Jews. The severity and extent of their suffering will be so great that, as we have already reminded ourselves of the words of the Lord Jesus: *Except those days should be shortened, there should no flesh be saved: but for the elect's sake those days shall be shortened (Matthew 24:22).* Notwithstanding the severity of their trials, the faithful remnant will treasure and keep the commandments of God; they will also retain, with joy in their hearts, the life testimony of the Lord Jesus Christ.

Chapter 13

v. 1. *And I stood upon the sand of the sea, and saw a beast rise up out of the sea, having seven heads and ten horns, and upon his horns ten crowns, and upon his heads the name of blasphemy.*

According to the most reliable Greek text, the first clause of this verse: *And I stood upon the sand of the sea,* should be verse 18 of the previous chapter. Furthermore, the descriptive detail of the beast is reversed; the verse should read: *And I saw a beast rising out of the sea, having ten horns and seven heads, and upon its horns ten diadems, and upon its heads, names of blasphemy.* Also, that the personal pronoun, *I*, in the verse, relates to John the seer, and not to the dragon. This understanding is strengthened by the fact that the dragon would have gone away to make war with the remnant of the woman's seed (Chapter 12:17).

This chapter, together with the previous and the one following, form a parenthesis between the first half-week, of Daniel's 70th week, and the second half-week which will be a time of: *great tribulation.* The chapter brings before us the two beasts which will feature greatly during this period.

The first beast, verses 1-10, will be a Gentile head, known variously as: *the little horn* (Daniel 7:8), *the coming prince* (Daniel 9:26) representing the revived Roman Empire, which will be noted for its cruelty and Satanic behaviour. The second beast, detailed in verses 11-18, will a reprobate Jew, known variously as: *the antichrist* (1 John 2:18), *the false prophet*, (Revelation 16:13), and, *the man of sin,* marked by apostasy (2 Thessalonians 2:3).

The sand of the sea shore on which John stands is a symbol of all the peoples of the nations of the world. Abraham, we may recall, was directed by God to offer his son Isaac as a burnt offering to God; albeit, a ram was offered in substitution. Because Abraham had not withheld his only son Isaac from God, God confirmed to him that his seed would be as the stars of heaven and as the sand of the sea shore (Genesis 22:17), symbols of incalculable multitudes. The beast rising out of the sea is undoubtedly the revived Roman empire. The sea from which the beast emerges symbolises the disturbed nations of the world.

The beast will have seven heads and ten horns crowned with (diadems), and upon his heads the name of blasphemy. This beast is distinct from, albeit related to, the red dragon John had already seen as a sign in heaven (chapter 12:3). But now, while standing on the sea shore, he witnesses the emergence of a beast from the nations of the world. It is a symbol of the revived Roman Empire which, in its original form, was the last of four world-wide kingdoms which began with the Babylonian kingdom under Nebuchadnezzar in 606 B.C. It was also the beginning of: *the times of the Gentiles* (Luke 21:24), which will continue until the Lord comes with power and great glory to establish His Millennial kingdom. The other two kingdoms which followed were the Medo-Persian and the Greek/Macedonian. The original Roman empire began in 27 B.C. and ended under the reign of its last emperor, Romulus Augustulus in 476 A.D.

The seven crowned heads do not refer to the seven hills upon which Rome is built, but rather to the seven kingdoms (nations) which in their time had overwhelmed Israel. The time span covering the world kingdoms is from when the nation was enslaved in Egypt under the Pharaohs to a time yet future, being the revived Roman Empire, comprising a confederacy of ten kingdoms (chapter 17:12). As Scripture is silent regarding the identity of the ten kingdoms, it would be unwise to hazard a guess as to which they may be.

Upon his heads the name of blasphemy. Notice the personal, single pronoun, *his*, confirming the overall power will be controlled by one person. The blasphemy occurs when the heads elevate themselves to that of gods, as did Nero in the 1st Century when he claimed the title: *the eternal one*. But the blasphemy will be more than this, for the heads will be guilty of every form of dishonour before God and man.

> **v. 2.** *And the beast which I saw was like unto a leopard, and his feet were as the feet of a bear; and his mouth as the mouth of a lion: and the dragon gave him his power, and his seat, and great authority.*

The beast, resembling a leopard, will reflect the character of the Greek/Macedonian empire for its speed in conquest. The feet of the beast, like unto a bear, will mirror the Medo-Persian empire which held its peoples with an iron grip. The beast, having the mouth of a lion, will signify its cruel and ravenous character, as was seen throughout the time of the Babylonian empire. Thus, the nature and action of the beast - the revived Roman Empire - will be a fusion of all the Satanic features which marked the previous three empires.

It will be the dragon (Satan) which will give the revived Roman empire its world-wide power, and arrange for the setting of a great throne from which it will exercise exceptional demonic authority.

> **v. 3.** *And I saw one of his heads as it were wounded to death; and his deadly wound was healed: and all the world wondered after the beast.*

The head John saw which had been wounded was the revived Roman Empire which, according to Biblical historians, followed the Greek/Macedonian empire circa 146 BC. and lasted until 476 AD. The last Roman emperor, Romulus Augustulus, reigned from October 475 AD to September 476 AD. He was deposed by a Germanic barbarian statesman, named Flavius Odoacer, who inflicted a deadly wound upon the Roman empire, thus ending its imperial dominance over the known Western world. John now sees this head as the revived Roman Empire restored through the agency of Satan, and notes that the world will wonder (be astonished) by its rise, power, and influence.

> **v. 4.** *And they worshipped the dragon which gave power unto the beast: and they worshipped the beast, saying, Who is like unto the beast? Who is able to make war with him?*

Such will be the high esteem of the beast by the world that the world, with the exception of the God-fearing, will worship (*do homage unto*) the dragon which will give despotic power to the beast. Because of the influential power of the beast, it too will be worshipped by the unregenerate world. So fearful will the devastating forces of the beast be that the world will challenge any who dare to oppose it (*make war against it*). The world itself will elevate the beast as a deity to be worshipped (*do homage unto it*), thereby compounding its wickedness.

> **vv. 5-6.** *And there was given unto him a mouth speaking great things and blasphemies; and power was given unto him to continue* (practise) *forty and two months. And he opened his mouth in blasphemy against God, to blaspheme His name, and His tabernacle, and them that dwell in heaven.*

There is little doubt that what John sees and hears was prophetically spoken of in Daniel 7:8 & 25, and relates to the revived Roman empire, defined by John as *the beast*. Power will be given to the beast by the dragon to wear out (*persecute and slay*) the saints. Although allowed of God, it will be inspired by Satan and limited by God to forty and two months, i.e., the last half of Daniel's 70th week. Meanwhile, pouring out of the mouth of the beast will be the most dreadful blasphemies; defaming, denouncing, railing, reviling, slandering, vilifying and dishonouring the name of Almighty God. Furthermore, the beast will denigrate the holy tabernacle, the sanctuary of God, and pour contempt, with blasphemies, upon the saints of God.

v. 7. *And it was given unto him* (the beast) *to make war with the saints, and to overcome them: and power was given him over all kindreds, and tongues, and nations.*

According to the original Greek text, the latter clause of this verse reads: *And authority was given to it over every tribe, and people, and tongue, and nation.*

It will be the dragon which gives the beast the incentive to war against the saints of God. The authority given to the beast by the dragon was to persecute the saints of every tribe, people, tongue and nation who do not, in the spiritual sense, dwell on the earth, but in spirit are citizens of heaven. Those who are earth dwellers are not persecuted by the beast, because the dragon already has them in his grasp. The term: *to overcome them,* implies that the suffering of the saints will be unto natural death, but spiritually, unto eternal life, in contrast to eternal death for all unregenerate. Malachi wrote: *They that feared the Lord spake often one to another: and the Lord hearkened, and heard it, and a book of remembrance was written before Him for them that feared the Lord, and that thought upon His name. And they shall be Mine, saith the Lord of hosts, in that day when I make up My jewels (treasures)* (Malachi 3:16-17).

v. 8. *And all that dwell upon the earth shall worship him, whose names are not written in the book of life of the Lamb slain from the foundation of the world.*

In this verse, there is a clear case for distinguishing between the God-fearing who will be living on the earth and worship God and the ungodly who dwell upon the earth and worship the beast. The God-fearing, living on the earth, are persecuted and chastened by the beast, even unto death, but they are prepared to die rather than surrender their faith in Christ; for heaven is their home. The earth-dwellers who worship the beast reject God's overtures of love and the salvation He offers. Such live just for today and give no thought about their eternal destiny; hence, their names will not be found written in the Lamb's book of life. The final judgment on their Godless life as they stand before the Great White Throne will be condemnation; their destiny will be Hell, Gehenna, the lake of fire for all eternity.

vv. 9-10. *If any man have an ear, let him hear. He that leadeth into captivity shall go into captivity: he that killeth with the sword must be killed with the sword. Here is the patience and the faith of the saints.*

This warning, to give ear to what the Spirit of God has to say, is as important for the God-fearing today, as it will be in the time of: *great tribulation,* when the saints of God may be called upon to suffer unto death for the sake of the testimony of Christ. For today, we would heed the words of the apostle Peter: *If, when ye do well, and suffer for it, ye take it patiently, this is acceptable with God* (1 Peter 2:20).

In the day of which John writes, the saints will be called upon not to resist the rule of the beast where there would be no conflict with their pure conscience before God. However, they must not be involved in attempts to quell strife and uprisings by holding guilty parties captive; to do so would be tantamount to resisting the beast, which they must not do. Furthermore, they must not be involved in any form of warfare, because their objective would be in conflict with the aims of the beast, and as a consequence they will suffer mortal death.

Here is the patience and the faith of the saints; this statement confirms that, as with the saints of God today, so with the saints in the time of: *great tribulation;* all are in the kingdom and patience of Jesus Christ, not the kingdom of power. We shall be in the kingdom of power with Christ throughout the Millennial age.

> **v. 11.** *And I beheld another beast coming up out of the earth; and he had two horns like a lamb, and he spake as a dragon.*

This beast is quite distinct from the first beast, in that it arises from out of the earth having only one head with two horns. Rising out of the earth indicates that it will come out from the established and settled state of government in Jerusalem of Isarel. This will be an apostate Jew, the false prophet, the antichrist, having the appearance of a gentle lamb with just two horns. He presumes to possess divine power, but his speech betrays him, for his words are those of a dragon. Comment has already been made about the Lamb of chapter 5:6, which is clearly the Lord Jesus, having seven horns and seven eyes which are the seven Spirits of God sent forth into all the earth.

Horns in Scripture usually speak of power, which this beast intends to exercise in merciless cruelty as the false prophet and the antichrist. He will arrogate to himself an exalted status, coupled with the authority and power given to him by the dragon. He will speak as a dragon, for his words will be demonic, brutal, and deceptive; and he will spare none who fails to conform to his edicts. There is no doubt this, *man of sin,* will act with determination to do his own will, in stark contrast to the Lord Jesus who ever delighted to do the will of His Father; ref. Psalm 40:8 and John 6:38. The Lord Jesus speaks of this antichrist as the one who will come in his own name and deceive reprobate Jews who will accept him with open arms (John 5:43).

> **v. 12.** *And he exerciseth all the power of the first beast before him, and causeth the earth and them that dwell therein to worship the first beast, whose deadly wound was healed.*

The power which will be exercised by this second beast, who is the false prophet, the antichrist, the man of sin, will be the same as that detailed for the first beast in verses 5, 6 and 7 of this chapter. He will know that his fellow beast has the allegiance and power of ten kingdom nations at his disposal, so will not wish to occasion him displeasure. Accordingly, the beast (an individual) will do anything to ingratiate himself with the first beast in order to preserve his life, status, and ambition. As the supremo of all religious thinking and practice on earth, he will direct all to worship the first beast which had a deadly wound to the head healed.

> **vv. 13-14.** *And he doeth great wonders* (signs), *so that he maketh fire come down from heaven on the earth in the sight of men. And deceiveth them that dwell on the earth by the means of those miracles which he had power to do in the sight of the beast; saying to them that dwell on the earth, that they should make an image to the beast, which had the wound by the sword, and did live.*

In 2 Thessalonians 2:3-4, Paul wrote prophetically about this antichrist, also known as: *the man of sin, the son of perdition;* how that by his acts he will deceive many. He will exalt himself in a demonic spirit of arrogance above the God of creation, and all that is divinely revered. The, *man of sin,* will establish a personal seat in the temple of God (the temple erected by apostate Jews, which God, in His time, will demolish) shewing himself that he is God. Such will be the dreadful Satanic character and hubris of the: *man of sin.* Furthermore, being under the total influence and power of the dragon, he will occasion unnatural incidents to occur, and even cause fire to come down from heaven for all to see and wonder, but it will be by Satanic power. Such evil power was exercised by Pharaoh's magicians via their enchantments, when Moses and Aaron stood before Pharaoh to plead for the release of the children of Israel from their bondage (Exodus 7 & 8). One is also reminded of the time when Elijah called upon the Lord to accept his sacrifice which had been saturated with water. Fire came down from heaven, it consumed the sacrifice, the wood and the stones, and licked up all the water (1 Kings 18:37-39). This was a miraculous demonstration of the power of Almighty God over the forces of nature, but the actions of the, *man of sin,* will be powered by Satan. This individual, the antichrist, possessing Satanic powers, will persuade the earth-dwellers to accept him as their supreme head. Whereupon, he will direct them to make an image, not of, but to the beast, and set it up in a prominent place. For the third time (verses 3, 12, & 14), we are told that the first beast had been seriously wounded unto death, and miraculously healed. In this verse, we are told how the beast was wounded; it was the sword, confirming that the first Roman empire ended violently; as will happen with this, the last Roman empire (Revelation 19:20-21).

v.15. *And he had power to give life* (breath) *unto the image of the beast, that the image of the beast should both speak, and cause that as many as would not worship the image of the beast should be killed.*

The power given to the beast was from the dragon, but such power could not give life to energise the image, for the giving of life is the prerogative of God alone. The giving of breath to the image that it might speak confirms it will be Satan's voice which the people will hear, just as occurs today in the practice of spiritualism, sorcery, and necromancy. That the image speaks will be taken as the power and authority given to command all that dwell upon the earth to worship the image; any who refuse will be sentenced to death at the behest of the image. At this time, the faithful remnant will not be persuaded to worship an idol, but will be ready to lay down their lives in defence of the truth of God in Jesus Christ. While these faithful ones may know the words of Moses in his decalogue (Exodus 20:3-5), they may not be familiar with the words of the apostle Paul, that: *Christ is the end of the law for righteousness to everyone that believeth* (Romans 10:4). Nevertheless, they will be saved.

> **vv. 16-17.** *And he causeth all, both small and great, rich and poor, free and bond, to receive a mark in their right hand, or in their foreheads: and that no man might buy or sell, save he that had the mark, or the name of the beast, or the number of his name.*

The one who *causeth,* is: *the antichrist, the false prophet, the man of sin, an apostate Jew,* who, under the influence of Satan, will direct that all mankind in all stations of life bear a mark of subservience to the first beast, the head of the revived Roman Empire. The mark upon the right hand will signify servitude and submission to the tyrannical rule of the beast; and the mark or name in the forehead will be a public acknowledgement of such servitude and unalloyed allegiance to the beast.

Just as the faithful remnant will refuse to worship the image, so they will likewise refuse to submit to bearing the marks or name of the beast on their bodies. They will refuse, knowing full well the consequences, for they will be denied the basic essentials for living; but their faith will rise above the harsh circumstances of this life, knowing that:

> *God is still on the throne,*
> *And He will remember His own.*
> *Though trials may press us,*
> *And burdens distress us;*
> *He never will leave us alone.*
> *God is still on the throne,*
> *And He will remember His own,*
> *His promise is true,*
> *He will not forget you;*
> *God is still on the throne.*
>
> Mrs. F W Suffield.

Today, the saints of God should be marked by a Godly disposition, and a walk pleasing to the Lord.

> **v. 18.** *Here is wisdom. Let him that hath understanding count the number of the beast: for it is the number of a man; and his number is six hundred threescore and six.*

The words: *here is wisdom,* has reference to the wisdom of God of which the apostle Paul speaks in his first epistle to the Corinthian church (chapter 2:7). Throughout the past centuries, man has applied his own wisdom in a vain attempt to work out the significance of the number of the beast, 666. Notwithstanding an existing multitude of reasoned explanations, to the spiritually minded, none appears as a valid and divine interpretation. However, it is clear that a divine wisdom and understanding of the number will be given to the faithful remnant at

CHAPTER 13

the time of: *great tribulation,* and not before. Meanwhile, we may accept the undisputed significance of the number 6 in Scripture, as symbolising man's weakness, coming one short of perfection which we have in the number, seven. The number of the beast, being: *Six hundred* threescore and six, may well signify the incontrovertible evidence of the total weakness of man after the flesh. The destiny of the beast (chapter 19:20), will also confirm his utter weakness against the power of Almighty God.

Chapter 14

v. 1. And *I looked, and, lo, a Lamb stood on the mount Sion* (Zion), *and with Him an hundred forty and four thousand, having His Father's name written in their foreheads.*

This chapter is the last of the three (12, 13 & 14) which form a parenthesis between the sounding of the seventh trumpet judgment and the pouring out of the first vial judgment. It is important to note that the series of seven distinct visions given in this chapter are not in chronological order, but have been penned in the order they were revealed to John.

The first vision is given in verses 1-5. The Lamb is the Lord Jesus, and the one hundred and forty and four thousand, a number which is symbolic, representative of the faithful remnant of Jews, of the tribe of Judah; they will have been saved out of: *great tribulation*. The one hundred forty and four thousand of chapter 7:4 is again a number which is symbolic, made up of twelve thousand from each of the twelve named tribes of Israel, sealed in their foreheads, but we are not told what the seal will be, whereas the one hundred forty and four thousand standing with the Lord Jesus on mount Zion will have the name of the Lord Jesus and the name of His Father written upon their foreheads, thereby confirming they belong to the Lord Jesus.

CHAPTER 14

vv. 2-3. *And I heard a voice from heaven, as the voice of many waters, and as the voice of a great thunder: and I heard the voice of harpers harping with their harps. And they sung as it were a new song before the throne, and before the four beasts* (living creatures), *and the elders: and no man could learn* (understand) *that song but the hundred and forty and four thousand, which were redeemed from the earth.*

Although the noun, *voice,* is the same in Greek for *noise,* and *sound*; the translators have given us, *voice, i*n the singular, thereby emphasising the unison of the chorus which will echo throughout the courts of heaven in praise of the Lord Jesus. Without doubt, the volume of the chorus will exceed that of the sound on earth of many waterfalls and exceed the sounds in the atmospheric heaven of great thunder claps, for they will be as nothing when compared with the volume of the heavenly chorus.

John hears the music of the harp and the singing of the harpers. The harp is the first musical instrument mentioned in the Bible (Genesis 4:21). Harp music is the most tranquil and soothing of all music. When God finished His creation, His great yearning was that it should exist in an atmosphere of calm and serenity. Alas, Satan, the archenemy of God, bewitched man and spoilt everything designed to reflect the glory of God.

We do not know how many strings were on David's harp, but harps today may have anything from 12 to 36 strings. David was a proficient player of the harp and in all probability when caring for his father's sheep he would play his harp in praise to God. Whenever Saul was distressed and almost out of his mind because of an evil spirit from God upon him, he would call for David to play the harp that he might be calmed and refreshed, causing the evil spirit to depart from him (1 Samuel 16:23). In Psalm 33:2, Israel was called to give praise to the Lord

Jehovah with the harp, and in Psalm 98:5, to sing unto the Lord Jehovah with the harp. Thus, the sound of the harp in heaven confirmed the tranquil state of our home above, to which we shall soon be transported.

And they sung as it were a new song before the throne, and before the living creatures, and the elders. The one hundred and forty-four thousand will sing the new song of heaven, but what will the song celebrate? We are not told, but it will no doubt include reference to the fact that they have been brought from the earth, and settled into the realm of eternal blessing. The words: *And no man could learn that song,* applies exclusively to the unregenerate.

> **vv. 4-5.** *These are they which were not defiled with women; for they are virgins. These are they which follow the Lamb whithersoever He goeth. These were redeemed from among men, being the firstfruits unto God and to the Lamb. And in their mouth was found no guile, for they are without fault.* N.B. The words: *Before the throne of God,* are an unwarranted interpolation.

We observe the four-fold identity of this faithful remnant: (1) They were undefiled. (2) They follow the Lamb. (3) They are redeemed being the firstfruits of God. (4) They are without guile and blameless. These faithful Jews had kept themselves morally pure by holy separation from the defiling habits and influences of the unregenerate world of mankind. The language: *for they are virgins,* is symbolic, and simply means that the faithful had not been corrupted by association with the aims and objectives of the world which is under condemnation; they remained wholly pure. Following the Lamb implies unswerving discipleship to the One who was rejected by the world and slain; they too will be prepared to suffer and die for their faith. God's answer to all who suffer for righteousness is their redemption, being the firstfruits unto God and to the Lamb. Finally, they will be found to be blameless, for the blood of Jesus Christ, God's Son, will have cleansed them from all sin; and being justified by faith, they will have eternal peace with God.

> **vv. 6-7.** *And I saw another angel fly in the midst of heaven, having the everlasting gospel to preach unto them that dwell on the earth, and to every nation, and kindred, and tongue, and people, saying with a loud voice, Fear God, and give glory to Him; for the hour of His judgment is come: and worship Him that made heaven, and earth, and the sea, and the fountains of waters.*

Here we have the second of seven distinct visions detailed in this chapter. An angel, being a heavenly messenger, flying in the midst of heaven, adds divine gravitas to the message: *the gospel of the kingdom,* which he brings to all sitting or settled on the earth. Christ is about to come and establish His Millennial kingdom and reign, but until He comes with power and great glory, the gospel message will continue to be preached. The message will be to every nation, kindred, tongue and people, reaching to the four quarters of the world. The title of the message: *the everlasting gospel,* confirms that it has ever been the longing of our creator God to have mankind, the product of His creation, in close communion with Himself. Accordingly, all that God has planned and instituted from the beginning has been to that end. Such is the mercy of God that, after the church has been raptured to heaven, the preaching of the gospel of the kingdom will continue until the Lord Jesus comes to this world with power and great glory.

We observe that the angel who announces the message will do so with a loud voice, thereby implying that all on earth shall hear, and should, in the fear of God, respond in giving Him glory in the spirit of repentance with faith. All who repent will be required to do homage unto their mighty Creator who formed the four essential elements of this creation: the heavens, the earth, the sea and the fountains of water, all the latent resources to sustain life on earth.

> **v. 8.** *And there followed another angel, saying,* (Great) *Babylon is fallen, is fallen, that great city, because she made all nations drink of the wine of the wrath of her fornication.*

This third vision in the chapter tells us of the fall of Babylon which will occur just before the Lord comes to establish His kingdom. The name *Babylon* carries the thought of confusion and tyranny which will characterise the corrupt church testimony following the rapture of the true church to glory (1 Thessalonians 4:16-17). Great Babylon, as she is Scripturally known, is the enslaver of God's people. When under the influence of the Jewish beast, all nations, with the exception of the faithful remnant, will be drunken with the intoxicating wine/poison of the fury of her wickedness, idolatry, fornication, and evil powers. The fulfilment of the words: *Babylon is fallen, is fallen,* will occur just before the Lord Jesus returns with power and great glory.

> **vv. 9-10.** *And the third angel followed them, saying with a loud voice, If any man worship the beast and his image, and receive his mark in his forehead, or in his hand, the same shall drink the wine of the wrath of God, which is poured out without mixture into the cup of His indignation; and he shall be tormented with fire and brimstone in the presence of the holy angels, and in the presence of the Lamb.*

Verses 9 to 12 detail the fourth vision of this chapter. The third angel announces, loud and clear, a divine warning to any who submit to the demands of the first beast who will insist that all should worship him and his image. The reference is to the authority of the revived Roman

Empire. Any who worship the beast and his image secretly in their heart will be identified by the mark of the beast, either in their forehead or in their hand. Furthermore, they will be known by their thoughts revealed in conversations, also by their actions.

The eternal destiny for all who bow down and worship the beast and his image is hell (Gehenna); a place which is so horrendous that the Lord Jesus defined the environment of the place as: *everlasting fire, prepared for the devil and his angels* (Matthew 25:41). It will be the time when divine judgment is no longer mingled with grace. Here John defines the judgment of the Lord, as drinking the wine of the fury of God, poured out unmitigated into a cup of His wrath, to occasion eternal torment in fire and brimstone, and witnessed before God's holy angels and the Lamb.

When God made man, it was never His intention that man should share the destiny planned for the devil and his angels; rather, that man should live for ever in the paradise of God. Alas, through man's disobedience, sin came in and put man under condemnation; he would, therefore, suffer the same fate as the devil and his angels. But God in His infinite mercy, had a plan whereby man might be redeemed. He would, in love give His Beloved Son to be a sacrifice for sin, and by the shedding of His precious blood, atone for the sins of man, and the sin of the world. This great and unique gift of God would ensure that man, if he repented of his sins before God and put his faith and trust in the Lord Jesus Christ, would have eternal life in heaven. Well might the redeemed say: *Thanks be unto God for His unspeakable gift* (2 Corinthians 9:15). A gift which the lexicons of human language cannot define in words.

> **vv. 11-12.** *And the smoke of their torment ascendeth up for ever and ever: and they have no rest day nor night, who worship the beast and his*

image, and whosoever receiveth the mark of his name. Here is the patience (endurance) *of the saints: here are they that keep the commandments of God, and the faith of Jesus.*

These two verses are a sure confirmation of the destiny and suffering of all who worship the beast and his image on earth, and who carry the identity marks of the beast on their bodies. They will not have rest day and night, for it will not be an environment in which one might eventually accept as being normal and therefore be at ease with it in time. No, the severity of the torment will never ease nor cease.

Here, refers to the end-time of the: *great tribulation* period; during which the saints of God will suffer the greatest test of endurance, even unto death as they faithfully adhere to the truth of God's Word: *As the truth is in Jesus* (Ephesians 4:21). From the beginning, man has either died in the Lord, or died in sin. To die in the Lord is to enter the paradise of God to await a glorious resurrection to glory. To die in sin is to await a resurrection to a fearful day of judgment, to appear before the Great White Throne and receive the just penalty for sin against God and His Christ (Revelation 20:11-15).

> **v. 13.** *And I heard a voice from heaven saying unto me, Write, Blessed are the dead which die in the Lord from henceforth: Yea, saith the Spirit, that they may rest from their labours; and their works do follow them.*

This one verse represents the fifth vision. Thus, all who die in the Lord are blessed of the Lord. *Rest from their labours,* tells us of their faithfulness in service and their patient endurance, even unto death. Theirs will be, as with all the saints of God in glory, an eternal rest of sublime tranquillity and peace. For the unsaved, their time in eternity will be in an environment of torment, turmoil, and pain. However, when the saints: *appear before the judgment seat of Christ* (2 Corinthians 5:10), all their faithful labours, which will have followed them, will be assessed by the Lord Jesus, and a due reward given. The fruit of their labours on earth will result in an on-going blessing among all who hear and accept the message of the gospel of the kingdom of Jesus Christ; thus: *their works will follow them.*

> **vv. 14-16.** *And I looked, and behold a white cloud, and upon the cloud one sat like unto the Son of man, having on His head a golden crown, and in His hand a sharp sickle. And another angel came out of the temple, crying with a loud voice to Him that sat on the cloud, Thrust in Thy sickle, and reap: for the time is come for Thee to reap; for the harvest of the earth is ripe. And He that sat on the cloud thrust in His sickle on the earth; and the earth was reaped.*

We come now to the sixth vision. *Behold a white cloud;* this is a symbol of the glory of the Lord and His holy, untarnished perfection, when He exercises judgment in righteousness. *On his head a golden crown,* signifying His supreme right and authority to initiate the commencement of the harvest. The sharp sickle in the hand will signify everything has been made ready for the final harvest from the earth; it will also signal the end of this present age. In chapter 3 and verse 13 of the book of Joel, we read: *Put ye in the sickle, for the harvest is ripe;* it is a prophetic statement made about this very event in God's time. In verse 15, we note another angel comes from out of the temple, the very presence of God. We have already noticed that previous angels have appeared from before or from around the throne of God (Chapter 5:11 & 7:11).

Coming from the temple of God will indicate the urgency and importance of the angel's mission which will be to cry with a loud voice: *Thrust in Thy sickle and reap … for the harvest of the earth is ripe.*

We also notice that the angel does not: *say with a loud voice*, but rather: *cries with a loud voice*. The cry is an earnest appeal to carry out the task expeditiously, for the harvest is over-ripe. The sharp sickle indicates that the action of the reaper will not be, as it were, with a blunt, indifferent tool, but with one sharper than any two-edged sword; swift, positive, discerning, and thorough; a symbol of the Word of God (Hebrews 4:12). The wheat harvest will not be an act of judgment at this stage, but simply the separation of the wheat from the tares. The wheat, representing the godly remnant, will be harvested and set aside for glory, but the tares, representing the apostates, will be stored to await their appearance for judgment before the Great White Throne (Revelation 20:11-15). The task, which will be carried out alone by the one sitting on the cloud, will be the fulfilment of the prophecy of the Lord Jesus in Matthew 13:38-42.

> **vv. 17-20.** *And another angel came out of the temple which is in heaven, he also having a sharp sickle. And another angel came out from the altar, which had power over fire; and cried with a loud cry to him that had the sharp sickle, saying, Thrust in thy sharp sickle, and gather the clusters of the vine of the earth; for her grapes are fully ripe. And the angel thrust in his sickle into the earth, and gathered the vine of the earth, and cast it into the great winepress of the wrath of God. And the winepress was trodden without the city, and blood came out of the winepress, even unto the horse bridles, by the space of a thousand and six hundred furlongs.*

These four verses detail the events of the seventh and last vision in the chapter; i.e., the gathering of the fruit of the vine. It will be seen that greater detail is given regarding the origin of this angel: *Another angel came out of the temple which is in heaven*. The apostate Jews had resorted to idolatry (Zechariah 13:2), and in their synagogues they sanctioned all manner of evil practices. Thus, the origin of this angel with a sharp sickle and with divine authority is significant in respect of the judgment of God which is about to fall upon the entire religious world, fulfilling Joel's prophecy; chapter 3:12-13.

Verse 18 tells us that another angel came out from the altar, the brazen altar, which had power over fire. The brazen altar reminds us of the death of Christ as our substitute and the ground of blessing today, but then, it will be the symbol of judgment on the ungodly. The angel, having power over the fire, implies that the intensity of heat will be controlled by the angel as directed by the Lord Jesus. In all God's judgments, there will be different degrees of punishment as confirmed by the Lord Jesus Himself regarding the eventual judgment which will fall upon Sodom and Gomorrah, detailed in the first three Gospels: Matthew 10:15; Mark 6:11; Luke 10:12. That this angel cries with a loud cry to the first angel confirms the urgency of the action which should be taken.

Just as the wheat harvest will cover the whole earth, so likewise the gathering of the fruit of the vine. However, we notice that in the gathering of the fruit of the vine, nothing will be set aside, for all will be cast into the: *winepress of the wrath of God.* The gathering of the clusters of fruit on the vine indicates that all the groups which make up apostate Christendom throughout the world, together with all who have worshipped the beast, will be cast into the great winepress of God's wrath. The greatness of the winepress is emphasised because it will receive all the ungodly, both Jew and Gentile throughout the world; all will suffer the great wrath of God's judgment, as detailed in verse 19.

It is important to note that in all the judgments of God during the tribulation period; i.e., the last week of the 70 weeks of years spoken of by the angel Gabriel to Daniel (Daniel 9:20-27), it is the wrath of God, being the fierceness of His righteous indignation, anger, and vengeance which will be expended upon the people. But when all the ungodly, from the beginning of time stand before the Great White Throne to be judged and sentenced for their sinful life (Revelation 20:11-15), it will not be to face the wrath and vengeance of God; rather, they will stand before the Lord Jesus Christ, God's appointed Judge (Acts 17:31), whose righteous judgments will be delivered with profound solemnity and dignity befitting the Throne of God. Such will know they have no excuse or cover for their sinful life; they will not protest against the judgment passed upon them as do people today when found guilty by a court of law, but will calmly accept the righteous and just penalty passed on them by the Lord Jesus.

The writer of the epistle to the Hebrew saints tells us that the nation (Judah) in their unbelief, trod underfoot the Son of God (Hebrews 10:29). In the prophecy of Isaiah 63:3, we read: *I have trodden the winepress alone; and of the people there was none with Me, for I will tread them in Mine anger, and trample them in My fury.* The detail of the last verse of this chapter 14 is confirmation that this is exactly what is going to happen to all the peoples of the world who will gather in Israel at the end of this age to demonstrate their total opposition to any thought of God and His Christ. The occasion will be the final battle of Armageddon, referred to in chapter 16:16.

The winepress will be trodden without the city. Such will be wrath of God in His judgment, that the blood from the winepress (instrument of judgment) will, figuratively speaking, flow as a mighty flood throughout the land of Israel, from Dan in the north to Beersheba in the south, approximately 200 miles, and to a depth rising to the bit of a horse's bridle. The beast, together with the *false prophet* who is also the *Antichrist,* will together be cast directly into the lake of fire, burning with brimstone (chapter 19:20), thus bringing to an end the current age. What the Holy Spirit has brought before us is the fact that God's judgments will cleanse the entire land of Israel of all evil and corruption; making it ready for the coming of the King (the Lord Jesus), to establish His Millennial kingdom.

All that follows as detailed in this and succeeding chapters up to and including chapter 19 will occur before the events detailed in chapter 11:15-17, and most definitely before the happenings recorded in chapter 14 when the Lord God Almighty will take to Himself great power and reign as King of kings, and Lord of lords, ref. chapter 19:16. This chapter and the following detail the third and last of the three sets of God's governmental judgments which He will pour out upon mankind during the week of tribulation, bringing to an end the present age.

Chapter 15

v. 1. *And I saw another sign in heaven, great and marvellous* (wonderful), *seven angels having the seven last plagues; for in them is filled up* (finished) *the wrath of God.*

The sign John saw in heaven was exceedingly great and marvellous; a definition not accorded to the previous two signs. The sign John now sees predicts the severest of all the plagues, the bowl (vial) judgments, which God will inflict upon the nations of the world, but more particularly upon Israel during the last three and a half years of the 70th week of years (Daniel 9:27). The Lord Jesus termed this period as: *great tribulation* (Matthew 24:21), which will conclude the fulfilment of the entire prophecy communicated to Daniel by the angel Gabriel, as recorded in Daniel 9:20-27.

v. 2. *And I saw as it were a sea of glass mingled with fire: and them that has gotten the victory over the beast, and over his image, and over his mark, and over the number of his name, stand on the sea of glass, having the harps of God.*

According to the most reliable Greek translations from original texts, the words in this verse: *and over his mark,* are an unwarranted interpolation and add nothing to our understanding about the details of those who will have yielded to the demands of the beast. Reference to: *the mark of his name,* in chapter 14:11, equates with: *the number of his name,* referred to in verse 2, which we know to be 666.

John now contemplates the third sign in heaven, having already seen two, also in heaven. The first was the woman (Israel) travailing to be delivered of her child, the Lord Jesus Christ (chapter 12:1-2). The second sign was the appearance in heaven of a great red dragon (Satan) which stood ready to devour the child as soon as it was born (chapter 12:3-4). Here, in verse 1 of chapter 15, we have the third sign which John sees in heaven.

John sees a sea of glass mingled with fire. This would remind us of the brazen laver and its foot which stood between the brazen altar and the door of the tabernacle. The priests were required to wash their hands and feet before exercising their priestly office (Exodus 30:18-20). The sea of glass is also the antitype of the molten sea which was an essential item in the furnishings of Solomon's temple (1 Kings 7:23). In our verse, those who had the victory over the beast and everything associated with him stand on the sea of glass, symbolising that not only are they eternally cleansed by both the blood of the Lamb and the Word of God, but that heaven will a place of settled calm and tranquillity, for nothing evil can possibly enter in to disturb the eternal peace (chapter 21:27). That they had triumphed through much tribulation will be signified by the sea of glass being mingled with fire.

The harpers harping with their harps, is a precious statement confirming that the soft, soothing, and harmonious music of the harp is what will echo throughout the courts of heaven for all eternity. In chapters 5:8; 14:2, and in this verse, the harp appears to be the only musical instrument referred to symbolically as being in heaven.

vv. 3-4. *And they sing the song of Moses the servant of God, and the song of the Lamb, saying, Great and marvellous are Thy works, Lord God Almighty; just and true are Thy ways, Thou King of saints* (nations). *Who shall not fear Thee, O Lord, and glorify Thy name? For Thou only art holy: for all nations shall come and worship before Thee; for Thy judgments are made manifest.*

The vision John has is of a great company of ransomed Jews singing the song of triumph which Moses and the children of Israel sang after they had successfully crossed the Red Sea. The song will be about how they had been saved by blood; the blood which was sprinkled upon the door posts and lintels of the homes in which they dwelt in Egypt (Exodus 12:5-8). Also, how they were delivered by the power of Jehovah when they landed safely on the eastern side of the Red sea.

The song of Moses, recorded in Exodus 15, tells how the Lord had triumphed gloriously over the enemy, throwing the horse and his rider into the sea. The: *Song of the Lamb,* will be the song of their redemption and subsequent blessings, achieved solely on the eternal efficacy of the blood of Christ shed on Calvary's Cross. It is worthy of note that the song of Moses in Exodus 15 and the song of the redeemed Jews in this chapter 15 of the Revelation represent the first and last songs in the Scriptures, and both have the same theme, having come through: *great tribulation.*

Great and marvellous (wonderful) *are Thy works, Lord God Almighty.* The works of the Lord from the beginning of time, throughout His life on earth and since His exaltation to the right hand of His Father in heaven are termed *wonderful,* because they are beyond comprehension to the unbeliever; but to the redeemed all is made plain by the indwelling power of God's Holy Spirit. Together, with all the saints of God, both in heaven and on earth, eternity will not be long enough to exhaust the praises due to the One, who loves us and gave Himself for us.

Just and true are Thy ways, Thou King of saints (nations). The redeemed remnant acknowledges that all the judgments which have fallen upon Israel down through centuries were righteous and true in their objective. The title: *King of saints,* is unscriptural, for nowhere in the Scriptures will such a title be found. On the other hand, the title: *King of nations,* is befitting the One who will in a coming day rule as King over all nations of the world. Jeremiah confirms this fact, for he records the words of the faithful in Israel who respond to the words of Jehovah concerning the Gentile nations around them: *Forasmuch as there is none like unto Thee, O Lord; Thou art great, and Thy name is great in might. Who would not fear Thee, O King of nations?* (Jeremiah 10:6-7). Psalm 86 is one of David's many prayers; where in verse 9 he says: *All nations whom Thou hast made shall come and worship before Thee, O Lord; and shall glorify Thy name.*

> **v. 4.** *Who shall not fear Thee, O Lord, and glorify Thy name? For Thou only art holy* (merciful): *for all nations shall come and worship before Thee; for Thy judgments are made manifest.*

An interrogative question, knowing that when the Lord Jesus reigns supreme, no-one on earth will refrain from worshipping Him, and glorifying His name as Saviour and Lord supreme. The last clause of the verse speaks of the unparalleled mercy of the Lord in the righteousness and openness of all His judgments.

> **vv. 5-6.** *And after that I looked, and, behold, the temple of the tabernacle of the testimony in heaven was opened: and the seven angels came out of the temple, having the seven plagues, clothed in pure and white linen, and having their breasts girded with golden girdles.*

In John's vision, he sees in heaven that the temple of the tabernacle of witness is open; not open that the blessings of God might flow out, but open in order that the judgments of God might proceed forthwith. In chapter 11:19, the seer beheld the ark of the covenant in God's temple, which was Israel's assurance of divine blessing. Now, the ark is no longer seen, for the final series of judgments are about to be poured out, not only upon Israel, but upon the entire world.

God's last judgments will be perfect, thorough, and complete. Coming forth from the temple will be seven angels, each will receive a golden vial (bowl) containing one of the seven plagues. What a sad mission for the angels of God! It was ever God's purpose that His angels should be messengers of divine blessing, as we read in Hebrews 1:14: *Are they not all ministering spirits, sent forth to minister for them who shall be heirs of salvation?* The angels here are clothed in pure white linen, with a golden girdle about their breast. The pure white linen will signify the perfect, untarnished character of the angels, divinely suited to carry out God's will. The golden girdles about their breasts will reflect divine righteousness in the execution of the judgments, and also indicate that divine affections will be restrained; albeit, the very essence of God's nature is Love (1 John 4:8).

> **vv. 7-8.** *And one of the four beasts* (living creatures) *gave unto the seven angels seven golden vials full of the wrath of God, who liveth for ever and ever. And the temple was filled with smoke from the glory of God, and from His power; and no man was able to enter into the temple, till the seven plagues of the seven angels were fulfilled* (completed).

Each of the angels receives a golden vial full of the wrath of God who liveth for ever and ever. The contents of the vials will be poured out in judgment on all the apostates who will experience dying for ever and ever. *And the temple was filled with smoke from the glory of God, and from His power.* The temple being filled with smoke at this time equates with the occasion, recorded in Exodus 19, when the Lord Jehovah came down to the top of the mount to speak to Moses, it was then that: *Mount Sinai was altogether on a smoke ... as the smoke of a furnace.* No one was permitted to come near the mount or to touch it; the penalty for doing so was death. God was going to speak to Moses about His Law (decalogue) for the nation to obey, together with the consequences if the Law was broken, for there was neither grace nor mercy in the Law.

Referring back to verse 8 of our chapter, instead of a cloud of the light and glory of the love of God filling and emanating from the temple, as recorded in 1 Kings 8:10-11, there will be smoke of fire to betoken His power and wrath in the execution of His judgments. Access to the presence of God to make appeal or to plead for mercy will no longer be possible, for the angels, in pouring out the seven last plagues, complete the judgments of God.

We shall notice in this chapter that the wrath of God in the pouring out of His judgments will no longer be restricted to one third of the earth, as will occur with the trumpet judgments (chapters 8-9), but will cover the entire world, and be more severe. Although there is an affinity between the trumpet judgments and the vial judgments, our studies will be confined to gaining a basic understanding of the vial judgments. The chapter makes plain the fearful measures God will employ in His final dealings with the wickedness of men. Furthermore, we should understand that the vial judgments must be seen as symbolic, and not literal as were the plagues of Egypt (Exodus 7–12).

Chapter 16

v. 1. *And I heard a great* (loud) *voice out of the temple saying to the seven angels, Go your ways, and pour out the vials of the wrath of God upon the earth.*

The loud voice implies that the entire world will hear the command God gives to the angels, designed to awaken all nations as to the severity and gravity of the judgments about to be poured out upon them. The loud voice coming out of the temple will be the divine command to the angels to now pour out their vials of the wrath of God upon the earth. None of these vial judgments will flow out as a gentle stream; rather, their flow will be tantamount to the bursting forth of a mighty flood upon the nations.

v. 2. *And the first went, and poured out his vial upon the earth; and there fell a noisome and grievous sore upon the men which had the mark of the beast, and upon them which worshipped his image.*

Men bearing the mark of the beast will suddenly be marked and afflicted by a pernicious, painful and distressing mental upheaval. Their disposition will become offensive and more rebellious, over which they will have absolutely no control. As they suffer the severe physical anguish of the vial judgment, their normal physiognomy may well change to render them unrecognisable. Furthermore, they will not experience any relief from the pain and torment, for the degree of suffering under the vial judgments will be unspeakably severe.

v. 3. *And the second angel poured out his vial upon the sea; and it became as the blood of a dead man: and every living soul died in the sea.*

In the original, and most reliable Greek translations, the noun *angel* in verses 3, 4, 8, 10, 12 and 17 does not appear. However, it must be said that the presence of the noun in no way adversely affects the truth of the text, but may in this case aid one's understanding.

The vial is poured out upon the sea, symbolically, the disturbed nations of the world. The sea becoming as the blood of a dead man means that any vestige of eternal life in the souls of men will have disappeared, thereby effecting both moral and spiritual death to all who will have declared their allegiance to the beast (the Roman power).

vv. 4-7. *And the third angel poured out his vial upon the rivers and fountains of waters; and they became blood. And I heard the angel of the waters say, Thou art righteous, O Lord, which art, and wast, and shalt be, because Thou hast judged thus. For they have shed the blood of saints and prophets, and Thou hast given them blood to drink; for they are worthy. And I heard another out of the altar say, Even so, Lord God Almighty, true and righteous are Thy judgments.*

In this vial judgment, the rivers are a symbol of the people's uninterrupted flow of normal business life. Spiritually, they may symbolise the ethics of Christian life which have become corrupted, defiled and apostate, and therefore dead. Rivers also symbolise prominent sources of governmental principles and influences which become corrupt, being a further cause of spiritual death. The fountains of water refer to everything which contributes to man's well-being and refreshment, but the judgment will occasion the very antithesis of well-being, and become the fount of spiritual death. The waters becoming as blood, symbolise death.

The angel of the waters, who oversees issues relating to all which is necessary for the refreshment and well-being of man on earth, speaks to confirm the righteousness of God's judgments. The angel continues to confirm that all who follow the beast and bear his mark on their bodies have shed the blood of the saints. Accordingly, and symbolically, they will be made to drink i.e., endure in their bodies the most unpleasant consequences of their murderous activities. The words of the angel: *For they are worthy*, implies that they will receive the just reward for their deeds (Hebrews 2:2).

John hears another voice, this time from out of the altar. In other words, the altar cries out on behalf of all the saints who had been unjustly slain, saying, *Even so, Lord God Almighty, true and righteous are Thy judgments.* Not a single soul in the whole of creation will be able to question the justice of the judgments measured out from the throne of God.

> **vv. 8-9.** *And the fourth angel poured out his vial upon the sun; and power was given unto him to scorch men with fire. And men were scorched with great heat, and blasphemed the name of God, which hath power over these plagues: and they repented not to give Him glory.*

In this fourth plague, the angel pours out the contents of his vial upon the sun, and not directly upon the people. The sun in turn now becomes a symbol of a supreme authority in government, an individual exercising tyrannical and oppressive power which greatly intensifies the pressures of life over and above what is normal and humanly bearable. Being scorched with a great heat signifies that men will bear the marks of such intense affliction. Alas, instead of the nations turning to God in the spirit of sincere repentance, they

will increase their rebellion by blaspheming the name of the Lord God Almighty, and mocking the probity and justice of His judgments.

> **vv. 10-11.** *And the fifth angel poured out his vial upon the seat* (throne) *of the beast; and his kingdom was full of darkness; and they gnawed their tongues for pain. And blasphemed the God of heaven because of their pains and their sores, and repented not of their deeds.*

It will have been noticed that the first four seal and trumpet judgments, together with the first four vial judgments, differ from the last three judgments in each of the three series. Here, with the last three vial judgments, we see they are clearly dissimilar in their objective to the first four. In the first four vial judgments, God's action in order fell upon the earth, the sea, the rivers, and the sun.

The outpouring of the wrath of God in the fifth vial is upon the seat (throne) of the beast, confirming that his power and diabolical influence, which Satan had given to him, will be rendered null and void forthwith. It is the beast, his throne and dominion which are the subject of this vial judgment. His kingdom will be plunged into moral darkness; mankind will be unable to discern between right and wrong, true and false, good and bad, wise and foolish. What will follow will be utter confusion and chaos throughout his kingdom. The beast himself will not be touched, for his destiny will be determined, along with the false prophet, when the Lord Jesus comes with power and great glory (Revelation 19:20).

They gnawed their tongues for pain (with distress). The tongue is that part of the anatomy of our mouth which enables us to form our words. The people of the kingdom of the beast will suffer unspeakable mental and physical pain and torment, and will struggle hard (gnaw with their tongues) to form words with which to blaspheme the God of heaven. The apostle James, in his epistle, tells us that the tongue: *is an unruly evil, full of deadly poison* (James 3:8); such is what will issue from the mouths of the tormented reprobates, but they will not repent of their deeds.

v. 12. *And the sixth angel poured out his vial upon the great river Euphrates; and the water thereof was dried up, that the way of the kings of the east might be prepared.*

We should note that in this verse what is forecast is literal, not symbolic. The great river Euphrates rises in the mountainous region of Armenia and Turkey. Turkey, by the erection of a series of dams, controls the flow of the river running south through Syria and Iraq to its confluence with the river Tigris, emptying out at Basra, into the Persian Gulf; a distance of 1780 miles. Furthermore, the great river Euphrates was the Eastern boundary of the Promised Land for the nation of Israel, with its Western boundary being the River of Egypt, which is the Nile with its seven main streams feeding into the Mediterranean Sea (Genesis 15:18 and Isaiah 11:15-16).

We may rightly ask; did the angel pour out his vial along the entire length of the Euphrates, or just at its source? Scripture is silent about this, but texts such as Matthew 24:7; Mark 13:8 and Luke 21:11, all referring to the same occasion, speak of the day when there will be earthquakes in unexpected places during the period of: *great tribulation*, which will be the time for the pouring out of the seven vial judgments. An earthquake in the mountainous region of Turkey could well stop or divert the flow of the Euphrates at its source, and thus occasion the drying up of the entire river. Although God has not told us how He will achieve His purpose, this one thing we do know, the Great Euphrates river will dry up, and thus open up the way for the kings from the rising of the sun to advance westward without let or hindrance to wage war against the holy city. The kings from the East may well include reprobates from Japan, China, Mongolia, and India, etc. etc. The title *kings*, may not necessarily refer to royalty; but maybe supreme dignities who hold high office in their respective countries.

> **vv. 13-14.** *And I saw three unclean spirits like frogs come out of the mouth of the dragon, and out of the mouth of the beast, and out of the mouth of the false prophet. For they are the spirits of devils, working miracles, which go forth unto the kings of the earth and of the whole world, to gather them to the battle of that great day of God Almighty.*

The habitat of frogs is the unclean, watery slime and mire of this world, with their movements during the darkness of night. Thus, the Spirit of God designates the character, source and movement of the unclean spirits; i.e., out of the mouths of the three powers, the trinity of evil; all in open rebellion against God and His Christ. The dragon is Satan, the overt and malicious enemy of God; the beast leads the revived Roman Empire, and, finally, the false prophet is a Jew, the man of sin who will draw reprobate Jews to himself and: *who will exalt himself, shewing himself that he is God* (2 Thessalonians 2:4).

What follows will be the corrupt and wicked activities of the trinity of evil: the dragon, the beast, and the false prophet, all setting themselves against the trinity of the Godhead; the Father, Son and Holy Spirit. The trinity of evil will have power permitted of God to perform miracles and remarkable signs, to persuade, influence and direct kings and republican rulers with their peoples throughout the world to assemble in readiness for battle against the Holy City. But it will be in total, moral, and spiritual darkness that all the nations will come to battle on that great day of God the Almighty. Micah, in his little prophecy speaks of the gathering of the Gentile nations against Jerusalem for battle (Micah 4:11-13).

> **v. 15.** *Behold, I come as a thief. Blessed is he that watcheth, and keepeth his garments, lest he walk naked, and they see his shame.*

In this little parenthesis, we have an example of the Lord's unparalleled love and mercy, in that He: *is … not willing that any should perish, but that all should come to repentance* (2 Peter 3:9). Thus, those who believe are exhorted to watch and keep their garments, which means that their works of righteousness must not be cancelled out or obliterated by works of the flesh, otherwise they will walk spiritually naked to their shame. However, souls who during the: *great tribulation* period repent and believe in the redemptive work of the Lord Jesus and His coming Kingdom are cautioned to watch for the day when the Lord will come with power and great glory with all His redeemed saints to establish His Millennial kingdom of which they will be a part. As Malachi prophesied: *They shall be Mine, saith the Lord of host, in that day when I make up My jewels; and I will spare them, as a man spareth his own son that serveth him* (Malachi 3:17). For the rebellious reprobate, the Lord will come as a thief, i.e., they will be unprepared, and the Lord's merciless judgment will fall upon them.

> **v. 16.** *And he gathered them together into a place called in the Hebrew tongue Armageddon.*

The translation of the noun Armageddon is: *The mountain of slaughter*, and is used symbolically to indicate the unparalleled destruction which will fall upon the enemies of the Lord Jesus. This verse simply tells us that the Lord will allow the nations of the world, from the East and from the West which are under the influence of the Roman Empire, to surround the land of Israel with the expressed purpose of destroying the nation and the beloved city, Jerusalem. According to Daniel 2:31-45, the Lord Jesus, as the 'stone' cut without hands, will smite the great image which Nebuchadnezzar saw in his dream, i.e., the revived Roman Empire, so that its power will disappear as chaff carried away by the wind. Daniel 12:1; tells us that: *There shall be a time of trouble, such as never was since there was a nation even to that same time: and at that time thy people shall be delivered, every one that shall be found written in the book* (Book of Life). This will be the fulfilment of the Lord's own words: *Except those days should be shortened, there should no flesh be saved: but for the elect's sake those days shall be shortened* (Matthew 24:22).

> **vv. 17-18.** *And the seventh angel poured out his vial into the air; and there came a great voice out of the temple of heaven, and from the throne, saying, It is done. And there were voices, and thunders, and lightnings; and there was a great earthquake, such as was not since men were upon the earth, so mighty an earthquake, and so great.*

We shall notice that the adjective *great (megas)* occurs seven times in the detail of this last vial; in each occurrence the word means *exceedingly great*, indicating the severest of all the vial judgments upon a rebellious world. Consequently, every feature of the judgment is defined as *great*. Satan, having been cast out of heaven (chapter 12:9), remains: *the prince of the power of the air, the spirit that now worketh in the children of disobedience* (Ephesians 2:2). Bearing in mind we are still in the realm of symbols, the vial being poured on the air signifies that the very environment in which man exists, moves, and has his being, will be polluted and corrupted by every thought and the immoral behaviour. The great voice from the temple of heaven, from the throne, saying: *It is done*, or, *It is over,* is the voice of God, and will be heard by all creation. It announces that the righteous judgments of Almighty God on the sinfulness of mankind after six thousand years is at long last over. In verse 18, the order of events recorded in the KJV is different to what is given in the original Greek translation. The order should read as follows: *And there were lightnings, and voices, and thunders, and a great earthquake, such as was not since men were upon the earth, so mighty an earthquake, and so great.* A simple explanation of the lightnings, voices, and thunders is given in the notes on chapter 4, verse 5.

Alas, many will, as they do today, ignore the opportunity to surrender their lives to a merciful God and enter by faith into the realm of eternal light. Instead, they will remain indifferent to God's gracious call to repentance, continue in sin, and so end up in the gloom of eternal darkness and suffering.

The emphasis on the earthquake as being great, and so great, is important. Never before, since creation, will there have been such an unprecedented political upheaval resulting in the total collapse of social order and authority. Governments throughout the world will be thrown into unresolvable chaos. One would expect that the magnitude of the breakdown of all forms of human restraint, discipline, and control in society, together with man's physical suffering as never before, would lead man to fall prostrate before God in the spirit of repentance, but no; man will intensify his blasphemy against God, and so confirm his fate to eternity in Gehenna.

vv. 19-20. *And the great city was divided into three parts, and the cities of the nations fell: and great Babylon came in remembrance before God,* *to give unto her the cup of the wine of the fierceness of His wrath. And every island fled away, and the mountains were not found.*

There is no doubt that *great Babylon* refers to Rome as the great centre of the Roman Empire. The great earthquake symbolises the complete breakup of the Roman Empire into three political factions. A major consequence of the upheaval will be that the Roman Empire's overall authority, power and influence will be dissolved, as symbolised by the tripartite political division of the great city. The cities of nations, which were under the control of Rome, will lose their identity through the absence of the infamous, political domination of the beast. While great Babylon will be destroyed, as detailed in the following two chapters, she will be remembered before God for her gross, unparalleled iniquity and rebellion and will be made to drink from the cup containing the wine of the fury of His wrath.

And every island fled away. The islands were, according to Scripture, sources of wealth and regions of prosperity (Isaiah 23:2 and Ezekiel 27:3-15) but will no longer exist. Islands were places to escape to from the traumas of life; they were cities of refuge, but there will be no escaping the wrath of God from the outpouring of His judgments.

With regard to the mountains disappearing, they are symbolic of prominent and dominant authorities overshadowing dependencies; such authorities will be humbled and brought low. As the end of the: *great tribulation* period draws near, there will be no governmental authority or legally restraining hand in any country of the world. Accordingly, the world will be in a state of total chaos and will remain so until the Lord returns with all His saints to establish His Millennial kingdom, in which: *The wolf and the lamb shall feed together, and the lion shall eat straw like the bullock: and dust shall be the serpent's meat* (Isaiah 65:25).

v. 21. *And there fell upon men a great hail out of heaven, every stone about the weight of a talent: and men blasphemed God because of the plague of the hail; for the plague thereof was exceeding great.*

In this last element of the judgments of God, emphasis is placed upon the adjective *great*. The great hail is symbolic, but with every hail stone given as the weight of a talent, it accentuates the fact that the impact of God's judgment upon man will be tantamount to a burden beyond the natural, physical, and mental strength of human beings to bear. It will crush them. However, rebellious man with Satanic strength, will resist all attempts of Almighty God to persuade them to repent.

The chapter before us and the following detail the judgments which shall befall Babylon before the events given in chapter 14 verses 8–20 but after the judgment of the seventh vial in chapter 16:17-21. This sequence of events is further confirmation that the details of the visions and their purpose are not given in the chronological order in which the events will occur. Acceptance of this fact will help to ensure an accurate understanding of all that follows in this book. We shall see that this chapter is in two parts; the first part covers verses 1–6, in which we get a description of the great harlot; the second is verses 7-18, where we have the detail of the Satanic activities of the beast, the ten kingdoms, and the harlot, all in unison against the Lamb.

Chapter 17

vv. 1-2. *And there came one of the seven angels which had the seven vials, and talked with me, saying unto me, Come hither; I will shew unto thee the judgment of the great whore* (harlot) *that sitteth upon many waters: with whom the kings of the earth have committed fornication, and the inhabitants of the earth have been made drunk with the wine of her fornication.*

That one of the angels came from heaven to call John to follow confirms that in this vision he is now on earth observing events as they appear before him. The great harlot is the religious element of the Satanic activities of the beast, i.e., the revived Roman Empire. The whoredom of the great harlot will be her spiritual prostitution, support and fusion with the moral corruption in the world. The waters upon which the great harlot sits are symbolic of all countries of the earth; i.e., peoples, multitudes, nations and tongues, and signify her universal and spiritually corrupt influence over them. Details of the judgment of the great whore is given in chapter 18:8. *The kings of the earth have committed fornication.* That is, kings and their peoples will be seduced, and become besotted by the great harlot's evil, intoxicating attractions and her intercourse with world affairs. They will freely enter into what will be a coalition of the corrupt business systems of the world. Likewise, the earth-dwellers will, by the conduct of the harlot's narcotic and seductive behaviour and idolatry, become totally confused and incapable of judging between right and wrong, i.e., they will be morally drunk. This will be the measure of the great harlot's momentary, yet evil, influence in world affairs.

> **vv. 3-4.** *So he carried me away in the spirit into the wilderness: and I saw a woman sit upon a scarlet coloured beast, full of names of blasphemy, having seven heads and ten horns. And the woman was arrayed in purple and scarlet colour, and decked with gold and precious stones and pearls, having a golden cup in her hand full of abominations and filthiness of her fornication.*

It was the angel of verse 1, under the control of the Spirit of God, which carried John away in spirit into the wilderness. We should note that the wilderness (desert place) offers no refreshment for the thirsty soul, and no spiritual food for the hungry soul, but spiritually is typical of the environment in which the beast and the great whore (harlot) exist; i.e., arid and barren. The scarlet coloured beast on which the woman (symbol of Babylon) sits is the insignia of the Roman Empire, confirming that the woman, the religious element, will for a time be in total control of all events on earth. The colour scarlet signifies that the world regime will be marked by moral corruption, blood-shed and cruel tyranny, coupled with a malicious outburst of unparalleled blasphemy against God, thereby establishing beyond all doubt the inherent nature of the unregenerate man who fears neither God nor man.

Having seven heads and ten horns. Here, the seven heads of the beast upon which the woman sits symbolises the great city Rome, which was built upon seven mountains, and controlling ten kingdoms which will be impotent and uncrowned for a time. The harlot who is referred to in verse one of this chapter symbolises the great city Rome which has usurped the position it has taken and abused the Name and Authority of Christ.

v. 4. *And the woman was arrayed in purple and scarlet colour; and decked with gold and precious stones and pearls, having a golden cup in her hand full of abominations and filthiness of her fornication.*

Everything about the woman (godless, religious profession of the day) will be designed to be admired and entrap the unwary. The purple colour of her robes will signify an assumed imperial status. The scarlet colour normally signifies the moral glories and qualities of one's way of life, as in the Lord Jesus; here the colour reflects the immoral qualities of the woman's life. Today, the Roman Catholic Church adorns its clerics with robes of the same colours to set forth before men their earthly status, albeit, there is nothing of divine significance in their dress. Whatever colours they employ, none reflects anything which is for the glory of God. The woman will carry ornaments of gold and precious stones, symbolising the wealth of the earth, and pearls, being the wealth of the sea, i.e., pearls from oysters, thus, claiming the wealth of earth and sea as hers by right. In her hand a golden cup full of abominations and the filth of her fornication. The woman's occupation will be to offer from her cup the corrupt fruit of her loathsome works.

The child of God should be marked by the very antithesis of everything which marks the nature and character of the woman, a harlot. The disposition of our walk should manifest the eternal relationship we have with the King of kings and Lord of lords (purple colour). The testimony of our path of service should be marked by the moral excellencies which were evident in the pathway of our Blessed Saviour (scarlet colour). Gold speaks of the righteousness and glory of God; thus, our lives should yield the peaceable fruit of righteousness. The spiritual significance of the precious stones and pearls which are secured by great endeavour, suffering and cost, have reference to the great truths of Holy Scripture which likewise are acquired by sacrificial study of the Word of God. Our cup, which is our personal vessel, should ever be full of divine refreshment and ready to give drink to any soul thirsting for the Word of God (Matthew 10:42).

v. 5. *And upon her forehead was a name written, MYSTERY, BABYLON THE GREAT, THE MOTHER OF HARLOTS AND ABOMINATIONS OF THE EARTH.*

Although there are some translations from the original Greek text which give the full title of the woman in the *lower-case* script, there does appear to be a very special reason why the Spirit of God, through His servants, has boldly emphasised the name of the woman. Surely, it is that we might fully understand the gross wickedness of all the forces which are, and will be set against God, His Son, and the saints of God. The name *MYSTERY*, applies to everything hitherto hidden about the evil activities of the woman; they will be exposed to the full, and herself judged according to the righteousness of God. The title, *Babylon*, comes from the original title of the city Babel (Genesis 11:9), lying on the East side of the great river Euphrates in the region of Biblical Chaldea (Shinar), now Eastern Iraq. The appellation *great*, to the title Babylon, was first given by Nebuchadnezzar as recorded in Daniel 4:30, when he was lifted up with pride and arrogance about his achievements. It was while he was soliloquising that a voice from heaven announced a seven-year judgment upon him, as detailed in the following verses of the same chapter. The next occasion when the title *great*, is applied to Babylon, is in Revelation 16:19. However, here in this verse, the title *BABYLON THE GREAT* emphasises the enormity of the impact the evil, religious system has and will have upon the entire world. That the woman should be called, THE MOTHER OF HARLOTS, confirms she is the progenitor of all the grave consequences her adulteries (idolatry), and of her unbridled fornication, i.e., her uninhibited fusion with evil systems worldwide. Finally, she is identified by the worst of all titles, and called the: ABOMINATIONS OF THE EARTH. We note that the plural tense is employed in order to highlight the multiplicity of the woman's obnoxious activities and influence upon the earth. She, and what she represents as before the eye of God, is detestable, disgusting, immoral, loathsome, vile and offensive to God.

> **vv. 6-7.** *And I saw the woman drunken with the blood of the saints, and with the blood of the martyrs of Jesus: and when I saw her, I wondered with great admiration. And the angel said unto me, Wherefore didst thou marvel? I will tell thee the mystery of the woman, and of the beast that carrieth her, which hath the seven heads and ten horns.*

In our study, we are still in the time of the: *great tribulation* period. John now sees the woman (Babylon) inebriated with the blood of saints and martyrs of Jesus. The sight of the drunken woman confirms to John that multitudes of the saints of God world-wide will have sacrificed their lives in defence of the testimony of Jesus Christ. Having died for their faith, they now await a glorious resurrection. Meanwhile, although our text states that John, *wondered with great admiration,* we should understand that John does not admire what he sees; rather, he is astonished and wonders with a great wonderment (amazement), but why? There is no doubt the seer is overwhelmed by the scale of the massacre of the saints of God by those who supposedly stood for Christianity; it pains his heart deeply. The angel questions John as to why he marvelled (wondered). John does not reply. The angel, by acknowledging that what John had seen and heard was an enigma to him, prepares to reveal the mystery of the woman and the beast which carried her. We should understand that the woman, symbol of the Roman Church, is not literally carried by the beast, but that the beast reflects the character of pagan Rome which the woman represents.

> **v. 8.** *The beast that thou sawest was, and is not; and shall ascend out of the bottomless pit, and go into perdition: and they that dwell on the earth shall wonder, whose names were not written in the book of life from the foundation of the world, when they behold the beast that was, and is not, and yet is.*

We have already established that the beast, according to the Scripture, represents the civil authority of the revived Roman Empire that was, and which followed the Grecian/Macedonian empire in 27 B.C. It continued until 476 A.D. when the last Emperor, Romulus Augustulus, was deposed by Flavius Odoacer. This was the occasion when the beast (Roman Empire) was wounded to death (chapter 13:3). Flavius Odoacer later became King of Italy. Thus, the term: *and is not*, applies to the present time. However, in God's time, the wounded beast will be healed (chapter 13:3 & 12), i.e., the Roman empire revived. As this verse 8 confirms, it will ascend out of the bottomless pit which is the abyss, the source of every conceivable evil force. The words: *And go into perdition* (destruction), refers to the doom of the beast, together with the false prophet as confirmed in chapter 19:20.

And they that dwell on the earth shall wonder. This is the last of several references in this book about those who dwell upon the earth. The statement refers to all whose names are not written in the Book of Life from the foundation of the world, who will have no place in heaven. The earth-dwellers will wonder at the beast, and being drawn to it by its power and influence, as to a magnet, will worship it, as confirmed in chapter 13:8 and 12.

> **v. 9.** *And here is the mind which hath wisdom. The seven heads are seven mountains, on which the woman sitteth.*

The mind which hath wisdom, refers to the communication of the mind of God by His Spirit; on this occasion, to John. It is an accepted fact that the topography of the region where the city of Rome is established is comprised of seven mountains; thus, it is the city of Rome upon which the woman (Babylon) sits. It is there where she will exercise her demonic influence and idolatry over Christendom.

> **vv. 10-11.** *And there are seven kings: five are fallen, and one is, and the other is not yet come; and when he cometh, he must continue a short space. And the beast that was, and is not, even he is the eighth, and is of the seven, and goeth into perdition.*

These seven kings are distinct from the ten kings, referred to in verse 12, all of whom have horns, being a symbol of power which they will have for a brief time. The seven kings relate to consecutive Gentile, despotic regimes covering vast areas of the Western world. At the time of John's exile on the Isle of Patmos, five of the regimes had fallen, but the sixth was in power, and continued to 476 A.D. The seventh king (empire) may well have reference to the Napoleonic era 1799–1815; an empire controlling vast areas of Europe, Asia, and North Africa, and supported by the Roman Church. Napoleon survived the anarchy of the French Revolution and came into prominence as suddenly as was his sad demise; which confirms what the Scripture says: *He must continue a short space.* Now, I would not press acceptance of this explanation for the seventh kingdom/empire, but Scripture clearly indicates that such a kingdom did exist, and only lasted for a short space of time. The eighth, yet future, will be the revived Roman Empire termed "the beast" which, as we have already noted, relates to a secular empire, not ecclesiastical. When it comes into prominence, it will bear all the hallmarks of the previous seven kings, but with increased merciless ferocity. It will enforce all the Satanic objectives of the first seven kings, including idolatry, and will exercise and encourage gross profanity against God and the Lord Jesus Christ. The beast will continue to persecute the saints of God, even unto death. However, the end of the beast is guaranteed, for it will be cast into the Lake of fire, Gehenna (chapter 19:20).

vv. 12-13. *And the ten horns which thou sawest are ten kings, which have received no kingdom as yet; but receive power as kings one hour with the beast. These have one mind, and shall give their power and strength unto the beast.*

The ten horns which John saw were not attached to the beast, but seen as coming with the beast. The horns symbolise ten kings, each initially without a designated kingdom, but with a measure of power lasting just one hour which they surrender to the beast; they nevertheless represent the revived Roman Empire. Whilst Scripture is silent as to exactly which kingdoms are referred to, we may safely assume that according to the original empire, the greater part of Western Europe, parts of Asia and North Africa will be involved. We then have in verse 13, the remarkable statement that: *These have one mind.* This confirms that all ten kingdoms will, in mind and purpose, be controlled and influenced by Satan, and in unison surrender their power and strength to the beast. It has been suggested that the current European Union is the embryo of the revived Roman Empire, but this must surely be far from the truth of Holy Scripture, for Scripture is silent as to which current countries will comprise the revived Roman Empire. Long before the beast appears on the political scene of this world, all the saints will have been raptured away to glory. Indeed, the saints in glory will be spectators of all subsequent events occurring on earth; it is these events we have been considering.

> **v. 14.** *These shall make war with the Lamb, and the Lamb shall overcome them: for He is Lord of lords, and King of kings: and they that are with Him are called, and chosen, and faithful.*

The war referred to in the above verse will be the battle of Armageddon, mentioned in chapter 16:14 and in chapter 19:11-21. It will take place after the great harlot has been disposed of by the beast and the ten kingdoms (horns), as detailed here in verse 16. The war, involving the beast and the ten kingdoms, will be against the Lamb, the King of kings, and Lord of lords, and will take place when He comes with power and great glory, with tens of thousands of His saints, called, chosen, and faithful. The Lamb, with a single stroke of the sword of His mouth, will overcome all.

> **v. 15.** *And he saith unto me, The waters which thou sawest, where the whore* (harlot) *sitteth, are peoples, and multitudes, and nations, and tongues.*

This verse confirms that the Satanic influence of the harlot will spread world-wide. The waters symbolise the disturbed nations of the world. The fact that the harlot is sitting implies she is resting complacent in the belief she has accomplished her evil objective. There is little doubt there will not be a people, multitude, nation nor tongue on earth which will be immune from the toxic malevolence occasioned by the Satanic activities of the harlot.

vv. 16-18. *And the ten horns which thou sawest upon* (and) *the beast, these shall hate the whore* (harlot), *and shall make her desolate and naked, and shall eat her flesh, and burn her with fire. For God hath put in their hearts to fulfil His will, and to agree, and give their kingdom unto the beast, until the words of God shall be fulfilled. And the woman which thou sawest is that great city, which reigneth over the kings of the earth.*

We remind our hearts that the ten horns (kingdoms) are symbols of ten secular nations under the control of the beast. The beast symbolises the secular part of the revived Roman Empire. The harlot symbolises the corruption in Christendom within the empire. It will be God who by divine wisdom and purpose will put it into the hearts of the ten horns (kingdoms) and the beast to hate the harlot and to dispose of her. They will first make her desolate and naked, that is she will be deserted by all who are normally at her disposal and command. They will then strip her of her status and titles, for she will no longer sit as queen of a realm. The eating of her flesh will be tantamount to consuming for themselves all the evil and corrupt practices which marked her reign, and then surreptitiously employing them for their own gain. The burning of the harlot will be the disposing of every feature of her life and practice.

The actions of the ten horns and the beast will be in unison, and accord with the will of God, albeit, they will not be aware of the divine objective, for they will act in unbelief. Finally, we get confirmation that the woman will be a symbol of a perverted religious system, which will have its centre in Rome. Rome will be the corrupt, ecclesiastical metropolis of the world. The system will continue to usurp authority, abuse the name of the Lord Jesus Christ, and exercise kingship over the nations of the world; but God's judgment awaits!

In this chapter, we have the last mention of Babylon. Like a great millstone, it will with violence be cast into the sea – dispersed among the nations of the world - to be found no more, verse 21. Babylon is the woman who symbolises the utter corruption of the Christian testimony. With her seat in Rome, she is guilty of the most heinous crimes against the saints of God, but more seriously against God and His Beloved Son, the Lord Jesus Christ. Although the name, *that great city* i.e., Babylon, disappears from subsequent pages of this book, all involved in its set-up and operation will eventually appear for judgment before the Lord Jesus Christ at the Great White Throne (chapter 20:11-15).

Chapter 18

v. 1. *And after these things I saw another angel come down from heaven, having great power; and the earth was lightened with his glory.*

These things, refer to the multiplicity of evil works and the corruption of Babylon, as symbolised by the woman; also, her eventual end as detailed in the previous chapter. *Another angel from heaven with great power,* is clearly the Lord Jesus. With the exception of Simon the sorcerer, who was a servant of Satan (Acts 8:10), no other angel or person in the New Testament is credited with *having great power.* The testimony of such great power will be evidenced by the light of the glory of His Person which will lighten the earth.

vv. 2-3. *And he cried mightily with a strong voice, saying, Babylon the great is fallen, is fallen, and is become the habitation of devils, and the hold of every foul spirit, and a cage of every unclean and hateful bird. For all nations have drunk of the wine of the wrath of her fornication, and the kings of the earth have committed fornication with her, and the merchants of the earth are waxed rich through the abundance of her delicacies.*

It is the purpose of God that the entire world should hear the voice of the Lord Jesus. It is most likely that the world will have never before heard a voice of such power and authority. All creation will be affected by the judgments God will pour out upon all who dwell upon the earth. Babylon is given the title *great,* because of the grave impact her infectious and deadly iniquities will have upon the entire world. The repeat of the words: *is fallen,* is divine confirmation that the judgment on Babylon and her consequent demise, i.e., loss of world-wide power and influence, will be irreversible. The realm in which Babylon will continue to exist – for she will not have been destroyed at this stage in God's dealing with her – will be a den of iniquity, for it will represent everything that is foul, putrescent, and hateful. The unclean and hateful birds must surely apply to individuals in the service of Satan who fly from place to place spreading corruption of every kind.

The nations of the world will become totally confused, having been taken in by the subtleties of the woman (Babylon). They will, with indifference and total disregard for what is right, imbibe all the tangible provisions the corrupt commercial world produces, and wax fat on the material richness of such transient luxuries. Rulers of the earth and traders will likewise fall prey to the subtle enticements of the woman and her inordinate way of life; they will also prosper in status and possessions, but for a short season only.

> **vv. 4-5.** *And I heard another voice from heaven, saying, Come out of her, My people, that ye be not partakers of her sins, and that ye receive not of her plagues. For her sins have reached unto heaven, and God hath remembered her iniquities.*

The strong voice of the Lord Jesus has been heard (verse 2). John hears another voice. It is the voice of God Himself laying claim to His people, and He addresses them accordingly: *Come out of her, My people.* During the time of great trial on the earth, there will be people who own God as the creator-God, and know the Lord Jesus Christ as Saviour. While many saints will have died for their testimony of faith, there will be other believers who will not be open witnesses of their faith, and may possibly be caught up in the affairs of the corrupt world and all that is counterfeit and idolatrous in the Christian testimony; it is to these God calls: *Come out of her, My people.*

Such is the unparalleled love of God, that He will be anxious for His people not to be caught up in the noxious affairs of the world and thereby infected by its plagues. In 2 Corinthians 6:14-18, the apostle Paul, addressing Christians who may be mixed up with the world and all it stands for, first reminds them that they are: *the temple of the living God;* he then boldly exhorts them not to have any physical, social, or commercial links with the defiled world, and, quoting the words of the Lord, writes: *Come out from among them, and be ye separate and touch not the unclean thing.* This is the counsel every child of God should heed today. The sins of the woman (Babylon) against God and His redeemed people will be so great that when they are joined together and piled one upon another, they will, metaphorically speaking, reach heaven (ref. Genesis 11:4). Accordingly, God has remembered her deeds of unrighteousness; divine judgment will follow in due course.

> **vv. 6-8.** *Reward her even as she rewarded you, and double unto her double according to her works: in the cup which she hath filled fill to her double. How much she hath glorified herself, and lived deliciously, so much torment and sorrow give her: for she saith in her heart, I sit a queen, and am no widow, and shall see no sorrow. Therefore shall her plagues come in one day, death, and mourning, and famine; and she shall be utterly burned with fire: for strong is the Lord God who judgeth her.*

As we read in chapter 17:17, it is God who will put it into the heart of the beast and the ten horns (the ten kingdoms comprising the revived

Roman Empire) to fulfil His will regarding the avenging judgment of the woman (Babylon). They will not be acting in a God-fearing way, but rather demonstrating their Godless hate for the woman, not forgetting all they will have suffered while the woman reigned supreme. In terms of suffering, they will administer to her double, even to the cup of her wrath. The judgment on the woman will be devastating; she will be powerless, stripped of her usurped royal status, and reduced to a state of penury; she will endure great suffering, and experience unspeakable grief. The woman's experience will accord with what Solomon said: *Pride goeth before destruction, and an haughty spirit before a fall* (Proverbs 16:18).

Such will be the severity of the judgment meted out by the ten kings; they will be likened unto plagues, famine, mourning, and death. Although the power-head of Babylon will be dissolved, the spirit of the system will continue up to the coming of Christ, who will come with power and great glory. At that time, corrupt Babylon will be utterly destroyed and burned with fire by the Lord God. However, all who surrendered to the spell of the woman (the Roman Catholic Church) and served her will eventually appear before the Great White Throne for judgment and sentence by the Lord Jesus Himself (chapter 20:11-15).

> **vv. 9-10.** *And the kings of the earth, who have committed fornication and lived deliciously with her, shall bewail her, and lament for her, when they shall see the smoke of her burning. Standing afar off for the fear of her torment, saying, Alas, alas* (woe, woe) *that great city Babylon, that mighty city! For in one hour is thy judgment come.*

The kings of the earth, referred to in this verse are distinct from the ten horns (political kingdoms) which succeeded in achieving the demise of the woman, having rendered her desolate and naked. However, these kings of the earth will be the chiefs of nations of the world who practised illegitimate business intimacy and contracts with the woman (moral fornication) to sustained their luxurious way of life. Her death and the collapse of her empire will be signalled by the smoke of her burning; i.e., a symbol of the world-wide dark clouds of business-depression and bankruptcy. The reaction of the kings, following the death of the woman, their weeping, wailing, and exclamation of grief in crying, Woe, woe, together with their recognition of Babylon as a great and mighty city, will serve to validate the level of their subjugation to, and endorsement of her evil achievements. Furthermore, their standing afar off will be seen as an act of disowning any responsibility for the total collapse of international business; also, of their fear of experiencing the same fate as that suffered by the woman. The statement: *For in one hour thy judgment is come,* confirms that at a given time according to God's calendar of events, Babylon will be disposed of once and for all, as given in verse 21 of our chapter.

v. 11. *And the merchants of the earth shall weep and mourn over her; for no man buyeth their merchandise any more.*

The merchants are the Wholesale Tradesmen throughout the world, whose markets for the sale of their goods will disappear without hope of recovery. Under God's hand, the woman will lose all her influence in world affairs, and this will adversely impact upon the business world, which is why the merchants will weep and grieve over her. Their sorrow will not be because they had high regard or love for the woman, for Babylon will have ruled with an iron fist, without compassion or sympathy, but because by her they lived luxuriously, a way of life which will come to an end.

vv.12-13. *The merchandise of gold, and silver, and precious stones, and of pearls, and fine linen, and purple, and silk, and scarlet, and all thyine* *wood, and all manner vessels of ivory, and all manner vessels of most precious wood, and of brass, and iron, and marble. And cinnamon, and odours, and ointments, and frankincense, and wine, and oil, and fine flour, and wheat, and beasts, and sheep, and horses, and chariots, and slaves, and souls of men.*

In these two verses we have the range of merchandise which nobody will be able to sell or buy because of the collapse of governmental fiscal systems, financial services, and banks throughout the world. In the wisdom of God, who by divine design allowed for the breakdown of the world's economy, we note that the range of merchandise listed in these two verses, covers 28 items including everything man could possible require for life on earth. We also note that the items are categorised into seven groups, the perfect number, for when God put man on earth, He had provided for his every need. God's provision for the trading of goods between people and nations was confirmation of His gift to the natural man (Ecclesiastes 5:19). Sadly, man has abused and misused every gift God has given for his well-being on earth.

The four items which comprise the first group are: *gold,* the glory and righteousness of God, 2 Corinthians 4:6; *silver,* which has to do with redemption, ref. Exodus 30; *precious stones,* believers are living stones built into a spiritual house, 1 Peter 2:5. The *pearls,* figure of the kingdom of heaven (saints of God), secured at great cost, Matthew 13:45-46; all items reflecting the natural wealth of earth and sea, which man has plundered, devalued, and misappropriated.

The second group is of four materials used for décor and dress. The *fine linen,* has to do with the purity and faithfulness of one's walk and testimony in the world, Revelation 19:8. *Purple,* is the imperial, kingly colour of Scripture. The holy fabrics in both the Tabernacle and the Temple included purple to mirror the imperial and royal status and dignity of the Lord Jesus as King of kings, and Lord of lords. Our walk and disposition in the world should leave none in doubt that we belong to a divine, royal family. *Silk,* is a fine, soft, lustrous fibre, derived from the cocoon of the silk worm, a Chinese moth, *Bonbyx mori.* The material reflects the glowing, unruffled gentleness of the Lord Jesus; features which should mark our character and behaviour before all men. The fourth and last item in this group is: *Scarlet.* In Scripture, Scarlet has always to do with the moral attributes of a person. In the Lord Jesus, we see in figure the distinct radiance of Scarlet in His uniquely divine and glorious disposition. When the Lord Jesus washed the feet of the disciples, it was an act that reflected His refulgent moral glory. Sadly, today, and in the coming day, the world to its shame woefully misuses the wonderful provisions of God, as portrayed by the woman in verse 4 of the previous chapter.

The third group of merchandise is of solid materials used for making items for one's comfort and every-day living. John also refers to the precious resources used for commercial and social buildings, but, as Scripture infers, nothing was used for the glory of God. The apostle Paul exhorted the Corinthian saints that: *Whatsoever ye do, do all to the glory of God* (1 Corinthians 10:31).

Verse 13 begins with listing four items which generate an attractive fragrance: cinnamon, odours (scents), ointments (sweet-smelling), and frankincense. We know that the Lord Jesus, wherever He went, occasioned and left in His wake a unique sweet-smelling fragrance to leave one in no doubt that the Lord had been in that place; such should be the effect whenever the saints meet together unto the Name of the Lord Jesus (Matthew 18:20). In the apostate church today and as it will be in a coming day, their incense burning will be a false indication of the presence of God.

CHAPTER 18

We next have six items to sustain the natural man. Wine, oil, fine flour, wheat, beasts and sheep. These represent not only what is essential to life but also the ephemeral luxuries of life which will be either unaffordable or unavailable; thus, man will starve.

The sixth group in this range of seven has to do with transport: i.e., horses and chariots. This implies that the movement of peoples and goods between countries and within countries will not be possible because of the absence of all modes of transport. The horses and chariots are symbols of every form of transport facility which will have been available before the time of: *great tribulation.*

Finally, the merchants who will control the markets of all commodities traded throughout the world, having been made rich by the corruption of the woman (Babylon), will wail because their slaves, the workhorses of industry and producers of their wealth, will no longer yield to their demands. Clearly, there will be a substantial social upheaval at all levels of society, with the merchants losing all control of man-power and bereft of the markets for their goods. With regard to ecclesiastical Rome which the woman symbolises, there will be an excessive increase in the unholy trafficking of the souls of individuals. As happens today, but in a more dramatic way, many souls will believe they can buy their salvation by contributing to the coffers of the Roman Catholic Church, which the woman represents.

Furthermore, such souls will be misled into believing there will be a reduction in the time they may spend in Purgatory, based upon the amount of money or assets they bequeath to the Roman Catholic Church upon their death. Purgatory is an imaginary place or state of soul, thought up by the Roman Catholic Church, where one is supposed to suffer for venial sins. Such teaching is grave and Satanic, for it leads people to believe they can escape hell, Gehenna, which will be their destiny if unsaved when they die. All this is tantamount to meddling with the souls of men.

v. 14. *And the fruits that thy soul lusted after are departed from thee, and all things which were dainty and goodly are departed from thee, and thou shalt find them no more at all.*

The voice of God (verse 4) will be heard by the God-fearing, saying: *Come out of her, My people.* That same voice is now addressing the nations of the world. At this time, they will be longing for and expecting the mature, ripe fruits of their annual endeavours, but they will nowhere be found for it will be a time of great famine. Also, their eyes will long to behold what is magnificent and sumptuous in the world, but such things will never be found for every element of luxury which gave soul satisfaction to the natural man will have disappeared. In these verses, 11, 12, & 13, we have brought before us the consequence of the governmental judgment of Almighty God upon the woman, and upon all who benefitted from her immoral conduct. Even at this late time, toward the end of the 3.5 years of: *great tribulation*, there will be many throughout the world who are God-fearing and who will be preserved in their faith. They will be brought safely through to the time of the coming of the Lord Jesus, who will come with all His saints in power and great glory, to herald in the Millennial reign of Christ. In verse 14, the voice of the Lord God addresses the woman, confirming to the woman that it is the hand of God in judgment that has brought about her demise.

vv. 15-16. *The merchants of these things, which were made rich by her, shall stand afar off for the fear of her torment, weeping and wailing. And saying, Alas, alas that great city, that was clothed in fine linen,* and purple, and scarlet, and decked with gold, and precious stones, and pearls! For in one hour so great riches is come to naught.*

In verse 10 of our chapter, it is said of the kings (rulers) of the earth that they stood afar off, fearing they too might suffer the torment inflicted upon the woman. Here, in verse 15, it is the merchants who will stand afar off from the sound and sight of the woman's torment, weeping and wailing, fearing they too might be caught up in the woman's suffering. Notwithstanding the dramatic and cataclysmic collapse of the world economy following the judgment of the woman, the kings of the earth and the merchants will shew no disposition of repentance before God for having collaborated with the woman's evil objectives and actions.

True, the merchants will grieve because of the abysmal degradation of their once luxurious living standards, but their exclamation of grief will not be sympathy for the woman, but a selfish, ungodly reaction to their unexpected state of penury. The first sentence of verse 17 should be at the end verse 16. The manner and speed with which Babylon will fall – not destroyed at this time, that will happen later – will startle the world, for the fall will be cataclysmic and disastrous for the entire commercial world. All the wealth and luxuries which marked the *great city* will disappear at a time and hour of God's choosing. It will not be phased.

> **vv. 17-19.** *And every shipmaster, and all the company in ships, and sailors, and as many as trade by sea, stood afar off, and cried when they saw the smoke of her burning, saying, What city is like unto this great city! And they cast dust on their heads, and cried, weeping and wailing, saying, Alas, alas* (woe, woe) *that great city, wherein were made rich all that had ships in the sea by reason of her costliness! For in one hour is she made desolate.*

The earlier verses of this chapter relate to events occurring in countries which will be in a settled state, and controlled by kings and rulers. The verses now before us have reference to the unsettled areas of the world, i.e., countries which are in constant turmoil, like the oceans of the sea. As symbols, every shipmaster is likened unto a king or ruler of an unsettled country. The sailors would be the workers of such countries; those who trade parallel the business merchants and the travellers, the general population. In unison, they likewise stand afar off, not wishing to be caught up in the judgment which will have befallen Babylon. Whenever a cataclysmic disaster strikes at home or abroad, and adversely impacts upon one's life, the world will speak of: *a cloud of doom falling upon people*. At this time, it will be the judgment of God upon Babylon which will occasion the clouds of despair and which will disrupt the life of the great city. What happens to the great city will so alarm the people that they will mourn and sorrow, not because they loved the city, but because of the loss of those things which contributed to their luxurious way of life. The world will certainly wonder with shock and amazement that within a predetermined hour or period of time international trading businesses will have collapsed so dramatically and with such dire consequences that their properties and estates will have been made desolate and laid waste. Well might they express their grief and sorrow with tears and wailing, acknowledging their woes, and metaphorically casting dust upon their heads. Sadly, their reaction will not be repentance before God, neither will it be in any way a recognition of God acting in judgment, for just like the unregenerate world today, they will remain indifferent to the God of mercy and grace. There will, however, be a vast company of God-fearing individuals on earth who, although affected by the upheaval of society, will nevertheless remain faithful and steadfast, looking forward to the coming kingdom in which Christ will reign supreme.

v. 20. *Rejoice over her, thou heaven, and ye* (saints) *and holy apostles and prophets; for God hath avenged you on her.*

For some inexplicable reason, the reference to *saints* is left out in the King James Authorised Version. The inclusion of the saints is important for our understanding of all who comprise the denizens of heaven, i.e., the angels, the saints, the holy apostles, and the prophets. For the second time in this chapter, there is a voice from heaven. In verse 4, the voice from heaven will be a call to the saints on earth to separate themselves from the corruption of the world. The second call will exhort the saints in heaven to rejoice because the righteousness of God will have been vindicated. The rejoicing by all the saints in heaven will continue throughout the golden ages of eternity. The saints of God do not and will never rejoice in the destiny of unsaved souls. The Lord God has said: *Vengeance is Mine; I will repay* (Romans 12:19).

vv. 21-23: *And a mighty angel took up a stone like a great millstone, and cast it into the sea, saying, Thus with violence shall that great city Babylon be thrown down, and shall be found no more at all. And the voice of harpers, and musicians, and of pipers, and trumpeters, shall be heard no more at all in thee; and no craftsman, of whatever craft he be, shall be found any more in thee; and the sound of a millstone shall be heard no more at all in thee; and the light of a candle shall shine no more at all in thee; and the voice of the bridegroom and of the bride shall be heard no more at all in thee: for thy merchants were the great men of the earth; for by thy sorceries were all nations deceived.*

It is noteworthy that the divine manner in which Babylon will finally be dealt with and disposed of for all time will be the action of a mighty angel. The mighty angel will excel in the strength and power attributed to Babylon, which is frequently referred to as *great* because of her Satanic power and influence throughout the world. The millstone illustrates how the pernicious influence and teachings of the so-called Christian church, which is Babylon the woman, have, and will continue to have free course, rolling from country to country, crushing all opposition to its relentless pursuit.

Cast into the sea. This statement implies that the judgment of God will occasion Babylon, as a corrupt system, disappearing from the face of the earth. It is admitted that a great deal of the prophetic language in this book is symbolic; e.g., *the sea,* symbolising the disturbed nations of the world. However, in this instance, *the sea,* is figurative of a region where something will sink, be lost and disappear out of sight for ever, and never to be found. Such words confirm that God will be thorough in His judgments.

Thus with violence shall that great city Babylon be thrown down. This statement implies that while Babylon will have been powerful and influential throughout the world, God's judgment upon the system will be the exercise of His unmitigated wrath, thereby dissolving its power and influence for ever. Moreover, the perpetrators and followers of the cult of Babylon will not escape their final judgment and destiny. They all will appear before the Lord Jesus, at the Great White Throne of judgment, to account for their deeds, including their rejection of the Lord Jesus Christ as the Saviour of the world. Because their names will not be found in the book of life, they will be cast into the lake of fire which is hell, Gehenna. Ref. Chapter 20:11-15.

No more at all. This statement occurs six times through verses 21–23. The number six in Scripture signifies man's weakness, falling short of perfection which is the number seven in Scripture. In these three verses we discern that following the demise of Babylon, all the normal activities which contribute to a reasonable quality of life for man in the unregenerate world will not only cease, but disappear from the face of the earth, thus confirming that every aspect of life for man after the flesh and all he stands for will disappear. In all this, we see the fulfilment of the prophecy of Isaiah 13:19-22; verse 19 reads: *And Babylon, the glory of kingdoms, the beauty of the Chaldees' excellency, shall be as when God overthrew Sodom and Gomorrah.*

For thy merchants were the great men of the earth. The merchants will be controlled by Babylon, the religious and ecclesiastical system which, as we have seen, will eventually be judged and disposed of for ever. Merchants at the time will be deemed great men of the earth not only because of their domination of world markets but also because of the manner of their behaviour, having been bewitched and misled by the impact upon them of the drug-like teachings of Babylon, i.e., the woman, the false church. Furthermore, Babylon will have a devastating impact upon the nations of the world which will be madly intoxicated by her corruptions and adulteries, but she will not escape the day of judgment which God has predetermined, when all mankind will be judged by the One whom He has appointed (Acts 17:31).

v. 24. *And in her was found the blood of prophets, and of saints, and of all that were slain upon the earth.*

The seer continues to speak of Babylon and the record of her atrocities, especially against the saints of God. Every drop of blood shed in pursuit of her murderous endeavour will be accounted for at the Great White Throne of judgment (chapter 20:12). The statement: *And of all that were slain upon the earth,* is confirmation that the blood of every godly person slain, from righteous Abel (Genesis 4:8) to the last saint slain before the Lord comes with power and great glory, will be accounted for before the judge of all the earth. When He comes, it will be to establish His Millennial Kingdom, and there will be no further unjust killings.

Up to this time, John had been given a preview of all that will happen on earth and in heaven following the rapture to heaven of the saints of God of all dispensations. In chapter 4 of this book, Old and New Testament saints are already seen in heaven as represented by the four and twenty elders.

Chapter 19

vv. 1-3. *And after these things I heard a great voice of much people in heaven, saying, Hallelujah; Salvation, and glory, and honour, and power, unto the Lord our God: for true and righteous are His judgments: for He hath judged the great whore, which did corrupt the earth with her fornication, and hath avenged* (inflicted a punishment for) *the blood of His servants at her hand. And again they said, Hallelujah. And her smoke rose up for ever and ever.*

After these things. This statement refers to the judgments of God upon Babylon, the woman/whore/harlot, representative of the false church, and upon kings, merchants, and all traders who will have committed industrial fornication with the woman, i.e., the illicit trading in goods and activities. According to chapter 18:21, the great city Babylon, which symbolised the system, will be summarily judged and disposed of for ever and ever, but all mankind involved in her activities, will await their final judgment before the Great White Throne (chapter 20:11-15).

John hears a loud voice, just one voice confirming the unity of the innumerable company in heaven, acclaiming the righteous judgments of Almighty God upon Babylon and her corrupt system. Such, will occasion an outburst of praise in heaven: *Hallelujah; Salvation, and glory, and honour, and power, unto the Lord our God.*

Alleluia, in our Authorised Version of the Bible, is the Latin equivalent to the Hebrew, *Hallelujah* (praise ye the Lord). The term is an interjection of praise occurring just four times in the first six verses of this chapter, the only chapter in the entire New Testament where the interjection, *Hallelujah* is to be found, for which there is a very good reason. In verse 1, we have the widest possible circle of praise; heaven will be occupied for the first time since creation, with all the redeemed who will be engaged in an eternal anthem of praise, worship, and thanksgiving. According to verse 2, it will be the saints who will acclaim the incontrovertible justice of God's judgments upon the whore who will have corrupted the earth with her fornication, and shed the blood of millions of God-fearing souls.

In the third verse we have the second mention of *Hallelujah,* this time celebrating the evidence, confirmed in chapter 18:18, that the great whore (harlot) and all her works have been utterly burned with fire. The whore will have been responsible for all the corruption in the Christian profession, and accountable for the untimely deaths of many faithful saints of God. Such will be the joy of the people in heaven to know that the judgment of the whore is complete and eternal, they will again cry aloud: *Hallelujah.* Furthermore, the smoke arising from the judgment of the woman will be the undeniable evidence of the total and everlasting disposal of her. It will be the righteous judgments of Almighty God, perfectly executed, which will occasion the heavenly Hallelujahs.

v. 4. *And the four and twenty elders and the four beasts* (living creatures) *fell down and worshipped God that sat on the throne, saying, Amen; Hallelujah.*

In this verse we have the third mention of *Hallelujah.* Four and twenty elders and the four beasts (living creatures) join in their Hallelujahs, falling down and worshipping God who is sitting upon the Throne. It is God sitting upon His throne, because He at this time will be judging the activities of all involved with corruption in Christendom and their overt opposition to all His ways in judgment. The saints in heaven will generate a paean of praise which will echo throughout its courts. The four and twenty elders are the divinely elected representatives of all the redeemed. Thoughts on the significance of the living creatures are given in the study of chapter 4, verses 6 – 8. In those verses, we noted that the living creatures symbolised the heads of God's world-wide creation, together with His attributes as seen in the Person of His Son. The King, as in the Lion; the perfect Servant, as in the Ox; the perfect image of God, in the Man; and the heavenly character of Christ in the Eagle. It will be a wonderful day when all the divine attributes of creation function in unison, and are brought into line with the mind and will of God.

v. 5. *And a voice came out of the throne, saying, Praise our God, all ye His servants, and ye that fear Him, both small and great.*

The fourth mention of *Hallelujah* is in verse 6. This verse embraces all the inhabitants who will be on earth throughout the Millennial reign of Christ. The voice of an angel being heard from out of the throne will add to the authority and power of the One commanding all to: *Praise our God*. This directive will not be given to the saints in heaven, for they continually praise and worship the One who loved them and washed them in His own blood, and made them a kingdom, priests to God the Father; for they render to Him the glory and the might to the ages of ages; ref. Revelation 1:5-6.

Neither will the saints in heaven be classified small and great. So, it is to all God's servants, small and great on earth, to whom the command is given to: *Praise our God*. Their praise will focus on the righteousness and triumph of God's judgments of the whore.

vv. 6-8. *And I heard as it were the voice of a great multitude, and as the voice of many waters, and as the voice of mighty thunderings, saying, Hallelujah: for the Lord God omnipotent reigneth. Let us be glad and rejoice, and give honour to Him: for the marriage of the Lamb is come, and His wife hath made herself ready. And to her was granted that she should be arrayed in fine linen, clean and white: for the fine linen is the righteousness(es) of saints.*

John hears the response of a great multitude in unison on the earth praising God; their voice as the sound of many waters (nations), and as the voice of mighty thunderings (the sound of praise from the resurrected saints, shaking the heavens) saying: *Hallelujah: for the Lord Omnipotent reigneth,* confirming that the Lord has initiated His Millennial reign on earth. In verse 7, it is the voice which was heard from out of the throne (verse 5), commanding all on earth to: *Praise our God.* That voice will call for all the saints on earth and in heaven to rejoice and give honour to the Lord because the moment for the marriage of the Lamb will have come. We know from Ephesians 1:4 that the church was betrothed to Christ in eternity past. Paul, writing to the saints at Corinth, impressed upon them the importance of being exclusively loyal to Christ, for he was anxious to ensure that the church would be presented to Christ as a chaste virgin (2 Corinthians 11:2). We should today cherish the precious truth that, in the past eons of eternity, not only were we chosen in Christ, but also betrothed to Him to be His bride. The marriage of the Lamb will occasion the greatest chorus of praise in heaven since the incarnation of the Son of God, when: *There was a multitude of the heavenly host praising God, and saying, Glory to God in the highest, and on earth peace, good will toward men* (Luke 2:13-14).

His wife hath made herself ready. Following the rapture of the saints to glory, the church as the Bride of Christ will be made ready for the marriage by first appearing before the Judgment Seat of Christ (the Bema, seat of manifestation), to give account of the deeds done (practised) in the body; see Romans 14:10 and 2 Corinthians 5:10. The redeemed will delight to see all that was contrary to the mind of God in their lives on earth forever cancelled out by the efficacy of the blood of Christ. What will be highlighted before the Bema will be their works of righteousness under the power of the Holy Spirit of God; for such works they will be rewarded.

So, the wife will have made herself ready. Accordingly, it was: *granted that she should be arrayed in fine linen, clean and white: for the fine linen is the righteousness(es) of saints.* It is clear from the teaching of Philippians 3:9 that through our faith in Jesus Christ, the righteousness of God has already been bestowed upon us, which should have been evident in our pilgrim pathway on earth. Accordingly, the robes of righteousness, referred to in our verse 8, are not what God has put upon the saints, but are garments made of all the silver coloured threads of fine, pure linen, woven together to reflect every righteous act and faithful service carried out in love for their Saviour during the time of one's testimony on earth. A pertinent question we might ask ourselves each day is: What silver thread of fine linen (act of righteousness) will we produce which might be sown into the garment of righteousness we shall wear in glory?

> **vv. 9-10.** *And he saith unto me, Write, Blessed are they which are called unto the marriage supper of the Lamb. And he saith unto me, These are the true sayings of God. And I fell at his feet to worship him. And he said unto me, See thou do it not: I am thy fellow-servant, and of thy brethren that have the testimony of Jesus: worship God: for the testimony of Jesus is the spirit of prophecy.*

It was the voice of an angel which came out of the throne (verse 5) which now commands John to write: *Blessed are they which are called unto the marriage supper of the Lamb.* Although the marriage supper of Bridegroom and Bride will be private and in heaven, testimony of the event will be confirmed when the Lord Jesus comes with power and great glory with all His saints to establish His Millennial kingdom. The title, Lamb, belonging to our blessed Lord, will be the designation by which we shall for ever be reminded of the One who was the Lamb of God's providing (Genesis 22:8 the type and John 1:29 the antitype), to bear away the sin of the world. It truly will be a heavenly joy for all who are invited to the marriage supper of the Lamb. The invite will be to all the Old Testament saints whom John the Baptist identified, with himself, as friends of the Bridegroom (John 3:29).

At this time, with the Lamb and the Bride being brought before us, Scripture no longer refers to the four and twenty elders who together represented Old and New Testament saints; their last mention is in verse 4 of this chapter. We should notice the glorious conclusion of their combined identity; they fall down and worship God who sits upon the Throne, saying: *Amen, Hallelujah.* Well might we also sing with joy in our hearts, the lovely hymn:

> *Lamb of God, Thou now art seated,*
> *High upon Thy Father's throne.*
> *All Thy gracious work completed;*
> *All Thy mighty victory won.*
> *Every knee in heaven is bending*
> *To the Lamb for sinners slain.*
> *Every voice and heart is swelling;*
> *Worthy is the Lamb to reign.*
> J.G. Deck.

CHAPTER 19

These are the true sayings of God. It is of supreme importance to every child of God who reads: *The Revelation of Jesus Christ,* that they accept and believe all that is written to be the inspired truth of God: *As the truth is in Jesus* (Ephesians 4:21). So vital is it for a divine understanding of all God, by His Spirit, has revealed to us in this book, that we are twice more reminded of the divine authenticity of what is written. In chapter 21:5, John is directed to write: *For these words are true and faithful.* We are then told that one of the seven angels which had the seven vials full of the last seven plagues (21:9), said to John, referring to all which had been revealed to him and which he had heard: *These sayings are faithful and true (22:6).*

And I fell at (before) *his feet to worship him.* John is so overwhelmed by what he has heard and what has been revealed to him that he falls to worship at the feet of the one he believed was the Lord. Instantly, the angel commands John to do no such thing, because it would be tantamount to idolatry. Whereupon, John is urged to bow in homage to God, acknowledging that the testimony of Jesus is the spirit of prophecy.

> **v. 11.** *And I saw heaven opened, and behold a white horse; and He that sat upon him was called Faithful and True, and in righteousness He doth judge and make war.*

This verse introduces us to the event long awaited for by the faithful remnant of the Jews and believing Gentiles who survive: *great tribulation. And I saw heaven opened*; it is not a door opened for an individual to come out, but heaven itself will be opened to allow the Lord to come forth with power, might and great glory, with ten thousand times ten thousand, and thousands of thousands of His saints (Jude 14). The white horse (not literal) is symbolic of triumph in warfare, for surely there will occur on earth the greatest war of all time; a unique war with casualties on one side only, the side of the enemies God and His Christ; enemies who will be totally vanquished. It will be the Lord Jesus Himself, sitting upon the horse (symbol of victory and power), who will be in total control of all proceedings to guarantee the holy triumph over all the forces of evil.

Faithful and True. This title is and will ever be unique to the Lord Jesus, for no created being will be able to lay claim to such a divine accolade. In chapter 3:14, the designation: *faithful and true,* emphasises the divine attributes of the Lord Jesus. Here in verse 11, the adjectives: *Faithful and True,* should be read as nouns, highlighting the divine titles God has bestowed upon His beloved Son.

In righteousness He doth judge and make war. Up to this point in time, it will have been God Himself who judged His enemies in righteousness and exercised divine action. Now, as recorded, it will be the Lord Jesus who will in righteousness judge all His foes. There will be no indiscriminate action, no miscarriage of justice, no prejudice or favour, but justice exercised in its pure and divinest form. There certainly will be violent opposition to the Lord's actions, but He will triumph gloriously, for in righteousness He will overcome and trample all His foes beneath His feet.

v. 12. *His eyes were as a flame of fire, and on His head were many crowns; and He had a name written, that no man knew, but He Himself.*

The most reliable translations read: *His eyes are a flame of fire,* leaving out the comparative conjunction, *as,* which is correct where it occurs in chapters 1:14, and 2:18. Here, the Lord will be acting in judgment. Symbolically, His eyes, a flame, will burn away the darkest of disguises and pierce the thickest blankets of concealment, to reveal all the histories of man's wickedness, exposing them ready for judgment. The many crowns (diadems) upon His head symbolise supreme authority in relation to the righteous judgments the Lord will make. However, the diadems on the seven heads of Satan who is represented as the: *great red dragon* in chapter 12:3 and the ten diadems on the horns of the beast, in chapter 13:1, all symbolised usurped authority and power energised by Satan. The Lord will have a name written which no one knows but Himself. It is clear that the name referred to is not: Faithful and True, verse 11, neither is it the: Word of God, verse 13, nor will it be any other name to be found in our Bible currently attached to the Lord Jesus. God, in His wisdom, has given to His beloved Son a name which is incomprehensible, beyond the wit of man, and certainly beyond the lexicons of human language to express or define. Furthermore, there is no assurance given in the Word of God that we shall ever know the name, for it is hidden in the vaults of heaven. Any attempt by man to define such a name would be tantamount to peering into the *Ark of the Covenant,* which could have very serious, spiritual consequences; see 1 Samuel 6:19.

v. 13. *And He was clothed with a vesture dipped in blood: and His name is called The Word of God.*

What we read in Isaiah 63:1-6 confirms that the Lord's, *vesture dipped in blood,* as spoken of in this verse, does not refer to His sacrificial work on Calvary's Cross. Rather, to the result of His Holy judgments when, in His righteous anger He tramples His foes beneath His feet in the wine-vat. Thus, His garments will be red as the garments of those who normally tread the wine-vat, becoming stained with the juice of the grape. The statement in our verse that: *He was clothed with a vesture dipped in blood,* is, of course, symbolic language; nevertheless, it is intended to convey the severity and consequence of the Lord's judgments.

And His name is called The Word of God. We read in the opening of John's Gospel: *In the beginning was the Word, and the Word was with God, and the Word was God.* In this divine appellation, the Greek for 'Word' is *Logos*, and signifies that the entire mind, heart, will, and purpose of God would be expressed in the Lord Jesus Christ as He came into Manhood. It is worthy of note, that the name: *The Word of God,* is quite distinct from any meaning of relationship to God, neither does the name denote status nor title, but it is an indication of the surpassing greatness and importance of all that would be expressed in the testimony of the Lord Jesus, as Son of Man on earth. Thus, the meaning of the Lord's title: *The Word of God*, will be fully worked out in all that follows, for the glory of God.

v. 14. *And the armies which were* (are) *in heaven followed Him on white horses, clothed in fine linen, white and clean.*

It is good to remind ourselves from time to time that what we are reading in these chapters is the record of what John saw and heard on a Lord's Day while exiled on the Isle of Patmos. John may well have understood that the visions he had were symbolic of actual events which will definitely occur in God's time. The armies which are referred to in this verse will comprise of all the Old and New Testament saints who will have been raptured to heaven prior to the commencement of the seven-year tribulation period (1 Thessalonians 4:16-17), together with the saints who suffered and died during the time of tribulation.

The Lord alone, who leads the armies, will appear to be clothed in a vesture dipped in blood, signifying that His mission is warfare, when blood will be shed among the enemies of God and His Christ; a war in which He will triumph gloriously. The saints who follow will likewise be symbolically on white horses, representing triumph though righteousness, for they will be clothed in garments of fine linen, white and clean. This event will be the actual realization of the prophecy by Enoch made circa 5,000 years earlier and recorded by Jude in his epistle, verses 14-15.

> **vv. 15-16.** *And out of His mouth goeth a sharp sword, that with it He should smite the nations: and He shall rule them with a rod of iron: and He treadeth the winepress of the fierceness and wrath of Almighty God.*

The sharp sword out of the mouth of the Lord will be His Word; its effect will be as given in the epistle to the Hebrews, chapter 4:12. *For the Word of God is quick, and powerful, and sharper than any twoedged sword, piercing even to the dividing asunder of soul and spirit, and of the joints and marrow, and is a discerner of the thoughts and intents of the heart.* The only weapon the Lord will use against the enemies of God will be the sharp sword of His mouth. The Word of the Lord will demolish to smithereens the greatest and most powerful weapons man will have in his arsenal.

The verb *smite* in our verse implies that the Lord's dealings with the opposing nations of the world will not be a long, drawn-out battle, but by just one powerful word they will be fatally struck down. The statement: *And He shall rule* (shepherd) *them with a rod of iron,* relates to the Millennial reign of Christ when He will reign in righteousness. Satan will be bound in the bottomless pit for the one thousand years, ensuring there will be no opposition to the rule of Christ, who will reign with His saints (chapter 20:6). Shepherding the peoples of the world with a rod of iron, signifies that the Lord will exercise absolute, unyielding, sovereign authority throughout the world.

And He treadeth the winepress of the fierceness and wrath of Almighty God. The expression: *Treading the winepress,* equates with the saying used today: *Stamping out evil.* The function of the winepress symbolises the out-pouring of the righteous vengeance of Almighty God. In the day to which we are referring, the Lord will, with unmitigated vengeance, stamp out every trace element of religious wickedness, rebellion, and apostasy. Writing prophetically of the Lord Jesus, Isaiah records these words: *I have trodden the winepress alone; and of the people there was none with Me: for I will tread them in Mine anger, and trample them in My fury; and their blood shall be sprinkled upon My garments, and I will stain all My raiment* (Isaiah 63:3).

v. 16. *And He hath on His vesture and on His thigh a name written, KING OF KINGS, AND LORD OF LORDS.*

The appearance of the Lord Jesus will be so majestic that none will fail to recognise Him. Furthermore, upon His vesture and upon His thigh He will bear a composite name to leave none in doubt as to His status, supremacy, power, and authority. As uncreated, He is, and ever will be paramount, above all creation.

vv. 17-18. *And I saw an angel standing in the sun; and he cried with a loud voice, saying to all the fowls that fly in the midst of heaven, Come and gather yourselves together unto the supper of the great God;* (it should more correctly read: *the great supper of God*) *that ye may eat the flesh of kings, and the flesh of captains, and the flesh of mighty men, and the flesh of horses, and of them that sit on them, and the flesh of all men, both free and bond, both small and great.*

An angel standing in the sun. It immediately comes to mind that the angel will be speaking with the supreme authority - as symbolised by the sun - given by God when he summons all the fowls of the air to gather themselves together to the great supper of God. This will be in stark contrast to the marriage supper of the Lamb, an event which will occasion great joy and praise throughout the courts of heaven.

CHAPTER 19

What now follows should be understood as an event which is not symbolic but which will literally occur. Why, we might ask, is this supper called the great supper of God? A supper is usually the last meal of a day. This meal, provided by God for all the carnivorous birds whose sphere of flight is the mid-heavens (atmospheric heavens), will signal the great end of God's dealings with man after the flesh. It is not without significance that for the disposal of all the literal flesh of the unregenerate slain of mankind at this time, God will employ the unclean, carnivorous birds mentioned in Leviticus 11:13-14.

Accordingly, there will be no dignified obsequies for rebellious man; rather, the unclean disposing of the unclean, from kings of realms, to beggars on dunghills. It is important to remind our hearts that it will take seven months for the house of Israel to bury the skeletal remains of the dead in their land, thereby ensuring the land will be cleansed according to God's standard (Ezekiel 39:12), and ready for the One who, as King of kings and Lord of lords, will reign in righteousness for a thousand years (chapter 20:4 & 6).

> **v. 19.** *And I saw the beast, and the kings of the earth, and their armies, gathered together to make war against Him that sat on the horse, and against His army.*

This verse specifically relates to the greatest of all wars, the war against Him that sits upon the horse, and against His army; it will be the battle of Armageddon, referred to in chapter 16:16. In accord with the Scriptural calendar of events, the battle will occur at the end of *great tribulation* period, coincident with the coming of the Lord with all His saints. All the world's human and material resources will have been mobilised by the kings of the earth, from the North, East, South and West. They will assemble for the greatest one-sided battle of all time, a battle against the Lord of Creation, the Faithful and True who sits upon the white horse, symbolising triumph through righteousness. The ten kingdoms representing the revived Roman Empire will, in title, have been be fused with the beast. However, the kings of the earth referred to in this verse relate to the kingdoms of the world which, with their armies, join forces with the beast and false prophet, also known as the antichrist, for what they will believe to be the final war of all wars, but it will end in their total destruction, without a single survivor.

v. 20. *And the beast was taken, and with him the false prophet that wrought miracles before him, with which he deceived them that had received the mark of the beast, and them that worshipped his image. These both were cast alive into a lake of fire burning with brimstone.*

The beast, an individual supremo of the Gentile forces, and the false prophet, a distinct personality, also known as the antichrist and head of religious apostasy, will be singled out for their summary removal from a scene of unparalleled hostile activity around Jerusalem. The false prophet will be guilty of deceiving millions of souls by performing miracles with Satanic power, and by enforcing all to receive the mark of the beast as a guarantee of uninterrupted life. Furthermore, the false prophet will denigrate the Godhead and the Lord Jesus by compelling men to worship the image of the beast, coupled with a threat that any who refuse should die (chapter 13:15). These two arch-enemies of God and the Lord Jesus will not pass through the normal article of death but will be cast alive into the lake of fire, burning with brimstone. They will be the first occupants of the place of eternal darkness, of weeping, gnashing of teeth and excruciating pain, prepared for the devil and his angels (Matthew 25:41); it will also be the destiny of all unregenerate souls following their appearance before the Great White Throne (chapter

20:11-15). In due course, Satan will be the third person to suffer the same fate (chapter 20:10).

> **v. 21.** *And the remnant were slain with the sword of Him that sat upon the horse, which sword proceeded out of His mouth: and all the fowls were filled with their flesh.*

As mentioned earlier, this war will be unique in the entire history of mankind. Although all the hostile powers will be assembled ready for battle against the Lord and His beloved city, we might ask ourselves: why is there no account of the war? The answer is that there will be no hand to hand conflict. While not a single soul of the faithful remnant on the Lord's side will die, at the very moment Satan signals his forces to commence their assault, the Lord, by the sword (word) of His mouth will consume the myriads of His enemies in death. Thus, will end the one-sided battle of Armageddon; all the adversaries of the Lord Jesus, except Satan, will have been dealt with. Once Satan is locked away, the healing and cleansing of the land will commence with the fowls of heaven devouring the flesh of the slain, and the skeletal remains, buried by the faithful remnant.

Chapter 20

vv. 1-3. *And I saw an angel come down from heaven, having the key of the bottomless pit and a great chain in his hand. And he laid hold on the dragon, that old serpent, which is the Devil, and Satan, and bound him a thousand years. And cast him into the bottomless pit, and shut him up, and set a seal upon him, that he should deceive the nations no more, till the thousand years should be fulfilled: and after that he must be loosed a little season.*

The *key, bottomless pit*, and *the great chain*, are symbols. Under the guidance of God, the angel holding the symbolic key will unlock access to the bottomless pit (the abyss) into which Satan and his angels will be cast. It is a region of utter darkness in the greatest depths and distance from God, and from where it will be impossible for Satan to exercise any influence on mankind. The great chain symbolises the great divine power which will hold Satan and his angels secure in the abyss for one thousand years. Satan, as a fallen angel, has a four-fold name which fully defines his character and evil attributes. "The dragon" relates to the ferocity, cruelty, and destructive nature of the beast. "That old serpent" is noted for his subtlety, deception, and poisonous influence. "The Devil" is the great traducer, beguiler, and dissembler. "Satan", the archenemy of God, the merciless adversary, the accuser of the brethren. Until Satan is bound for the one thousand years, he will remain the prince of this world (John 12:31), the god of this world (2 Corinthians 4:4), and the prince of the power of the air (Ephesians 2:2). The divine seal guarantees Satan's impregnable imprisonment.

N.B. In our studies to date, we have referred to the one-thousand-year reign of Christ as "the Millennium". Now, while it is freely admitted that such a noun does not appear in the Scriptures, its use in the written and verbal ministry of the Word of God should not disturb the saints, for its use in no way undermines the teaching of Holy Scripture regarding the eventual reign of Christ. There are other expressions, which are not found in the Scriptures, yet freely used by the Lord's servants in their ministry to enrich our understanding of the Word of God. e.g., The Deity of Christ; the Incarnation; Eternal Sonship *et. al.*. May our gracious Lord preserve us from dismissing, out of hand, such reverential expressions relating to the uniqueness of the Son of God.

> **v. 4.** *And I saw thrones, and they sat upon them, and judgment was given unto them: and I saw the souls of them that were beheaded for the witness of Jesus, and for the word of God, and which had not worshipped the beast, neither his image, neither had received his mark upon their foreheads, or in their hands; and they lived and reigned with Christ a thousand years.*

We have three distinct groups of saints brought before us in this verse. It is good to be reminded that the wisdom of this world should never be sought in one's endeavour to understand the teachings of the Word of God. Failure to acknowledge this vital fact will undoubtedly lead us to wrong conclusions about the symbols which the Holy Spirit has freely used throughout the Scriptures.

First, John sees thrones and those who sat upon them. There is little doubt that those sitting on the thrones are the four and twenty elders, representing all the Old and New Testament saints, already referred to in chapter 4:4. The New Testament saints comprise the church, the bride of Christ, while the Old Testament saints will be the friends of the Bridegroom at the marriage of the Lamb. The authority to judge (to make divine decisions) will be given to them; this will accord with the words of the apostle Paul to the saints at Corinth: *Do ye not know that the saints shall judge the world and ... angels?* (1 Corinthians 6:2-3). But here and now, in this day of God's grace to the world, a child of God should never prosecute a suit in a court of law, saved or unsaved, no matter how grave an issue. Let us ever follow the example of our Blessed Lord: *Who, when He was reviled, reviled not again; when He suffered, He threatened not; but committed Himself to Him that judgeth righteously* (1 Peter 2:23). The Lord Jesus in His High Priestly prayer, when referring to the saints of God, said: *They are not of the world, even as I am not of the world* (John 17:14). May our gracious Lord help us to live in accord with these precious words.

The second group referred to in this verse is spoken of as: *The souls of them that were beheaded for the witness* (testimony) *of Jesus, and for the word of God*. This clause in verse 4 should, more correctly, read: *And the souls of those beheaded on account of the testimony of Jesus, and on account of the word of God* (New Translation, JND). The correction will help us to more clearly identify the three groups of saints referred to in the verse. This is the group of saints, Jew and Gentile, who will believe and accept the Gospel of the Kingdom which will be preached following the rapture of the Church to glory. The Gospel of the Kingdom relates to the Millennial Kingdom on earth to be established by the Lord Jesus following His coming with power and great glory (Matthew 24:30). During the interval of time, between the rapture of the church and the appearance of the beast from out of the sea (nations of the world) detailed in chapter 13, a faithful, believing remnant of both Jew and Gentile will suffer severe persecution, even unto death; such are referred to in chapter 6:9-11. It will be when the fifth seal judgment is opened that John sees their souls under the altar (brazen alter), and hears their cry: *How long, O Lord, holy and true, dost Thou not judge and avenge our blood on them that dwell on the earth?*- chapter 6:10. In reply to their plea: it is said to them: *That they should rest yet for a little season, until their fellow servants also and their brethren, that should be killed as they were, should be fulfilled.*

We come now to the third group of souls referred to in the fourth verse: *Which had not worshipped the beast, neither his image, neither had received his mark upon their foreheads, or in their hands.* Clearly, this section of the verse refers to the faithful remnant of both Jew and Gentile who during the latter half of Daniel's seventieth week (Daniel 9:25-27) will experience even greater tribulation than those who will have gone before and whose souls John will have already seen under the Altar (chapter 6:9). Following the appearance upon the scene of the beast which arises from out of the sea (from among the nations of the world), as detailed in chapter 13:1-8, the severity of the trials inflicted upon the saints will increase dramatically. Such trials will be further intensified by the appearance and activity of another beast, this time from out of the earth, in other words, from among unregenerate Jews in Israel. He will be a reprobate Jew.

As we have already seen in our earlier studies, this second beast will have the appearance of a tender lamb, but will make no attempt to conceal his malignity, for he will be the false prophet, the antichrist, the man of sin who will exercise great and deadly influence over the first beast. Having persuaded the first beast to have an image made of himself, the false prophet will then compel all mankind to worship the image, with the threat of death to any who refuse.

Furthermore, in order to buy and trade, and thereby live, all must receive the mark of the beast on the right hand or upon the forehead. The mark will signify the commitment and dedication of the individual to the will of the beast. Thus, the third group of saints referred to in our verse will be those who flatly refuse to yield to the edicts of the false prophet, and will readily suffer the consequences. Nevertheless, they will be resurrected along with the second group of our study to live and reign with Christ.

> **vv. 5-6.** *But the rest of the dead lived not again until the thousand years were finished. This is the first resurrection. Blessed and holy is he that hath part in the first resurrection: on such the second death hath no power, but they shall be priests of God and of Christ, and shall reign with Him a thousand years.*

The rest of the dead, refers to all the unregenerate souls, from the time of Cain (1 John 3:12) to the moment of the coming of the Lord Jesus with all His saints to establish His Millennial Kingdom and reign as King of kings, and Lord of lords. These will remain in their graves throughout the reign of Christ for the one thousand years, after which, they will be raised to appear before the Great White Throne as detailed at the end of our chapter.

The statement: *This is the first resurrection,* requires clarification. We have already noted, from following the calendar of events in the Scriptures, that all the Old and New Testament saints were raptured to heaven when the Lord Jesus came to the clouds and called all His own to Himself. Those who were in the grave were resurrected, and those still alive were caught up and changed into the likeness of the Blessed Saviour (1 Corinthians 15:51-52, also, 1 Thessalonians 4:16-17).

According to the Lord's own words (John 5:29), there are just two resurrections referred to in the Scriptures; an incontrovertible fact referred to by Paul when standing before the most noble Felix: *There shall be a resurrection of the dead, both of the just and unjust* (Acts 24:15). **N.B.** the words: *of the dead,* do not appear in the original Greek Text. Thus, the resurrection of the Old and New Testament saints, together with the last two groups of saints referred to in verse 4 of our chapter is, by divine definition, the first resurrection, because the end result will be the same for all the redeemed saints, i.e., eternal rest, and joy in heaven with our Lord and Saviour, Jesus Christ.

Blessed and holy is he that hath part in the first resurrection: on such the second death hath no power. The saints of God have been blessed with every spiritual blessing in the heavenly places in Christ, ref. Ephesians 1:3. Furthermore, God has chosen us that we should be holy and without blame before Him in love. Our security in Christ is the assured guarantee that the second death will have no power over or upon us. As priests, the saints will be worshippers of God and the Lord Jesus Christ, and heaven will be filled with His praises throughout the golden ages of eternity. *They live and reign with Christ a thousand years,* refers to all the saints of God, previously raptured to glory. The *second death* refers to the eternal destiny, hell, Gehenna of all unregenerate souls after they have appeared before the Great White Throne; verse 14 of this chapter.

> **vv. 7-10.** *And when the thousand years are expired, Satan shall be loosed out of his prison, and shall go out to deceive the nations which are in the four quarters of the earth, Gog and Magog, to gather them together to battle: the number of whom is as the sand of the sea. And they went up*

on the breadth of the earth, and compassed the camp of the saints about, and the beloved city: and fire came down from God out of heaven, and devoured them. And the devil that deceived them was cast into the lake of fire and brimstone, where the beast and the false prophet are, and shall be tormented day and night for ever and ever.

We have seen in our studies to date that a great number of the visions John had and recorded under the guidance of the Holy Spirit are, in fact, symbols of actual persons, things, and events both current and prophetic. However, we have also noted that some of the data John has given are not symbolic but are actual, as in the case of the one-thousand-year reign Christ, known as the Millennium. If we do not accept the literal meaning of one thousand years, we shall not understand the significance of the statement that Satan will be loosed out of his prison at the end of the one-thousand-year period.

During the Millennium, Christ will reign in righteousness with an iron rod (chapter 19:15). With Satan being bound, the natural feelings of man's heart will be supressed by the power of the rule of Christ. However, as soon as Satan is released from the abyss, his evil influence will once again control the hearts of all who have not accepted Christ as the King of kings and Lord of lords during His one-thousand-year reign. Satan and his entourage will immediately go about to deceive the nations of the world with the intention of making a final assault on the saints of God and the beloved city, Jerusalem. The nations from the four quarters of the earth, being thoroughly deceived by Satan and energised by his power, will assemble for battle in their millions on all sides of the beloved city, the city of the great King, who is the Lord Jesus Himself. But before a single assault is made on any saint of God, fire will descend out of heaven from God to devour them, and not one will escape God's summary judgment.

CHAPTER 20

It is worthy of note that in 2 Thessalonians 2:8, prior to the one-thousand-year reign of Christ, it is the Lord Himself who consumes His enemies with the spirit (should read breath) of His mouth, for the Lord Jesus will be in supreme control of all events in the heavens and on earth. Here, in verse 9, it is God who pours out fire from heaven to consume all His foes. Then will begin the eternal state wherein righteousness will forever dwell and: *God* will *be all in all* (1 Corinthians 15:28).

Finally, the universal activities of Satan covering a period of seven thousand years since creation will be brought to an ignominious end when he is cast, without judgment, directly into the lake of fire and brimstone where, together with the beast and false prophet, they will be tormented day and night for ever and ever. The term: *Lake of fire and brimstone,* merits elucidation. The beast and the false prophet are still alive in the environment of Gehenna after one thousand years. So, Gehenna is not a consuming fire, rather a place of extreme, unrelenting and eternal torment. If we refer back to Exodus 3 and the occasion when the angel of the Lord appeared unto Moses in a flame of fire out of the midst of the bush, we are told that although the bush burned with fire, it was not consumed. The spiritual meaning of the vision was that the bush represented Israel in Egypt; the fire was a symbol of the torment and trial the nation was passing through under tyrannical oppression by the Egyptians, but the nation could not be consumed because the Lord Jehovah was in the midst of His people.

Now, while Israel was eventually delivered from the bondage of Egypt, there will be no such deliverance nor relief for the beast, false prophet, and Satan from the torment of Gehenna. Referring to the words: *Day and night,* we know that in eternity time will not be measured in days, for in the new earth and new heaven, there will be no night (chapter

21:25). Furthermore, in Gehenna, there will be no light, but rather a darkness which can be felt (Exodus 10:21). While the Lord Jehovah was with the nation of Israel in their trial, all who end up in the darkness and torment of Gehenna will be alone for ever.

> **v. 11.** *And I saw a great white throne, and Him that sat on it, from whose face the earth and the heaven fled away; and there was found no place for them.*

One thousand years earlier when the Lord came with tens of thousands of His saints, it was to judge the living; here, the Lord will come to judge the dead. John sees: *A great white throne.* The adjective *great* signifies the unique, incomparable supremacy of the divine court; *white* confirms the righteousness of the divine judgments, while the noun, *throne,* speaks of the dignity, right, and authority of the One who sits upon it to pass judgment.

From whose face (countenance) *the earth and the heaven fled away.* The Greek word for fled is, *pheugo,* which carries the thought of vanishing out of sight. John's vision of the Son of Man as recorded in chapter 1:16, reads: *His countenance was as the sun shineth in his strength.* The earth and heavens, defiled by sin, could not therefore stand in the light of the Lord's glory. They vanish from John's vision. At this point, the words of the Lord Jesus in John 5:28-29, regarding the unregenerate will be fulfilled, for the saints will have already been raised and glorified. But the dead who have done evil, will hear the Lord's voice and will come forth unto the resurrection of damnation.

> **v. 12.** *And I saw the dead, small and great, stand before God; and the books were opened: and another book was opened, which is the book of life: and the dead were judged out of those things which were written in the books, according to their works.*

The adjectives: *small and great* confirm that those raised for judgment will range from the noblest king and emperor to the beggar on the street, all whose names were not found written in the book of life. The words: *stand before God,* should read: *stand before the throne,* which is referred to in the previous verse as: *a great white throne.* It is upon this throne that the Lord Jesus will sit to judge the risen dead, small and great. There will be none too great to escape or be excused from standing before the Judge of the Supreme Court of the Universe and none too small and insignificant to be over-looked by the One who sees all (Genesis 16:13).

And the books were opened. This is symbolic language confirming that in the library of God's mind, there are records of the works of every ungodly person who has trod this earth, from the first to the very last person born after the flesh. The reason why we have books in the plural is confirmation that in God's library there are records of the lives of all the unsaved from the seven dispensational periods of this world's history, including the present day of grace and beyond.

The first dispensation was that of Innocence, ending with Adam and Eve being put out of the Garden of Eden (Genesis 3:23-24). The second was that of Conscience. Because of the wickedness of man, who had his conscience seared by Satan, God judged the world with a whelming flood, saving only Noah and his family (Genesis 7:23). The third dispensation was that of Human Government which failed with the judgment of Babel (Genesis 11:5-9). The fourth was patriarchal, the assured Promise (Genesis 12:1-3), ending with the bondage of the nation of Israel in Egypt. The fifth was that of the Law, ending with the judgment of God for sin being expended/exhausted upon the Saviour of the world upon Calvary's Cross (Romans 10:4). The sixth dispensation is the present Day of Grace, which will end when the Lord comes from heaven with all His saints, with power and great glory to establish His Millennial Kingdom (Jude 14). The final and seventh dispensation will be the Kingdom Reign of Christ, ending with the disposal of Satan directly into the Lake of fire where he will join the beast and false prophet (verse 10 of our chapter) and his followers who will join him after they have appeared for judgment before the Great White Throne. The foregoing data will help us understand why God has several books listing the wicked from each of the seven dispensations.

And another book was opened, which is the book of life. This book which God has in the library of His mind bears the names of all the redeemed, for God will reveal to us personally the record he holds of our testimony on earth. There will be no question of judgments for our failures, this is because they will have already been answered for by the atoning blood of our Saviour. What will be brought before us is the divine estimate of our service, witness, and testimony; we shall then be awarded accordingly. As with the judgment of the wicked, where there will be levels of punishment (Luke 10:12 & 14) so, with the Christian, there will be degrees and size of award (Luke 19:16-19).

We should not overlook the significance of the 'one book of life'. God knew that resulting from the subterfuge of Satan, there would arise many religious sects, all claiming to exist on the authority of God and His Word. The apostle Paul identified the seed of such heresy in the church at Corinth and, led by the Spirit of God, nipped the problem in the bud. Today, in the religious sects of Christendom, of which there are many, the majority of their doctrines are dangerously misleading, and counterfeit to the Word of God.

Sadly, there are many millions of souls who are totally immersed in the Satanic doctrines of such groups. Their leaders promulgate that acceptance of their teachings will be the individual's passport to heaven. Alas, it will not be, for their destiny after this life will be Gehenna, the Lake of Fire, unless they have repented of their sins before God, and put their faith and trust in the Lord Jesus Christ. Satan will have blinded their hearts and minds to the extent that they become unaware of the fact that unless they are born again they will not go to heaven after this life, but to hell, having been righteously judged according to their works. Thus, we can understand why there will be just one *book of life* which will list, not only the Old Testament saints, but the names of all who, on the basis of the teaching of Holy Scripture, have put their faith and trust in the finished work of Redemption, a work uniquely accomplished by the Lord Jesus Christ.

v. 13. *And the sea gave up the dead which were in it; and death and hell delivered up the dead which were in them: and they were judged every man according to their works.*

The sea as a symbol represents the disturbed world in general. Here, the reference to the sea is literal, for since creation, millions of people have lost their lives at sea. All the Old and New Testament saints will have already been raised and are in glory. It is a fact that many, many thousands of unregenerate individuals plan for when they die to have their bodies cremated and the ashes cast into the sea. In the majority of cases the objective will have been the hope of escaping a resurrection to appear before the Lord for judgment of their ungodly life, a truth which they do not believe but fear it might be true. Such souls think that by having their bodies reduced to ashes, it will be impossible for their bodies to be reconstituted, disregarding the fact that God made Adam from the dust of the earth (1 Corinthians 15:47).

Death and hell delivered up the dead which were in them. This statement requires a little explanation. We know that when a person dies, it is the separation of spirit, soul and body. Their spirit goes back to God who gave it (Ecclesiastes 12:7). Their soul goes either into Paradise (Luke 23:43), or hell, Gehenna for the unsaved (Luke 16:23). Their physical body is buried. So, death takes care of the body, and Paradise or Hell (Hades) retains the soul, until both destinies are required to release their charges to appear before the Judgment Seat of Christ, or the Great White Throne to be judged according to their works.

v. 14. *And death and hell were cast into the lake of fire. This is the second death.*

Having defined death as the separation of spirit, soul, and body, death and hell in this verse are viewed as depositories for the bodies and souls of the unregenerate. The apostle Paul has written: *The last enemy that shall be destroyed is death* (1 Corinthians 15:26). In writing these words, the apostle had in mind the glorious eternal state when: *God shall wipe away all tears from their eyes; and there shall be no more death, neither sorrow, nor crying, neither shall there be any more pain: for the former things are passed away* (Revelation 21:4). Death is the very antithesis of life and, therefore, defined as an enemy which will be annulled when, with hell, both are cast into the Lake of fire. At the present time, death takes care of the body, hell retains the soul, but as depositories, they will no longer be required. We should note, there is no mention of pain and suffering, for they are God's provision for the retention of bodies and souls: *unto the resurrection of damnation* (John 5:29 last clause).

Today, the Satanic art of necromancy is on the increase. People are anxious to know if their loved ones are safe on the other side of death, for, innately, they have a fear of the judgment of God falling upon their loved ones. By attending meetings for the practice of witchcraft, sorcery, etc., they believe that the voices they hear are those of their loved ones, whereas in actual fact they are hearing the voice of Satan imitating the voice of whoever they are seeking to contact. Hearing such voices, unregenerate people mistakenly believe it is sure evidence that their loved ones are not in hell, and take comfort in their heart and mind. Neither Satan nor his angels have access to the souls of people who have died; they are secure and inaccessible, under the control of the Lord, and will remain so, until raised in resurrection for judgment and eternal condemnation.

This is the second death. In the original Greek text, the words: *The lake of fire,* are added with significant authority. The second death is the final destiny of all who appear before the Great White Throne for judgment; they will be cast into the lake of fire which burneth for ever and ever, ref. verse 10.

v. 15. *And whosoever was not found written in the book of life was cast into the lake of fire.*

It has already been mentioned that the Book of Life is in the library of God's holy mind. The names which fill the pages of the divine record can never be erased, but every person who has walked on earth whose name is not found in the Book of Life will be consigned to the Lake of fire. While the first eight verses of the following chapter really belong to this chapter; we shall proceed in our studies of the verses as under chapter 21.

The best and most reliable authorities on the original Greek text of: *The Revelation of Jesus Christ,* teach that the first eight verses of chapter 21 should rightly be the end verses of chapter 20, which bring to a close the record of God's dealings with this world, and the introduction of the eternal state. Furthermore, from verse 9 of this chapter 21 to verse 5 of chapter 22 should be the whole of chapter 21, making verses 6-21 of chapter 22 the last chapter of the Bible. Notwithstanding, we shall consider the verses in the order in which they appear in the KJV version.

Thus, the first eight verses of our chapter set out how things will be in the eternal state following the Millennium. It has often been remarked that very little is recorded in the Bible about the eternal state. However, here in the first four verses of our chapter, we do have some details of that blessed environment, wherein, as the apostle Paul wrote: *That God may be all in all* (1 Corinthians 15:28), which is a clear reference to the eternal state. Peter writes about what the saints of God should be occupied with when he says: *We… look for new heavens and a new earth, wherein dwelleth righteousness* (2 Peter 3:13).

As a matter of interest, it would be worth detailing some facts about the original text of the Bible, as recorded in Walter Scott's book, *Story of our English Bible*. In the thirteenth century, the Roman Catholic Cardinal Hugo divided each of the 66 books of the Bible into chapters. In the fifteenth century, a Jewish Rabbi called Nathan, divided all Cardinal Hugo's chapters of the Old Testament into verses. In the sixteenth century, a French printer by the name of Stephens arranged all the New Testament chapters into verses. The first English Bible with chapters and verses was known as the Bishops' Bible. The current King James Authorised Version was first published in 1611. Notwithstanding some misplaced breaks in the chapters and a few Scriptural faults in translation from both the Hebrew and the Greek text; the well-loved KJV is still highly valued, and much used today.

Chapter 21

v. 1. *And I saw a new heaven and a new earth: for the first heaven and the first earth were passed away; and there was no more sea.*

John has a sight of the cleansed heaven and cleansed earth. All the features of the old atmospheric and starry heavens, in which Satan and his angels had sway, will have been cleansed of the evil influence they exerted. Isaiah prophesied: *Behold, I create new heavens and a new earth: and the former shall not be remembered, nor come into mind* (Isaiah 65:17; also 66:22). As we have already said, very little is recorded about the new heaven and new earth. However, we may be certain they will be divinely suited for God's purpose, reflecting His glory and majesty which will endure throughout the golden ages of eternity. Peter in his second epistle (2 Peter 3:10 & 12-13) confirms there will be a new heaven and a new earth, wherein righteousness will dwell. The old heaven and earth in their original state will no longer exist, the earth having been made anew by the fiery judgment of Almighty God.

And there was no more sea. In our earlier studies of this book, we have seen that mention of the sea has reference to the troubled, disturbed nations of the world. For example, in chapter 13 we are told that the beast, symbol of the revived Roman Empire, rises up out of the sea, a symbol of the unsettled nations of the world. Here, in our verse, the sea is meant to be understood as the literal sea which surrounds the continents of the world. So why, we may ask, will there be no sea in the new earth? Today, the oceans of the world play a vital role in maintaining the hygiene of the coastal regions of the world, where the refuse of the nations usually ends up. The twice daily tides, influenced by the moon, play a most important role in the disposal of the world's waste. Furthermore, we know that the sea contributes substantially to weather patterns around the world, providing rain for crops and plants in general; also drinking water to sustain life. Today, without water all life would cease to exist on earth. The life which would cease to exist is the temporal life of all things on earth, including man. The new earth will be peopled by all who feared and obeyed God during the Millennium; they will have glorified bodies, not requiring the resources of the old world to nourish them for they will be kept by the power of the Spirit of God. Just as the earth will have been made anew, so all who will dwell on the new earth will have been made anew by the Spirit of God; they will have bodies suited to the new, holy, and eternal environment (Philippians 3:21). In the enjoyment of eternal life, they will be sustained in every way by God.

v. 2. *And I John saw the holy city, new Jerusalem, coming down from God out of heaven, prepared as a bride adorned for her husband.*

Here we have the third of the three most important elements comprising God's new creation. In verse 1, we have a new Heaven and a new Earth, and, finally, a new Jerusalem. The church which has been in heaven comes down out of heaven. Coming out of heaven implies that the church has been in the third heaven, the heaven of heavens with Christ since being caught up. The new Jerusalem is, beyond doubt, the Bride of Christ. Since the church's rapture to heaven, it has appeared before the *bema* (judgment seat of Christ); each individual has been examined/appraised and awarded according to the measure of their faithfulness and service on earth. Thus, the bride is divinely prepared and adorned with garments pure white, and of pristine excellence, beauty and perfection; features representing her righteousnesses in testimony on earth as the Lord's servants (Ephesians 5:27). Remember, this has reference to the marriage which took place one thousand years earlier; yet still, the Bride will be seen in her initial, untarnished and resplendent glory, a glory which will endure for all eternity.

v. 3. *And I heard a great voice out of heaven saying, Behold, the tabernacle of God is with men, and He will dwell with them, and they shall be His people, and God Himself shall be with them, and be their God.*

The voice John hears is without doubt the voice of the saints in heaven, as will have been heard on five previous occasions. The references to the voices already heard are: chapters 11:15; 12:10; 14:2, and 19: 1 & 6. As we are here in the post-Millennial period, in the realm of eternity, there will be no reference to Jew and Gentile or of nations, tribes, tongues and peoples, but the voice will be heard by all in the new earth wherein righteousness will dwell.

Behold, the tabernacle of God is with men, and He will dwell with them. The tabernacle here is figurative of the entire company of Old and New Testament saints who have been in heaven with Christ. That the tabernacle is with men implies that the saints of God will be inseparably linked with men on the new earth, under the beneficent influence and presence of God Himself. As already mentioned, the glorified men on the new earth will be the faithful who came through the entire tribulation period, including all who, during that period, suffered death because of their faithful testimony. That the Eternal God will dwell, own, and ever be with men on the new earth and be their God is a glorious, unimpeachable asseveration of the divine objective, sealed in heaven away back in the past, limitless ages of eternity.

> **v. 4.** *And God shall wipe away all tears from their eyes; and there shall be no more death, neither sorrow, nor crying, neither shall there be any more pain: for the former things are passed away.*

God shall wipe away all tears from their eyes. Tears are the product of grief, sorrow, pain and sadness; happily, such causes will never exist in the new earth, for the eternal state will be marked by everlasting joy in the Lord God of all creation. The sweet Psalmist of Israel wrote: *In Thy presence is fulness of joy; at Thy right hand there are pleasures for evermore* (Psalm 16:11). All the causes and consequences of sin and death which occasion sorrow, crying, suffering and pain will no longer exist, for they will have passed into oblivion and every other vestige of the old creation will have disappeared for ever and ever. As for Satan, the author of all sin and human misery, he will have already been cast into the lake of fire, Gehenna, never to rise again.

> **v. 5.** *And He that sat upon the throne said, Behold, I make all things new. And He said unto me, Write: for these words are true and faithful.*

The one sitting upon the throne will be the omnipotent God, for the Lord Jesus, having put down all earthly rule and authority, with His enemies under His feet, will have committed all to God, that God may be all in all (1 Corinthians 15:24-28). Thus, it is God who will: *make all things new.* The current creation of God as from the time of Adam shall be dissolved, as prophesied by Peter: *The heavens shall pass away with a great noise, and the elements shall melt with fervent heat, the earth also and the works that are therein shall be burned up* (2 Peter 3:10). It is clear from chapter 20:11 that all this will occur when the final judgment of the dead, who will stand before the Great White Throne, is complete. Thus, it was that John saw a new heaven and a new earth, verse 1.

Why, we might ask, was John told to write the words: *Behold. I make all things new*? The old creation was the work of God by the power of His Word alone, as confirmed in Psalm 33:9: *For He spake, and it was done; He commanded, and it stood fast.* Also, in Psalm 148:5, speaking of the creation of God, the Psalmist writes: *For He commanded, and they were created.* The original creation was good; indeed, it was very good (Genesis 1:31).

Alas, Satan by his subtlety brought in sin to spoil the work of God on the land, in the sea, and in the air. So, God's declaration that He will make all things new was of such divine gravitas it confirmed that perfection would be the hallowed hallmark of His new heaven and new earth, wherein righteousness would dwell for ever and ever. What God will have produced will not be something which was old made new, but something altogether new in origin which will never decay nor grow old. John, by the Holy Spirit, is reminded of the divine veracity of all the words he has heard. Today, the saints of God should likewise take to heart that all God's words are true and faithful (Proverbs 30:5).

> **v. 6.** *And He said unto me, It is done. I am Alpha and Omega, the beginning and the end. I will give unto him that is athirst of the fountain of the water of life freely.*

God, having created the new earth and the new heaven and furnished them with His saints who will occupy the divine realms for ever and ever, alone could declare: *It is done.* What God will have done will be more than very good. It will be divine perfection as never seen before, save in the Person of His Beloved Son, the Lord Jesus Christ. As Man on earth He could say in His high priestly prayer: *I have glorified Thee on the earth: I have finished the work which Thou gavest Me to do* (John 17:4).

I am Alpha and Omega. I repeat what I have already written on verse 8, of chapter 1. Alpha and Omega are the first and last letters of the Greek alphabet; they are an example of all the alphabets which make up the lexicons of human language. We also have the fullest expression and complete definition of the Godhead in human language. The announcement of these divine titles, the dignity of the speaker, and the character of His utterances, demand our profound attention. God Himself is the speaker as He announces His own titles and glories. God is the source of all truth which has been revealed in the Person of His Son, Jesus Christ. The first words in this creation were from God: *Let there be light: and there was light* (Genesis 1:3). The last and final words of God in relation to the new creation will be: *It is done* (Revelation 21:6). Furthermore, in a coming day all honour and glory will centre in Him, the Omega. Everything necessary to be known about God and the Godhead has been recorded for man's blessing. No matter what depths of knowledge man may plumb, he can know nothing beyond what God has revealed through His Word.

The beginning and the end. The beginning and the end has to do with present creation. *In the beginning God created the heaven and the earth* (Genesis 1:1). We know from 2 Peter 3:10 that the heavens and the earth of this creation will in a coming day pass away with a great noise as the elements melt with a fervent heat. In verse 13 of the same chapter, we read that there is going to be a new heaven and a new earth wherein righteousness shall dwell. God speaks of Himself as: *The beginning and the end,* thereby confirming that there was nothing in existence before He brought the universe and this world into being.

CHAPTER 21

Neither will there be any traces left of this old universe and world after God has made everything new. God shall have achieved His purpose from the beginning, when in the end all glory will centre in His Beloved Son, and He is *all in all*. Nothing in the new heaven and new earth will ever fail.

I will give unto him that is athirst of the fountain of the water of life freely. In this latter part of verse 6, we move back into the present time. One is reminded of the narrative in John's Gospel, chapter 4; the Lord Jesus with the woman at the well. Initially, the woman was thirsty for the water to refresh her in this life, knowing full well that such water had but a transient benefit, and that she would have to return to the well, time and time again. Once the woman became aware that her personal, sinful life was an open book to the One speaking to her and that He was in fact the Messiah she had been expecting, she immediately returns to the town to tell others about the One she had met. Clearly, the woman had imbibed the: *Water of Life*, and became a well of water, springing up into everlasting life (John 4:14).

In Isaiah 55:1, we read of God's free gift of grace to the nations of the world, which is as applicable today as it ever was: *Ho, every one that thirsteth, come to the waters, and he that hath no money; come ye, buy, and eat; yea, come, buy wine and milk without money and without price.* This offer of the Water of Life to the sinner will cease when this present age comes to an end, which will be concurrent with the Lord Jesus coming to establish His Millennial kingdom.

> **v. 7.** *He that overcometh shall inherit all things; and I will be his God, and he shall be My son.*

Mention of the overcomer confirms that the time spoken of is the latter days of: *great tribulation,* when the God-fearing will be severely tested for their faith. They will be encouraged to hold fast to their faith, to stand resolute against the enemy, and to look beyond their present circumstances. The reward will be the inheritance of all things. The *all things,* relate to all the glories which will fill the eternal state, some of which are detailed in verses 3 and 4 above. *And I will be his God,* confirms that in the eternal state nothing will come between us and God in our unending praise and worship. The courts of heaven will eternally echo with the sound of praise: *Unto Him that loved us, and washed us from our sins in His own blood, and hath made us a kingdom, priests unto God and His Father; to Him be glory and dominion for ever and ever. Amen.*

And he shall be My son. From the moment of our conversion to Christ, we were born again as a child of God; we were also adopted as sons of God; i.e., born a child, adopted a son into God's family. Today, as a child of God, we should live our lives day by day in total dependence as a child, under the guidance of the Holy Spirit of God, owning that here on earth we are in the school of God as disciples (learners). Our relationship with God as sons by adoption carries personal responsibilities in relation to our testimony, walk, and ways.

Furthermore, it is important to know and understand that we are not yet in the place of sonship, but we are in the privilege and blessing of sonship. Meanwhile, we are waiting to be taken into the very circumstance of sonship (Romans 8:23), the moment when God's purpose will be fulfilled, i.e., *and he shall be My son.*

John Nelson Darby wrote the following, which sums up the glorious hope in our hearts:

CHAPTER 21

And is it so? We shall be like Thy son!
  Is this the grace which He for us has won.
Father of glory, thought beyond all thought,
  In glory, to His own blest likeness brought.

Nor we alone, Thy loved ones all complete
  In glory round Thee, there with joy shall meet,
All like Thee, for Thy glory like Thee, Lord,
  Object supreme of all, by all adored.

v. 8. *But the fearful, and unbelieving, and the abominable, and murderers, and whoremongers, and sorcerers, and idolaters, and all liars, shall have their part in the lake which burneth with fire and brimstone: which is the second death.*

This verse, together with 1 Corinthians 6:9-10 and Revelation 22:15, lists all the categories of unregenerate mankind, whose destiny is the lake of fire, which is the second death. With regard to the duration of the second death, there will be no review on the sentence passed; God will not be merciful to all suffering the torment of Gehenna. The judgment of God on the rebellious sinner is an everlasting punishment, just, equitable, and without alleviation. For the saints of God, there will degrees of reward as the Lord Jesus advised His disciples: *For the Son of man shall come in the glory of His Father with His angels; and then He shall reward every man according to his works* (Matthew 16:27).

Likewise, for the unsaved there will be various levels of punishment, all according to the gravity of the individual's sinful life. Speaking of the cities which had rejected His message of love, hope, and salvation, the Lord Jesus said: *Woe unto thee, Chorazin! Woe unto thee, Bethsaida! For if the mighty works had been done in Tyre and Sidon, which have been done in you, they had a great while ago repented, sitting in sackcloth and ashes. But it shall be more tolerable for Tyre and Sidon at the judgment, than for you* (Luke 10:13-14).

This verse 8, being a summary of the destiny of the ungodly, concludes the prophecy of the eternal state for both the saved and unsaved. Although we are told very little about the eternal state of the new earth and new heaven, wherein righteousness will dwell throughout the ages of eternity, the following Scriptures give us the briefest of references to God's plan for all the redeemed: John 14:2-3; 1 Corinthians 15:24-28; Ephesians 3:21 and 2 Peter 3:13; they are, however, divinely sufficient for an understanding of what the Lord Jesus has prepared for us who wait for Him:

While very little is said about heaven in the Scriptures, we do know, by faith, it is a place of eternal bliss where everything will reflect the unparalleled excellence of the glory and perfection of the Lord Jesus Christ in God. It will be in such an environment that the saints will dwell throughout the golden ages of eternity.

v. 9. *And there came unto me one of the seven angels which had the seven vials full of the seven last plagues, and talked with me, saying, Come hither, I will shew thee the bride, the Lamb's wife.*

As we have already noted from chapter 4 of this book, all that has been heard and seen by John has not been recorded in the chronological order as the events will ultimately occur, but have been set in the Scriptures by the Holy Spirit in accord with the mind and will of God. What follows here from this verse 9 does not follow on from the verses immediately preceding it, but retraces our steps to the beginning of the Millennial age.

In verse 1 of chapter 17, John was shown the judgment (sentence) of the great whore (harlot) who sits upon many waters, i.e., peoples and nations of the earth; a very solemn moment, just prior to the 1,000-year reign of Christ. But here, in this verse, it is a most joyous moment for John, he is shown the bride, the Lamb's wife, in all her glory, the glory of Christ. After the 1,000 years, the bride will have retained all the glory of pristine excellence with which she was arrayed at the time of her marriage to the Lamb; she will be sustained in it for ever and ever.

> **v. 10.** *And he carried me away in the Spirit to a great and high mountain, and shewed me that great city, the holy Jerusalem, descending out of heaven from God.*

John is still wholly taken over by the Holy Spirit of God, who now transports him spiritually to a great and high mountain. Nothing around him will obscure the glorious vision he will have of the holy Jerusalem (the church, the bride of Christ) descending to take up her role of reigning with Christ throughout the Millennium. However, when, in verse 2, John saw the holy city, the new Jerusalem coming down out of heaven from God, that occasion was at the beginning of the eternal state, at the conclusion of the Millennial age.

The adjective *great,* preceding the noun *city,* in our verse, is an unwarranted interpolation. The holy city, the new Jerusalem, requires no superlative to define it as it descends out of heaven from God. The first clause of verse 11, which reads: *having the glory of God,* should rightly be set as the last clause of verse 10. The holy city, Jerusalem, the bride, the Lamb's wife will be enveloped in heavenly glory, adorned with the glory of God, and be without equal in the creation of God.

> **v. 11.** *And her light was like unto a stone most precious, even like a jasper stone, clear as crystal.*

The light of the Lamb's wife will be of such luminosity, it will outshine all other lights in the universe; its effulgence will equate with the radiating glory of a jasper stone, and be transparent as crystal. But why: *like a jasper stone*? It is important to know that the jasper stone of Scripture was a crystal-clear, translucent white, micro granular quartz. While the mineral jasper may be found in a variety of colours, self or mixed, it is generally accepted by God-fearing theologians of yesteryear that the jasper stone of Scripture is a crystal-clear white diamond.

> **v. 12.** *And had a wall great and high, and had twelve gates, and at the gates twelve angels, and names written thereon, which are the names of the twelve tribes of the children of Israel.*

In our on-going consideration of the vision by the angel who had the seven vials full of the seven last plagues, we must remember John is recalling the sight of symbols of the holy city, being the new Jerusalem, the bride of Christ, etc. Indeed, all that is brought before us from verse 9 of our chapter, to verse 5 of chapter 22 has, in symbols, to do with the time of the Millennium. *A wall great and high.* A symbol signifying that the holy city, the glorified church, will be completely insulated from the ingress of evil intent and infection. It will also be inaccessible to the forces of evil, thus, confirming that the church will be presented to Christ: *a glorious church, not having spot or wrinkle, or any such thing; but that it should be holy and without blemish (Ephesians 5:27).*

And had twelve gates. Numbers referred to in the Scriptures have specific meaning. The number twelve, for example and without exception, signifies government and administration. Thus, throughout the Millennium there will be perfect government and administration under the control of the Lord Jesus, together with the saints of God. As with Christ, the saints will not reside on the earth, but over the earth.

Symbolically, the gates manned by angels will preclude the risk of anything that defiles entering the holy city, but will allow for the ingress and egress of the saints during the 1,000-year reign of Christ. The reason for the presence of the angels is that they are and will be the executors of the judgments of God. In Biblical days, the gate of a city was the place of judgment, where justice was dispensed. Ref. Genesis 19:1; and Ruth 4:1.

And names written thereon, which are the names of the twelve tribes of the children of Israel. The names of the twelve tribes of Israel written upon the gates will not only be confirmation of the nation's entitlement to the full, unlimited blessing of the Millennial age, but will also establish the territorial rights of each family to their God-given inheritance. There will be no dispute about who owns what, for all will be blissfully content to enter into and enjoy their eternal rest as prophesied by Amos: *Behold, the days come, saith the Lord, that the ploughman shall overtake the reaper, and the treader of grapes him that soweth seed; and the mountains shall drop sweet wine, and all the hills shall melt. And I will bring again the captivity of My people of Israel, and they shall build the waste cities, and inhabit them; and they shall plant vineyards, and drink the wine thereof; they shall also make gardens, and eat the fruit of them. And I will plant them upon their land, and they shall no more be pulled up out of their land which I have given them, saith the Lord God* (Amos 9:13-15). Micah the prophet also confirmed the time of blessing for Israel: *They shall sit every man under his vine and under his fig tree; and none shall make them afraid: for the mouth of the Lord of hosts hath spoken it* (Micah 4:4).

> **v. 13.** *On the east three gates; on the north three gates; on the south three gates; and on the west three gates.*

Bearing in mind we are still in the realm of symbols, Israel will understand the significance of the allotment of the families on the four sides of the city. In Numbers, chapter 2, we have the detail of a divinely ordered arrangement of the camp of Israel whenever it settled throughout its wilderness journeys. The camp will have occupied hundreds of hectares of land. The tribes, in four groups of three, were set equidistant from the four sides of the Tabernacle, which will have been the centre point of the camp. The Millennium will be marked by a divine harmony between the nations. Their focal, central point for praise, worship, and thanksgiving will be the Lord Jesus Christ. There will be a spirit of unparalleled forbearance in the animal kingdom, and a beautiful galaxy of colour and fragrance in the plant kingdom. All this will gloriously feature the sovereignty of the Lord Jesus Christ during His one-thousand-year reign (Isaiah 11:6-9; and 35:1-2).

v. 14. *And the wall of the city had twelve foundations, and in them the names of the twelve apostles of the Lamb.*

A wall built without a foundation will never stand. However, this symbolic wall has twelve separate foundations. Why? It certainly does not imply that the wall will be built piecemeal; neither does it infer that it will be built under the auspices of twelve separate groups of people nor indeed attributed to twelve different workers. Rather, it will be built by the Holy Spirit of God with sure and everlasting foundations. This is confirmed by the writer to the Hebrews, when referring to the hope Abraham had by faith: *For he looked for a city which hath foundations, whose builder and maker is God* (Hebrews 11:10). That the names of the twelve apostles of the Lamb will appear in the foundations is confirmation the structure will be based upon the ministry: *Of the apostles and prophets* (of the New Testament), *Jesus Christ Himself being the chief corner stone* (Ephesians 2:20). The twelve foundations will be fused together as one by the twelve gates. The apostle Paul wrote: *Other foundation can no man lay than that is laid, which is Jesus Christ* (1 Corinthians 3:11). The names of the twelve apostles of the Lamb will be indivisibly fused with the name of the Lamb. The term: *of the Lamb*, is significant, for it confirms that throughout the golden ages of eternity we shall never forget the Blessed One who answered to God for our sins and the sin of the world. The remembrance of that unique work of redemption will ever be the theme of praise throughout the courts of heaven.

> *Thou, Thou art worthy Lord,*
> *Of glad untiring praise.*
> *The Lamb once slain shall be adored,*
> *Through everlasting days.*
> *Worthy! We cry again,*
> *Worthy for evermore;*
> *And at Thy feet, O Lamb once slain,*
> *We worship, we adore.*
>
> Miss C.H. von Poseck

Last, but not least, the twelve foundations speak of, and confirm, there will be perfect government and administration throughout the Millennial age.

v. 15. *And he that talked with me had a golden reed to measure the city, and the gates thereof, and the wall thereof.*

It is still the angel which had the seven vials full of the seven last plagues who is talking to John. The golden reed being in the hand of the angel indicates that things to be measured are heavenly, whereas in chapter 7, John has an ordinary measuring reed to measure things to do with the Jewish economy on earth at the time of: *great tribulation*. We must keep in mind the fact that the visions John is having are of the heavenly city which is the church, the heavenly bride; such are symbols of God's divine and glorious plan. What is being vouchsafed to us at this time in the measuring of the city, the gates, and the wall is a spiritual impression of the greatness, glory, richness, and immeasurable vastness of the eternal state which will perfectly reflect the glory and majesty of God through our Lord Jesus Christ, for ever and ever.

> **vv. 16-17.** *And the city lieth foursquare, and the length is as large as the breath: and he measured the city with the reed, twelve thousand furlongs. The length and the breadth and the height of it are equal. And he measured the wall thereof, an hundred and forty and four cubits, according to the measure of a man, that is of the angel.*

Whether or not we accept Scriptural measurements of capacity: dry and liquid, length, money, or weights, it is clear there is a divine symmetry in the dimensions given for the city referred to in our two verses. Whatever numbers are given in the detail of the city and the wall, they are either exact multiples of twelve, or divisible by twelve precisely, thereby confirming perfection in divine government and administration. A wall always has reference to an enclosure of some kind for protection or to set a recognised boundary.

This symbolic wall is 1500 miles in length, in breadth, and in height; and is 72 yards thick, symbolising not only its unparalleled wonder and impregnability (verse 27), but rather, and more so, the durable and eternal character of the city which is the estate of the bride, the church in Christ. Furthermore, the dimensions convey to our finite minds the vastness of the Millennial kingdom, over which the Lord Jesus will reign in righteousness. The wisdom of man is quite incapable of grasping the magnitude of God's ways in grace, nor is it able to plumb the depths of the wisdom of God (Romans 11:33). Moreover, the Holy Spirit of God would have us understand that when it comes to the detail of how He has defined the bride of Christ, it is beyond the wit of the natural mind to comprehend. Notwithstanding, God in His mercy has revealed such treasured truth to His saints, by His Spirit (1 Corinthians 2:9-10).

The words: *According to the measure of a man, that is, of the angel,* require a little explanation. The angel, carrying out the measurements, employs the same standards of measurement as used by man and reveals to John the precise dimensions of the city, gates, and walls. This is divinely designed to ensure man fully appreciates the glory and magnitude of the holy city, the new Jerusalem, coming down from God out of heaven.

> **v. 18.** *And the building of the wall of it was of jasper: and the city was pure gold, like unto clear glass.*

In chapter 4, verse 3, we have reference to the glories of God in Christ as seen in the precious jasper stone, which is the purest and finest form of diamond. When the pure, white light of the jasper stone is passed through a prism, the seven colours of the spectrum, red through to violet, are revealed, symbolising the multi-various attributes of God in Christ. Jasper was the last of the twelve precious stones set in the breastplate (Exodus 28:20), signifying a summary of all the glorious attributes of Jehovah which were divinely exercised to bring the nation of Israel safely into the promised Land (Exodus 3:8).

And the city was pure gold, like unto clear glass. The pure gold is symbolic of the righteousness of God; such gold will have withstood the intense heat of God's holy judgments. However, the righteousness of the saints is portrayed in garments, pure and white, cleansed, not by fire which would destroy them, but the precious blood of Christ. There is a unique transparency about the pure gold in that it is clear as glass, for it implies that absolutely nothing will be concealed of all the glorious features of Christ reflected in the bride of the Lamb.

vv. 19-20. *And the foundations of the wall of the city were garnished with all manner of precious stones. The first foundation was jasper; the second, sapphire; the third, a chalcedony; the fourth, an emerald; the fifth, sardonyx; the sixth, sardius; the seventh, chrysolite; the eighth, beryl; the ninth, a topaz; the tenth, a chrysoprasus; the eleventh, a jacinth; the twelfth, an amethyst.*

From verse 14 we noted that it is the names of the twelve apostles of the Lamb which will appear in the foundations of the symbolic wall, its construction being based upon the ministry: *Of the apostles and prophets of the New Testament.* Jasper was the last of the twelve precious stones in the breastplate, but here in verse 19, it symbolises all the attributes of Christ in the first foundation; even in the symbolic wall, our Lord must have the pre-eminence (Colossians 1:18). Sardius, a blood-red, precious stone was the first jewel in the first row on Aaron's breastplate where it signified that it was the blood of an innocent lamb which redeemed Israel from the bondage of Egypt. Likewise, the blood of Christ has redeemed us back to God (1 Peter 1:18-20).

The last foundation of the wall was garnished with Amethyst, a gem, dark purple to violet in colour, the seventh and last colour of the spectrum of light. White light, when dispersed by a prism, will display the seven colours of the rainbow in the sky. Red, orange, yellow, green, blue, indigo and violet. Purple-violet has ever been recognised as an imperial colour of the robes worn by monarchs and emperors on festive occasions. In John's Gospel, chapter 19:1-2, we read that when Pilate had cruelly scourged the Lord Jesus in his vain attempt to please the Jews, the soldiers, in mockery of our Lord's Kingship, put on Him a purple robe. Before leading the Lord Jesus out of the Praetorium to be crucified, the Sanhedrin, with one ulterior motive, directed the soldiers to remove the purple robe from Him, for they did not want the people lining the streets to believe that they, the Sanhedrin, had accepted the Lord Jesus as King of the Jews. However, God would have His way and directed Pilate to put a most poignant superscription over the cross: *JESUS OF NAZARETH THE KING OF THE JEWS.* (John 19:19). So, the Amethyst, the twelfth precious gem garnishing the twelfth foundation is a symbol of the fact that throughout the Millennium, the Lord Jesus will reign as King of kings, and Lord of lords.

v. 21. *And the twelve gates were twelve pearls: every several gate was one pearl: and the street of the city was pure gold, as it were transparent glass.*

There is a very sound reason why the Spirit of God has symbolised the twelve gates as twelve pearls, particularly as in verse 12 of our chapter each of the gates is named after one of the tribes of Israel. The oyster, which produces the pearl, is an edible marine bivalve mollusc, known as a gastropod. Oysters, which live on the sea bed, are the main source of pearls, albeit, they are produced by other mollusc, such as mussels and clams.

A pearl is initiated in an oyster when a minute grain of sand, or other material, gets lodged within the shell, causing severe irritation to the oyster. The oyster secretes a solution of calcium carbonate to cover the grain with a view to getting relief from the irritation, but, alas, the suffering persists, and the pearl continues to develop. The sea in Scripture is most frequently likened unto the disturbed nations of the world. Certainly, having just come through: *great tribulation*, they will be greatly disturbed, particularly the land of Israel, but through it all, the Lord will have secured a multitude of precious pearls to occupy His new Kingdom.

In Matthew 13:45-46, we have the Lord's sixth parable regarding the kingdom of heaven: *The kingdom of heaven is like unto a merchant-man, seeking goodly pearls: who, when he hath found one pearl of great price, went and sold all that he had, and bought it.* While the fifth parable, in Matthew 13:44, relates to Israel, this sixth parable is about the merchant-man finding one pearl of great price; i.e., the church, for which Christ gave Himself. Accordingly, the Lord has secured the right to have the church in moral suitability to Himself, so that when complete it will be presented: *to Himself a glorious church, not having spot, or wrinkle, or any such thing; but that it should be holy and without blemish* (Ephesians 5:27), just like a goodly pearl. When we consider the ministry in the first seven chapters of the Acts of the Apostles, it might rightly be said that like the precious pearl from the oyster, the church was born out of much trial and suffering.

And the street of the city was pure gold, as it were transparent glass. What a lovely thought, just one street along which symbolically the redeemed shall walk in divine unison, all one in Christ, as our Lord prayed in His high-priestly prayer: *That they all may be one; as Thou, Father, art in Me, and I in Thee, that they also may be one in Us ... that they may be one, even as We are one: I in them, and Thou in Me, that they may be made perfect in one* (John 17:21-23). The *pure gold*, confirms that the city, the church, has been through the crucible of fire to rid it of all dross; for nothing that defiles could possibly exist in the city which is to reflect the glory of God. Never again will it be necessary to wash one's feet, for we shall for ever walk in the righteousness of God, on the golden street of the city of our God.

The words: *as it were transparent glass*, signify that nothing will mar the clarity of all the glories of God and His Christ which will eternally radiate through the saints. The glass is not a mirror, but pure, clear, and untarnished. Today, whenever we perceive that a person has a hidden agenda, we employ the expression: *I can see right through them.* We speak metaphorically, of course, as discerning their concealed intentions. In glory, the saints will be divinely transparent, for there will be nothing unworthy in us to hide from the all-seeing eye of Almighty God.

v. 22. *And I saw no temple therein: for the Lord God Almighty and the Lamb are the temple of it.*

In the Old Testament, the Temple was the centre of worship for the people of God; prior to that, it was the Tabernacle. Within both there was: *the most holy place,* concealed by a veil through which none could enter save the high priest, and that, just once a year, and not without blood. At the end of the three hours of darkness on the Cross, the Lord Jesus dismissed His spirit and committed it into the hands of His Father; immediately, the veil of the Temple was rent in two from top to bottom. Thus, J. G. Deck wrote:

> *The veil is rent; our souls draw near*
> > *Unto the throne of grace;*
> *The merits of the Lord appear,*
> > *They fill the holy place.*
>
> *Within the holiest of all,*
> > *Cleansed by His precious blood,*
> *Before the throne we prostrate fall,*
> > *And worship Thee, O God.*

Today, the saints of God have divine access at any time into the presence of God by the Holy Spirit. Whenever God's children meet together for prayer, praise, worship, and ministry, they rightly claim that the Lord Jesus, by the power of the Holy Spirit, is in their midst, and that they are in the: *most holy place*. In which case, it ever becomes them to be aware that they are on holy ground whenever they are gathered together unto the Name of the Lord Jesus. In order to be wholly taken up by the Holy Spirit, they symbolically remove their shoes, which are tokens of pilgrimage, and focus their thoughts on things spiritual to accord with the mind of heaven. There should ever be a disposition of holy dignity and reverence among the saints when meeting together in the Lord's Name.

Heaven requires no physical Temple, for the immeasurable realm of heaven is filled out with the glory of the Lord God Almighty and the Lamb, who are the Temple, from which we shall never go out. Solomon's Temple, which once occupied an area approximately 27 x 9 metres (90 feet long X 30 feet wide), is superseded by the eternal Temple which now fills out the entire expanse of heaven. The royal courts of heaven will, for all the ages of eternity, echo with the praises of the redeemed. What a glorious prospect lies before us!!

> **vv. 23-24.** *And the city had no need of the sun, neither of the moon, to shine in it: for the glory of God did lighten it, and the Lamb is the light thereof. And the nations* (of them which are saved) *shall walk in the light of it: and the kings of the earth do bring their glory and honour into* (to it) *it.*

Heaven is the realm of glory, way beyond the stars of heaven; hence, the light of the sun and moon will not be required, for their purpose is to give light to the earth by day and night. The light of the glory of God and the Lamb will be the light of the heavenly city. We may recall the occasion when the apostle Paul was on his way to Damascus to persecute the saints of God; suddenly, he saw a light from heaven above the brightness of the sun shining about him, and blinding him for three days (Acts 9). That was the light of the glory of God and the Lamb in which we shall dwell for all eternity. Heaven will be one long eternal day of light. *The Lamb is the light thereof.* These words would remind us of the intrinsic, shekinah glory of the Lord Jesus which was visible on the Mount, when the Lord was transfigured before three favoured disciples (Matthew 17:1-2). The shekinah glory is the dwelling glory which will envelop all the saints in heaven for all eternity.

We might note that in God's new heaven and new earth there will be no trace of the old creation, a creation which was spoiled by disobedience, and judged by water. It was further ruined by rebellion against God and His Christ; therefore: *the elements shall melt with fervent heat, the earth also and the works that are therein shall be burned up* (2 Peter 3:10). Furthermore, there will be no traces of the sinful nature of man, for all things will be new. The nations which occupy the new earth throughout the Millennium will walk in the light of the Lamb who will be the light thereof.

In verse 24, the words: *of them which are saved,* are an unfortunate interpolation which spoil the text. The words are quite meaningless within the context, for the Spirit of God would have us focus our attention on the kings of the earth bringing their glory and honour to the city, which is Christ reigning with His bride over the earth. In no way could the kings of the earth contribute to the city's light and glory by bringing something 'into' it. All divine light and glory have their origin in God, through Christ.

> **vv. 25-26.** *And the gates of it shall not be shut at all by day: for there shall be no night there. And they shall bring the glory and honour of the nations into* (should read: *to it*).

Gates have always to do with either ingress or egress. When shut, a gate signals security and safety, offence and defence. But in the city of the living God (Hebrews 12:22), no such safeguards will be necessary. There will be just one way in to the long, eternal day of glory, joy, security and peace; where the sound of praise will echo throughout the courts of heaven for ever and ever. Darkness will never be known, for the saints shall for ever be in the light and presence of the glory of their blessed Lord and Redeemer.

They shall bring the glory and honour of the nations to it. This refers to the kings of the earth, as detailed in verse 24. Throughout the Millennial age, the kings, while not in or part of the city, will unceasingly render due praise, glory, honour, and worship to the King of kings of the heavenly city.

> **v. 27.** *And there shall in no wise enter into it anything that defileth, neither whatsoever worketh abomination, or maketh a lie: but they which are written in the Lamb's book of life.*

The Spirit of God would make good to our souls that the holy city, symbol of the church, the bride of Christ, cannot possibly be defiled by any Satanic force. Satan, the author and embodiment of sin, will be bound in the abyss for the duration of the Millennium, after which, he will be set free for a short time. Details of his final exploits and doom are given in chapter 20:7-10. The holy city, illuminated with all the glorious attributes of Christ, will be divinely immune from the influence of anything abominable, deceptive, vile, and loathsome. The full and complete complement of the glorious city will comprise of all whose names are written in the Lamb's Book of Life.

The first five verses of this chapter more correctly belong at the end of

CHAPTER 21

chapter 21 to bring to a conclusion the unveiling (revelation) of the Lord Jesus Christ to John on the Isle of Patmos. In these verses, the Spirit of God is highlighting very important, additional features which will be evident throughout the Millennium. Furthermore, while some of the details shown to John are symbolic, as in verses 1 and 2, others, as in verses 3-5, are indeed literal. The Holy Spirit of God will guide us into all truth.

Chapter 22

v. 1. *And he shewed me a pure river of water of life, clear as crystal, proceeding out of the throne of God and of the Lamb.*

It is still the angel which had the seven vials full of the seven last plagues (chapter 21:9) who is with John and showing him: *a pure river of water of life.* Bearing in mind that: *the throne of God and of the Lamb,* is the source of all Millennial blessing, the: *pure river of water of life, clear as crystal,* symbolises the God-given, ever-flowing, super-abundant, unadulterated blessings and joys of divine life, which will be the holy provision for all the residents on earth throughout the Millennium. Furthermore, the pure river being clear as crystal, and flowing freely, confirms the transparency of the glorious, unalloyed purpose of God and the Lamb to identify fully with the Millennial earth.

v. 2. *In the midst of the street of it, and on either side of the river, was there the tree of life, which bare twelve manner of fruits, and yielded her fruit every month: and the leaves of the tree were for the healing of the nations.*

This is the street of pure gold: *as transparent glass,* referred to in verse 21 of the previous chapter (see my thoughts on the verse). A street is usually the thoroughfare of business; here, it is the divine channel (symbolic) along which God and the Lamb move in the fulfilment of their objective to sustain everlasting blessing to all throughout the Millennium. But the midst of this street will be the focal point to which the attention of all will be drawn, for there will be: *the tree of life*. This unique, fruitful tree will bear a different fruit each month of the year. Clearly, the: *tree of life*, being symbolic of the Lord Jesus, will sustain all the redeemed throughout the Millennial age. The twelve different fruits speak of the perfect administration of the divine blessings throughout each year; also, of the precious and varied attributes of the Lord Jesus with which the nations on earth will be blessed.

The leaves of the tree were for the healing of the nations. These words remind us that during the: *great tribulation* period; the nations of the world, and in particular the nation of Israel, were severely persecuted, injured and damaged physically and spiritually by Satan, the false prophet, and the beast. Accordingly, the nations will require divine physical and spiritual healing before they can enter fully into all the blessings of the Millennial Kingdom. The healing balm will come from feeding on the spiritual testimony (leaves) of the: *Tree of life,* which is the Lord Jesus Christ.

> **v. 3.** *And there shall be no more curse: but the throne of God and of the Lamb shall be in it; and His servants shall serve Him.*

The first being of this creation to be cursed by God was Satan (Genesis 3:14) and he will the last fallen angel of this creation to be summarily dealt with by being cast directly into hell (Gehenna) without appearing before a divine assize for judgment (chapter 20:10). God also cursed the ground because of Adam's disobedience (Genesis 3:17). The earth, being blighted, brought forth every offensive plant, which today compete with man's endeavour to cultivate economic crops. The earth is still plagued by such plants which are termed, pernicious.

During the Millennium, the ground will bring forth its fruits as God planned and created (Genesis 2:9). For example: *Instead of the thorn shall come up the fir tree, and instead of the brier shall come up the myrtle tree* (Isaiah 55:13). God's plan is that curses of any kind shall no longer exist or be contemplated.

Nothing of a corrupt nature could possible exist in the presence of: *the throne of God and of the Lamb.* The words: *shall be in it,* implies that the holiness of the Godhead will pervade the entire sinless environment of the Millennial age during which Satan will be bound in the bottomless pit.

His servants shall serve Him. All in heaven (the holy city, new Jerusalem) and all on earth will readily acknowledge themselves bondmen (*servants Gk. = Doulos, bondman*) to Jesus Christ, and in love and devotion will act in priestly service throughout the ages of eternity. Our worship will be on the highest plane to the One whose glory fills the realms of heaven, for we shall for ever be enveloped in our Lord's unique, dwelling glory. Thus, the priestly service will be the praise, worship, and thanksgiving of all the saints in unison; its harmonious chords reverberating throughout the courts of heaven for ever and ever.

v. 4. *And they shall see His face; and His name shall be in their foreheads.*

This Scripture confirms the prophecy of Zechariah 12:10, which reads: *They shall look upon Me whom they have pierced;* and in John 19:37, we read: *They shall look on Him whom they pierced.* The next time the world sees the Lord Jesus will be when He comes from heaven with power and great glory with all His saints (Jude 14). Then: *every eye shall see Him, and they also which pierced Him: and all kindreds of the earth shall wail because of Him* (chapter 1:7). All nations of the world, on seeing the Blessed One, will lament and mourn, for their conscience will smite them with a sense of guilt for having supported the rejection and crucifixion of the Lord Jesus, the Messiah of Israel.

Our Lord in manhood reflected a unique, intrinsic, moral glory. Alas, the unregenerate heart and mind of the Jewish nation, saw no beauty in Him to desire Him (Isaiah 53:2). Now, the faithful remnant of the nation, seeing Him in all His glory and power, desire and honour Him. *His name in their foreheads,* implies that having been converted (Romans 11:26), they will be totally committed to thinking and testifying about the only One who is the King of kings, and Lord of lords. Their minds will be filled with nothing save what is due to the Lord Jesus in terms of praise, worship, and thanksgiving for ever and ever.

> *O GLORIOUS Lord! what thoughts Thy mind did fill,*
> *When from Thy God Thou cam'st to do His will!*
> *How deep, indeed, the joy that filled Thy heart –*
> *That myriad sons with Thee should find their part!*
>
> *O blessed Lord, what treasured thoughts unfold*
> *In light divine, as we Thy face behold!*
> *Now on our view, unbounded glories break,*
> *That speak Thy fame, and songs eternal wake.*
>
> H. F. Nunnerley

v. 5. *And there shall be no night there; and they need no candle, neither light of the sun; for the Lord God giveth them light: and they shall reign for ever and ever.*

As we have proceeded in our studies of: *The Revelation of Jesus Christ,* we have noted that the greater part of the unveiling of the Lord Jesus Christ has been presented in symbolic form. Here, in this the last verse of the unveiling, we have four statements which the Holy Spirit will help us understand, being symbols of future events. First, we must accept that in this verse the angel is still speaking to John, and is referring to the heavenly city, the environment in which the glorified saints, the bride of Christ, shall dwell for ever and ever.

There shall be no night there, confirming that heaven will be one, long, eternal day of divine light. In the creation, darkness was the realm where God was not known, for the Spirit of God brooded over the dark waters. Darkness implies distance from God, but the saints could not be nearer to God than we already are in spirit; as the apostle Paul wrote: *Your life is hid with Christ in God* (Colossians 3:3). Thus, no night in the heavenly city.

And they need no candle (lamp). Here, a lamp is a symbol of the Word of God. In Psalm 119:105, we read: *Thy word is a lamp unto my feet, and a light unto my path.* In the heavenly city, there will be no need for prophetic Scriptures. While such were essential for one's pathway on earth, in the eternal state they will have no role, whatsoever. *Neither light of the sun; for the Lord God giveth them light.* The words: *The Lord God giveth them light,* should read: *The Lord God shall shine upon them.* The great created orb in the sky which lights the world day by day will pale to insignificance against the light of the glory of heaven, the radiant city of our God. The saints of God in heaven will be luminaries and reflectors of God's glory, as it will for ever shine upon them.

The fourth element of the verse is: *And they shall reign for ever and ever.* Such words are a glorious conclusion to the complete unveiling of the Lord Jesus Christ. The greatness of the honour, that we shall reign for ever and ever with our Redeemer, overwhelms us. Thus, we love to sing:

CHAPTER 22

How good is the God we adore,
  Our faithful, unchangeable friend:
Whose love is as great as His power,
  And knows neither measure nor end!

'Tis Jesus, the first and the last,
  Whose Spirit shall guide us safe home;
We'll praise Him for all that is past,
  And trust Him for all that's to come.

                                                J. Hart.

Verse 5 concludes the time of God's dealings with this creation in its last days. The day of God's grace to the world will have ended with the rapture of the saints to heaven (1 Thessalonians 4:16-17). Then, after an undefined lapse of time, there will be a seven-year period of world-wide tribulation, referred to in Daniel 9:27 and Matthew 24:15-26.

The last half-week of the seven-year period was termed by the Lord Jesus as: *a time of great tribulation.* Our Lord was referring to the time when the nation of Israel will suffer unspeakable pain, devastation, and death. Knowing how horrendous that time will be, our Lord said: *Except those days should be shortened, there should be no flesh be saved: but for the elect's sake those days shall be shortened* (Matthew 24:22). The 'elect' will be the faithful of the house of Israel.

Then follows the coming of the Lord Jesus with all His saints to reign over the earth for one thousand years (Jude 14 and Revelation 20:4). At the end of the one thousand years, Satan, being released from the bottomless pit for a short while, will energise the unregenerate of the nations of the world to rise up in rebellion against the Lord. Their numbers will be as the sand of the sea shore. They will surround the beloved city, Jerusalem, with the intention of demolishing it along with the saints. But they will make no impression whatsoever upon the city and the saints, for God will rain down fire from heaven, and devour them (chapter 20:9).

Next, all the unbelieving dead will be raised to appear before the: *Great White Throne,* and having been righteously judged, will be cast into hell, Gehenna, for ever and ever (chapter 20:11-15). When the Lord Jesus has brought the whole of creation under His control, He will deliver up the kingdom to God, even His Father, that God may be all in all (1 Corinthians 15:24 and 28). So, we come to the last chapter of this unique and most remarkable book; verses 6-21.

> **v. 6.** *And he said unto me, These sayings are faithful and true: and the Lord God of the holy prophets sent His angel to shew unto His servants the things which must shortly be done.*

There seems to be little doubt that the one speaking to John at this time is still the angel referred to in chapter 21, verse 9; and may well be the angel who delivered to John the unveiling of the Lord Jesus Christ (chapter 1:1). The faithful and true sayings refer to the full, divinely inspired record of the: *Revelation* (unveiling) *of the Lord Jesus Christ.* Regarding the universe, there is nothing more to be revealed of what God has purposed through the Lord Jesus Christ. Everything God deemed necessary for man to know has been revealed to, and rehearsed by, faithful prophets of Old and New Testament times, including the apostle John.

The things which must shortly come to pass, refers to all the details of the unveiling of the Lord Jesus Christ which have been disclosed to us from chapter 4 verse 1 to verse 5 of this chapter. We should treasure and hold these revelations in our hearts from day by day.

CHAPTER 22

> *For soon the happy day shall come,*
>   *When we shall reach our destined home,*
> *And see Him face to face;*
>   *Then with our Saviour, Lord and Friend,*
> *The one unbroken day we'll spend*
>   *In singing still His grace.*
>
>   S. Medley (amended)

v. 7. *Behold, I come quickly: blessed is he that keepeth the sayings of the prophecy of this book.*

In verse 6, the angel confirms to John the integrity and veracity of all he (John) had both seen and heard. Suddenly, the Lord Jesus interrupts the angel, stating that He is coming quickly. All the glories and wonders John has been absorbed in must never be allowed to eclipse the prospect of the Lord Jesus coming to rapture away to glory all the saints of God. The verb: *Behold*, which occurs many times in this last book of the Bible, is uttered in the imperative tense to draw attention to someone, or something, or to an event of great importance, such as the: *coming of the Lord Jesus for His own*.

The statement: *I come quickly*, occurs three times in this last chapter of the book. Here, the first mention relates to keeping alive in our hearts everything which has been revealed, so that we shall ever be ready for when the call from heaven comes, which will be: *A shout, with the voice of the archangel, and with the trump of God* (1 Thessalonians 4:16). The adverb: *quickly*, simply implies, at any moment. Accordingly, we should live from day to day in the spirit of expectancy, with the longing to be caught away and translated into the likeness of our Blessed Lord (1 John 3:2).

Blessed is he that keepeth the sayings. This is the sixth of seven assured blessings given to us in this book of the Revelation. This particular blessing is conditional on the believer keeping and treasuring in one's heart, mind, and soul, all that the Spirit of God has revealed in this book from chapter 4:1 to chapter 22:5. All that has been opened up to us is still prophecy. May God's gracious Spirit preserve us from letting slip anything God in His mercy has disclosed to us. Loss of the smallest detail, or our failure to understand the divine revelations, will leave us ill-prepared for when the assembling call of the archangel is heard, and the trump of God sounded (1 Thessalonians 4:16-17).

vv. 8-9. *And I John saw these things, and heard them. And when I had heard and seen, I fell down to worship before the feet of the angel which shewed me these things. Then saith he unto me, See thou do it not: for I am thy fellow servant, and of thy brethren the prophets, and of them which keep the sayings of this book: worship God.*

John was so overwhelmed by what he had both seen and heard that for a moment he took his eye off the Lord, and in his mind elevated the status of the angel to that of a deity to be worshipped. There was an earlier occasion when John did the same thing. Having been so awestruck by the prophetic vision of the glorious marriage of the Lamb, he fell at the feet of the angel to worship the one who had given him the preview. But the angel admonished John, saying: *See thou do it not (chapter 19:10).* This injunction is as applicable today as in the day when John was on the Isle of Patmos.

Christians should never bow down to senior clerics of national religions, such as those called bishops, archbishops, *et al.*, who claim to be on a higher spiritual plain, above the common people (Romans 12:3). To bow in reverence to such people would be tantamount to idolatry. However, in the secular world, Christians are exhorted to give honour to whom honour is due (Romans 13:7). The Lord Jesus Himself taught that we should honour our parents (Matthew 15:4), but not to worship any mortal being, for to do so would be idolatry. John is counselled to do homage (worship) God alone; this he will have done through and in the name of the Lord Jesus Christ.

> **v. 10.** *And he saith unto me, Seal not the sayings of the prophecy of this book: for the time is at hand.*

Reading this verse occasions our thoughts repairing to the book of Daniel, which is full of prophetic dreams and visions. In Daniel chapter twelve, verse four, following all his divine dreams and visions; Daniel is told to: *Shut up the words, and seal the book, even to the time of the end.* According to Daniel 12, at the end time, which was then afar off, there shall be a time of trouble, which the Lord Jesus titled, *great tribulation*. John is now told: *Seal not the sayings of the prophecy of this book* (Revelation): *for the time is at hand* (very near). The *time* referred to is the same as that indicated to Daniel, many hundreds of years earlier, i.e., the time of great trial which will fall upon the world, particularly upon the nation of Israel during the last 3.5 years of Daniel's 70th 'week of years' (Daniel 9:27), being: *great tribulation. The time is at hand,* signifies the imminence of the fulfilment of God's calendar of events, which will commence with the rapture of the church to glory.

> **v. 11.** *He that is unjust, let him be unjust still: and he which is filthy, let him be filthy still: and he that is righteous, let him be righteous still: and he that is holy, let him be holy still.*

This verse is confirmation that the time referred to in the statement is the close of the Day of God's Grace to the world. Here we have 2 x 2 groups of mankind who fill the earth. The *unjust,* will be those who have not been justified by faith in the Lord Jesus Christ, according to the teaching of Romans 5, verse 1. The definition, *filthy*, will apply to all who have not been cleansed of their sins in the precious blood of Christ.

In the second group of two, we have first the *righteous*, on whom the righteousness of God has been bestowed, that is: *upon all them that believe* (Romans 3:22). Finally, we have: *he that is holy*. In 1 Peter 1:15; we read: *As He which hath called you is holy, so be ye holy in all manner of conversation* (1 Peter 1:15). However, the tense in our verse is future; for when we are in glory, we shall for ever be with our Lord: *Holy and without blame before Him in love* (Ephesians 1:4).

> **v. 12.** *And, behold, I come quickly; and My reward is with Me, to give every man according as his work shall be.*

The angel speaking to John is again interrupted by the Lord Jesus with the wonderful statement of His coming again, and that He is coming quickly. The reason the Lord Jesus in love repeats the fact that He is coming quickly is to ensure the saints are spiritually retained in a state of expectancy. We should be ever looking up, away from this world to the heavenly realms of glory, from whence we look for our Saviour, the Lord Jesus Christ. May our gracious Lord preserve us from settling down in this scene of moral darkness.

And My reward is with Me, to give every man according as his work shall be. The just claim of the Lord Jesus that the rewards are with Him is confirmation of the words of the apostle Paul: *For we must all appear* (be manifested) *before the judgment seat of Christ; that every one may receive the things done in his body, according to that he hath done, whether it be good or bad* (2 Corinthians 5:10).

CHAPTER 22

The rewards the Lord Jesus will dispense to all the saints of God at the *Judgment Seat of Christ* will not be material, but spiritual. Our reward will be a filling up and enrichment of the measure of our apprehension of the worth and glories of Christ, commensurate with the level and integrity of our sacrificial service in His name. We might refer to the simile of the sweet Psalmist of Israel: *My cup runneth over* (Psalm 23:5). In heaven, every child of God will be like a cup, full and running over, but the cups will differ substantially in size according to the divine estimate and value of our spiritual service on earth. Think what a difference there will be in the size of the apostle Paul's cup, and that of the crucified, penitent thief; nevertheless, both will be full of the joy of heaven: *In Thy presence is fulness of joy; at Thy right hand there are pleasures for evermore* (Psalm 16:11).

v. 13. *I am Alpha and Omega, the beginning and the end, the first and the last.*

The correct reading of this verse, according to the best and most reliable translations from the original Greek text, is: *I am Alpha and Omega, the first and the last, the beginning and the end.* To the spiritual eye, it will be clear why this is the correct order of the Divine Titles. Thus, the announcement of these august appellations, their significance and the intrinsic authority, coupled with the dignity of the speaker demand our prayerful consideration. So, we confirm that our Lord Himself is the speaker as He announces His own titles and glories, albeit God is the source and the origin of all truth revealed through His Son, Jesus Christ. Furthermore, we should understand that the commencement of all divine testimony is in God, and ends in Christ, to whom all will gravitate. All honour and glory will centre in Him, the Alpha and Omega. Everything necessary to be known about God and the Godhead, has been recorded for man's blessing.

Alpha and Omega are the first and last letters of the Greek alphabet, which is an example of all the alphabets that make up the lexicons of human language. God, in His mercy, has communicated to us through His Word all that is necessary for man to know about His purpose and will for us and His creation. We are privileged to have in God's Word, the most comprehensive, detailed definition of the Godhead. No matter what depths of knowledge man may plumb, he can know nothing beyond what God has revealed through His Word.

The First and the Last, has to do with Jesus Christ personally. He was Foremost in time, order, place and importance, and in the final (last) state, every created intelligence will be made to own, honour, bow, and: *Confess that Jesus Christ is Lord, to the glory of God the Father* (Philippians 2:9-11).

In Proverbs 8:22-31, we read, prophetically of the Lord Jesus. There never was a man like Him, and never again will there be such a man; the Son of the Father's love: *The Lord* (God) *possessed me in the beginning of His way, before His works of old. I was set up from everlasting, from the beginning, or ever the earth was. When there were no depths, I was brought forth; when there were no fountains abounding with water. Before the mountains were settled, before the hills was I brought forth: while as yet He had not made the earth, nor the fields, nor the highest part of the dust of the world. When He prepared the heavens, I was there: when He set a compass upon the face of the depth: when He established the clouds above: when He strengthened the fountains of the deep: When He gave to the sea His decree, that the waters should not pass His commandment: when He appointed the foundations of the earth then I was by Him, as one brought up with Him: and I was daily His delight, rejoicing always before Him; rejoicing in the habitable part of His earth; and My delights were with the sons of men.*

He is the image of the invisible God, the firstborn of every creature. He was also the firstborn from the dead, that in all things He might have the pre-eminence (Colossians 1:15 & 18).

The beginning and the end. The beginning and the end have to do with present creation. Genesis 1:1: *In the beginning God created the heaven and the earth.* We know from 2 Peter 3:10 that the heavens and the earth of this creation will, in a coming day, pass away with a great noise as the elements melt with a fervent heat. In verse 13 of the same chapter, we read there is going to be a new heaven and a new earth wherein righteousness shall dwell. The beginning and the end intimate that all testimony on earth has its origin in God, and its end is His glory. Creation, providence, promise, history, prophecy, testimony, love and grace, all have their source and end in God. Nothing on the divine side can ever end in failure.

v. 14. *Blessed are they that do His commandments, that they may have right to the tree of life, and may enter in through the gates into the city.*

The opening clause of this verse in the KJV, is a serious mis-translation of the original Greek text. The clause should read: *Blessed are they that wash their robes* etc. This is the last of the seven blessings in this book, all of which are assured to believers in the Lord Jesus Christ. Accordingly, it is a very substantial reason why all the saints of God should prayerfully study the book, and seek to understand all that has been unveiled about God's Beloved Son.

We know from the teaching of the Gospel of the Grace of God that man will never be born again through faith in the Lord Jesus while attempting to keep the Sinaic law of God. This truth is confirmed in what the apostle Paul wrote to the saints in Rome: *For what the law could not do* (could not save a soul from a lost eternity), *in that it was weak through the flesh, God sending His own Son in the likeness of sinful flesh, and for sin, condemned sin in the flesh: that the righteousness of the law might be fulfilled in us, who walk not after the flesh, but after the Spirit* (Romans 8:3-4).

Blessed are they that wash their robes. This statement has reference to all who have put their faith and trust in the Lord Jesus Christ, and are spiritually cleansed by His precious blood. The washing of one's robes and being made white in the blood of the Lamb signifies the daily moral cleansing of a Christian's way of life, and their practical righteousness.

That they may have right to the tree of life. The *right*, referred to in this clause, was established and confirmed by the Lord Jesus (John 6:47-58). The tree of life is the Lord Jesus Christ. When Adam and Eve, whom God placed in the garden of Eden, sinned by disobeying God, they were immediately put out of the garden lest they should take of the *tree of life* and live for ever in sin. Cherubims with a flaming sword were set at the East of the garden to keep the way of the *tree of life*. Ref. Genesis 3:24. We now know that four thousand years later that metaphorical, flaming sword, was sheathed in the side of the Lord Jesus as He answered to God for our sins and the sin of the world. Thus, the way to the *tree of life* was opened to all who repent of their sins before God, and put their faith and trust in the atoning work of the Lord Jesus Christ.

The words: *and may enter in through the gates into the city,* take us back to verse 12 of the previous chapter. The symbolic gates into the city will be manned by angels to preclude the risk of anything that defiles entering the holy city, but will allow for the uninhibited ingress and egress of the saints of God during the 1,000-year reign of Christ.

CHAPTER 22

v. 15. *For without are dogs, and sorcerers, and whoremongers, and murderers, and idolaters, and whosoever loveth and maketh a lie.*

The Spirit of God hast given us a repeat list (see chapter 21:8) of the categories of unregenerate mankind who have not been cleansed by the precious blood of Christ, and who will never have title to nor gain access to the: *tree of life*. The sad destiny pronounced upon the unsaved when they appear before the Great White Throne (Chapter 20:11-15) will not be an act of vengeance by the Lord Jesus, neither will it be the exercise of a vendetta; when it comes to the righteous judgments by Almighty God, through Christ, it is absolutely impossible for such characteristics to feature in divine conclusions. All whose names are not found written in the *book of life* will be cast into the lake of fire, hell, Gehenna. There will be no protests, objections or appeals for review; all will accept the righteous judgment of the Lord Jesus. Neither will there be any relief from the eternal suffering occasioned by the fiery torment (Luke 16:19-31).

v. 16. *I Jesus have sent Mine angel to testify unto you these things in the churches. I am the root and the offspring of David, and the bright and morning star.*

What lowly grace we see in the way the Lord Jesus introduces Himself; *I Jesus.* We recall that the angel of the Lord told Joseph that his wife would bring forth a son, *and thou shalt call His name JESUS: for He shall save His people from their sins* (Matthew 1:21). What a precious name; a name God would have imprinted on the heart and conscience of every human being, for it is mentioned nearly one thousand times in the New Testament. Our Lord was born King of the Jews (Matthew 2:2); He died as King of the Jews (Matthew 27:37). One day, He is going to reign as King of the nation of Israel. The last time man saw that precious name in print was as a superscription over His Cross: *This is Jesus, the King of the Jews*. The next time the nation sees their King will be when He comes with power and great glory as King of kings, and Lord of lords (Matthew 24:30). It is clear that the angel whom the Lord Jesus sent was the one referred to in chapters 16:17 and 21:9, who had shown John many things of unfulfilled prophecy, including the bride, the Lamb's wife. Everything John had both heard and seen was to be communicated to the churches, that the saints might live in a state of preparedness for when the Lord Jesus comes to the clouds, to call home to heaven all the redeemed (1 Thessalonians 4:16-17).

I am the root and the offspring of David. David was the eighth son of Jesse, eight in Scripture speaks of resurrection. How very wonderful then, that God in His sovereign purpose chose David to be the progenitor of the Lord Jesus Christ who, speaking of Himself said: *I am the resurrection, and the life: he that believeth in Me, though he were dead, yet shall he live* (John 11:25). Thus, naturally, the Lord Jesus came from the root of David. Although David was the first divinely appointed king of Israel (1 Samuel 16:12-13), he was but a type of the One who would be born King of the Jews (Matthew 2:2).

The root of a plant is not only its anchor to hold it firm in the ground, it is also the source of water and nutrients for growth and maturity. The divine life of every believer is hidden with Christ in God (Colossians 3:3). Accordingly, Christ is the root and only source of spiritual nourishment to strengthen and sustain us well in our Christian profession. A firm anchorage in Christ will undoubtedly help us weather the storms of life in this morally dark world.

The bright and morning star. The appearance of, *the Bright and Morning Star,* has everything to do with the hope of the Church, the bride of

Christ. The saints are patiently waiting in faith for the coming of the Lord Jesus as, *the Bright and Morning Star,* which, when He comes will rapture us away to glory, will herald the beginning of our eternal day of rest in Christ. We note that the M*orning Star,* a symbol of Christ, is designated, *bright,* which indicates it will be gloriously radiant, eclipsing the light of all other heavenly bodies. It will be the intrinsic resurrection power, authority, and call of the Lord Jesus, which will snatch the saints away from earth to heaven; the dawn of a perennial day of glory, peace, and heavenly joy. The unregenerate will not witness the miraculous event.

In the prophecy of Malachi, we have reference to the Lord Jesus as, *the Sun of righteousness arising with healing in His wings (Malachi 4:2).* This prophecy relates to a time which will be subsequent to the rapture of the church. The lapse of time will be at least seven years, but probably considerably longer, when the Lord Jesus will come with power and great glory, with His saints, to established His Millennial Kingdom. Certainly, with the nations so recently sorely damaged and torn apart by: *great tribulation,* divine healing will prepare the nations to live in harmony for the duration of the Millennial age.

> **v. 17.** *And the Spirit and the bride say, Come. And let him that heareth say, Come. And let him that is athirst come. And whosoever will, let him take the water of life freely.*

We have in this verse two distinct groups of Christians, and one group thirsting for the word of God and invited to drink the water of life freely. However, the verse highlights the levels of spiritual preparedness for the coming of the Lord Jesus to the clouds to call the redeemed home to glory (1 Thessalonians 4:16-17).

First, *the Spirit and the bride say, Come.* This is a sincere response of the

Spirit and the bride on hearing the words of the Lord Jesus: *Behold I come quickly; and My reward is with Me … I am the Bright and Morning Star.* There is today, scattered throughout the world, a body of very dear saints of God who simply live and long for the time when they will be with and like their Lord in glory. They are fervent in prayer, faithful in service, patient in disposition, and wholly devoted to fulfilling God's will for them in this life. Their call to the Lord Jesus to come, is not a selfish ambition, but a yearning for the fulfilment of the desire of the Lord Jesus, which He expressed in His High Priestly prayer: *Father, I will that they also, whom Thou hast given Me, be with Me where I am; that they may behold My glory* (John 17:24).

And let him that heareth say, Come. This second group of saints is awoken by the words of the Lord Jesus given in verses 12, 13, and 16. Individually, they are prompted to respond in the only way a member of the bride of Christ should respond; that is, with deep sincerity of heart, they say: *Come.*

And let him that is athirst come. And whosoever will, let him take the water of life freely. We recall that at this time, of which John is writing, the church, the bride of Christ is still on earth and the day of God's grace has not yet ended. There will be many, many thousands of souls throughout the world, greatly disturbed by the breakdown of order in governmental, political, social, and educational establishments; also, in family life and society; they will yearn and thirst for relief from the stress of the natural life. However, unlike the first two groups, they do not, with the Spirit say, Come. Rather, God, in His mercy and willing that all might be saved, announces his final invitation to those thirsting for spiritual refreshment and eternal life; He says, Come. Those who are thirsty will respond, and in a spirit of repentance put their faith and trust in the

Lord Jesus Christ. Such will experience the assurance given by the Lord Jesus to the woman at Sychar's Well: *Whosoever drinketh of the water that I shall give him shall never thirst; but the water that I shall give him shall be in him a well of water springing up into everlasting life* (John 4:14).

> **vv. 18-19.** *For I testify unto every man that heareth the words of the prophecy of this book, If any man shall add unto these things, God shall add unto him the plagues that are written in this book: and if any man shall take away from the words of the book of this prophecy, God shall take away his part out of the book of life, and out of the holy city; and from the things which are written in this book.*

The words: *book of life,* in verse 19, are a mistranslation; the text should read: *tree of life.* I believe the words: *the prophecy of this book,* refer specifically to this last book of the Bible: *The Revelation of Jesus Christ.* Some spiritually competent expositors of the Word believe the text applies to the entire Word of God, and I would not vehemently dispute this, because all Scripture is given by inspiration of God (2 Timothy 3:16). However, my understanding is based on the truth that this book is unique; unlike any of the other sixty- five books of the Bible, it is the unveiling of the Lord Jesus Christ, and of how that God's purpose and counsel, will, in due time, be fulfilled through His Son.

Accordingly, what is most important today is the defence of the integrity and divine inspiration of the book: *The Revelation of Jesus Christ.* It is the Lord Jesus who is here speaking to all who have read the entire prophecy of the book and have in some measure understood what has been unveiled. This, to the God-fearing reader, will have proved to be a divine blessing. However, the Lord adds a very solemn warning of what will happen to any who attempt to add, embellish, or traduce the sacred Word of God. We have only to go to chapters 14 – 16 of this book to grasp the significance of the Lord's words: *God shall add unto him the plagues that are written in this book.*

Next, we have the consequences for any man who deletes any word, clause, or sentence from the book of this prophecy. The Greek word for, *words,* in this verse and the previous, is *Logos,* confirming it is the authoritative Word of God Himself which is here expressed. One can, therefore, understand the gravity of meddling with God's Word, either by adding to or subtracting from the record occasioned by divine inspiration. The penalties detailed in these two verses would suggest that the individuals have never belonged to the family of God, for God will confirm they have no part in Christ, the Tree of Life; neither will they be part of the holy city, the church, the bride of Christ. They surely fall into the category of those who are unregenerate: *Having a form of godliness, but denying the power thereof* (2 Timothy 3:5). However, tragically, there are in Christendom today, sects who are deleting or disregarding substantial portions of God's Word for the sole reason that the inspired ministry condemns their way of thinking and behavioural practices. Such groups will not escape the judgment of Almighty God.

v. 20. *He which testifieth these things saith, Surely, I come quickly. Amen. Even so, come, Lord Jesus.*

The words: *Even so,* in the KJV, do not appear in the original Greek text. The Lord Jesus continues to speak, while His divine attributes are once more confirmed by His incontrovertible testimony of all that has been unveiled. The adjective, *Surely,* is a strong affirmation that the Lord will come to the clouds to call His redeemed ones home to glory. The rapture of the church to glory will be an earth-shattering event for earth-dwellers; it will signal the end of God's Day of grace to this world. The Lord's coming for His own will not be a phased event, for when He calls, the rapture will occur within a nanosecond of time, or, as the apostle Paul has put it: *In a moment, in the twinkling of an eye* (1 Corinthians 15:52). The unregenerate of the nations of the world will awake to discover that millions of men, women, and children have disappeared from the face of the earth.

The faithful and watching Christian can be in little doubt that this current time of God's grace to the world is drawing inexorably to a close. Meanwhile, may we continue to take comfort from the words: *For yet a little while, and He that shall come will come, and will not tarry* (Hebrews 10:37). The immediate and sincere response of the bride to the Lord's last words: *Surely, I come quickly;* is: *Amen, come, Lord Jesus.*

v. 21. *The grace of our Lord Jesus Christ be with you all. Amen.*

John's succinct and tender doxology reveals his yearning for the saints of God to be daily spiritually strengthened in their faith while waiting for the adoption, to wit the redemption of our bodies.

> *We wait for Thee; thou wilt arise*
> *Whilst hope her watch is keeping;*
> *Forgotten then, in glad surprise,*
> *Shall be our years of weeping.*
> *Our hearts beat high, the dawn is nigh*
> *That ends our pilgrim story,*
> *In Thine eternal glory.*
>
> P. F. Hiller

Bibliography

An Outline of the Revelation	C. A. Coates
The Seven Churches	J. N. Darby
The Seven Churches	E. Dennett
Lectures on the Revelation	Dr. H. A. Ironside
Lectures on the Revelation	W. Kelly
The Revelation of Jesus Christ	W. Scott

THE REVELATION OF JESUS CHRIST